P9-EMR-670

# blue monday

THE KIDS
ARE ALRIGHT

cover colors by
**GUY MAJOR**

chapter one lettered by
**JEROMY COX**
chapters two-three lettered by:
**AMIE GRENIER**
"Sherlockette" lettered by
**GARY KATO**

gray tones by
**GUY MAJOR**
**STAISSI BRANDT**

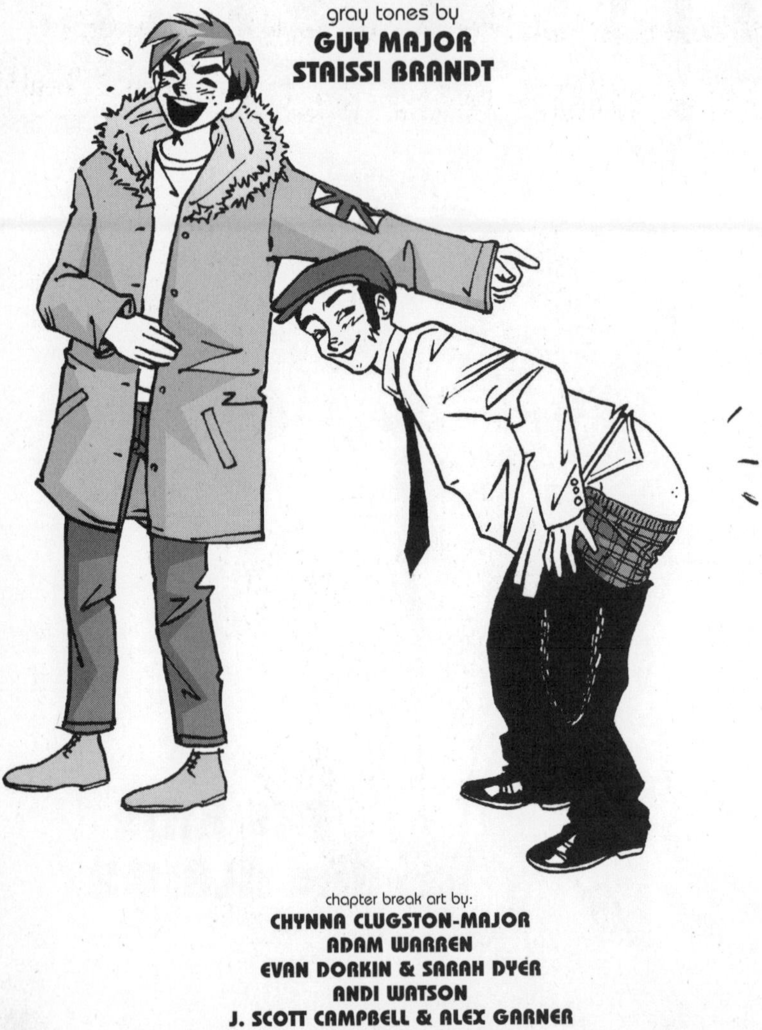

chapter break art by:
**CHYNNA CLUGSTON-MAJOR**
**ADAM WARREN**
**EVAN DORKIN & SARAH DYER**
**ANDI WATSON**
**J. SCOTT CAMPBELL & ALEX GARNER**

book design by **STEVEN BIRCH @ SERVO** & **KEITH WOOD**
edited by **JAMIE S. RICH**
assistant editing by **JAMES LUCAS JONES**

# blue monday ™

## THE KIDS ARE ALRIGHT

written and illustrated by

## CHYNNA CLUGSTON-MAJOR

Published by Oni Press, Inc.
**JOE NOZEMACK** publisher
**JAMIE S. RICH** editor in chief
**JAMES LUCAS JONES** associate editor

This collects issues 1-3 of the Oni Press comics series
*Blue Monday: The Kids Are Alright*™, as well as short stories from
various issues of *Dark Horse Presents* (Dark Horse Comics),
*Action Girl Comics* (Slave Labor Graphics), and
*Oni Double Feature* (Oni Press).

"That's the Spirit," "The Ants Come Marching," "The Curse of the
Jesus Head," "Contageously Yours," and "Stop, Schmop!" original-
ly edited by Sarah Dyer. "Sherlockette" originally edited by Bob
Schreck & Jamie S. Rich. All others edited by Jamie S. Rich

Blue Monday: The Kids Are Alright is ™ & © 2000, 2003 Chynna
Clugston-Major. Unless otherwise specified, all other material ©
2003 Oni Press, Inc. Oni Press logo and icon are ™ & © 2003
Oni Press, Inc. All rights reserved. Oni Press logo and icon artwork
created by Dave Gibbons. The events, institutions, and characters presented in this book are fictional. Any resemblance to
actual persons, living or dead, is purely coincidental. No portion
of this publication may be reproduced, by any means, without
the express written permission of the copyright holders.
A new rock family of wild nobility.

ONI PRESS, INC.
6336 SE Milwaukie Avenue, PMB30
Portland, OR 97202
USA

www.onipress.com

Second edition: May 2003
ISBN 1-929998-62-7

1 3 5 7 9 10 8 6 4 2
PRINTED IN CANADA.

# chapter one:
# "THERE'S NO OTHER WAY"

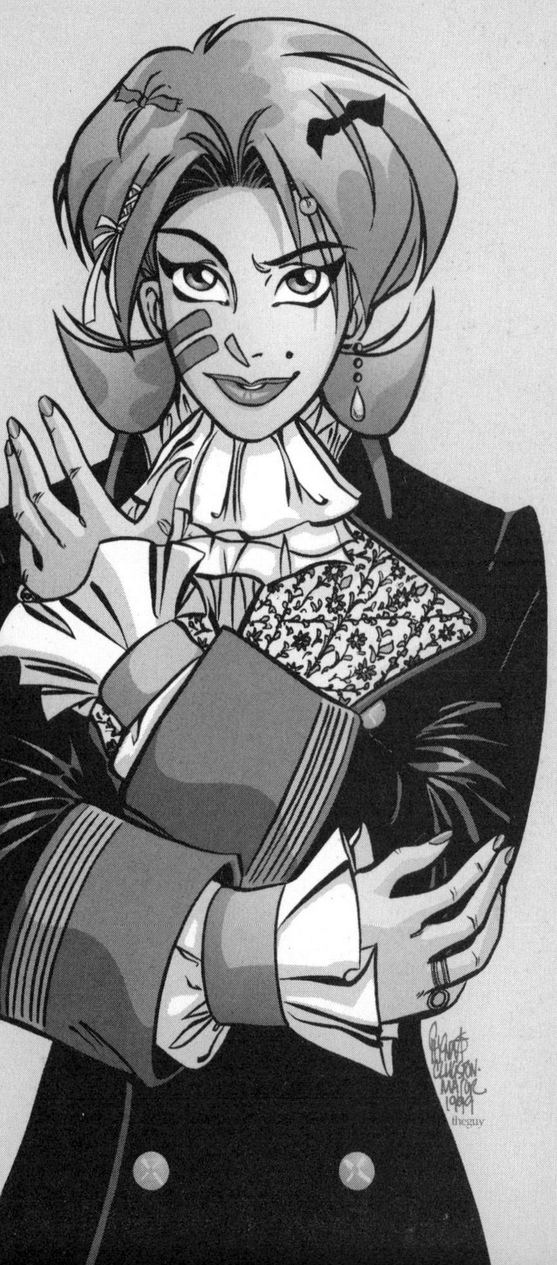
theguy

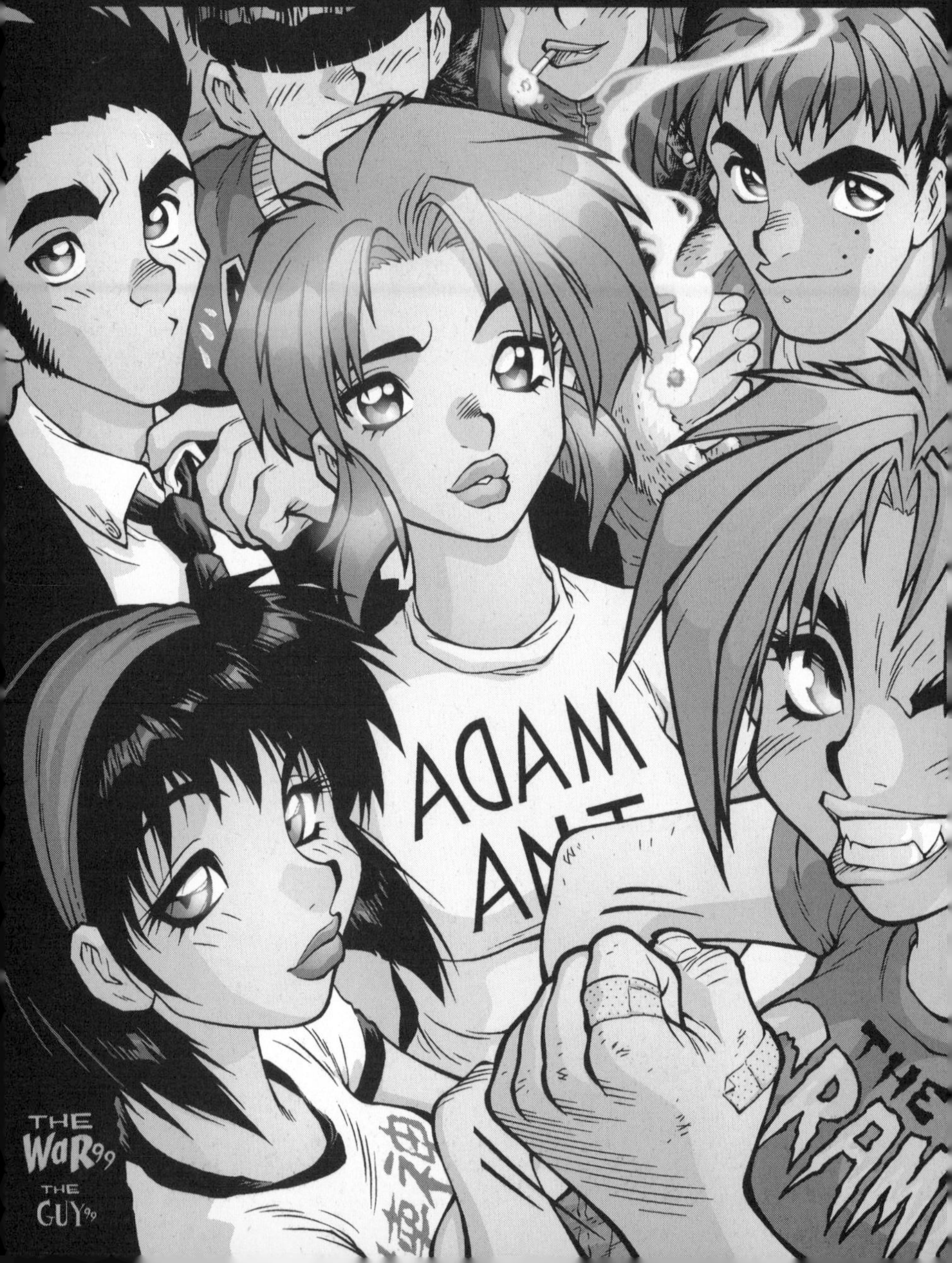
THE WaR99
THE GUY99

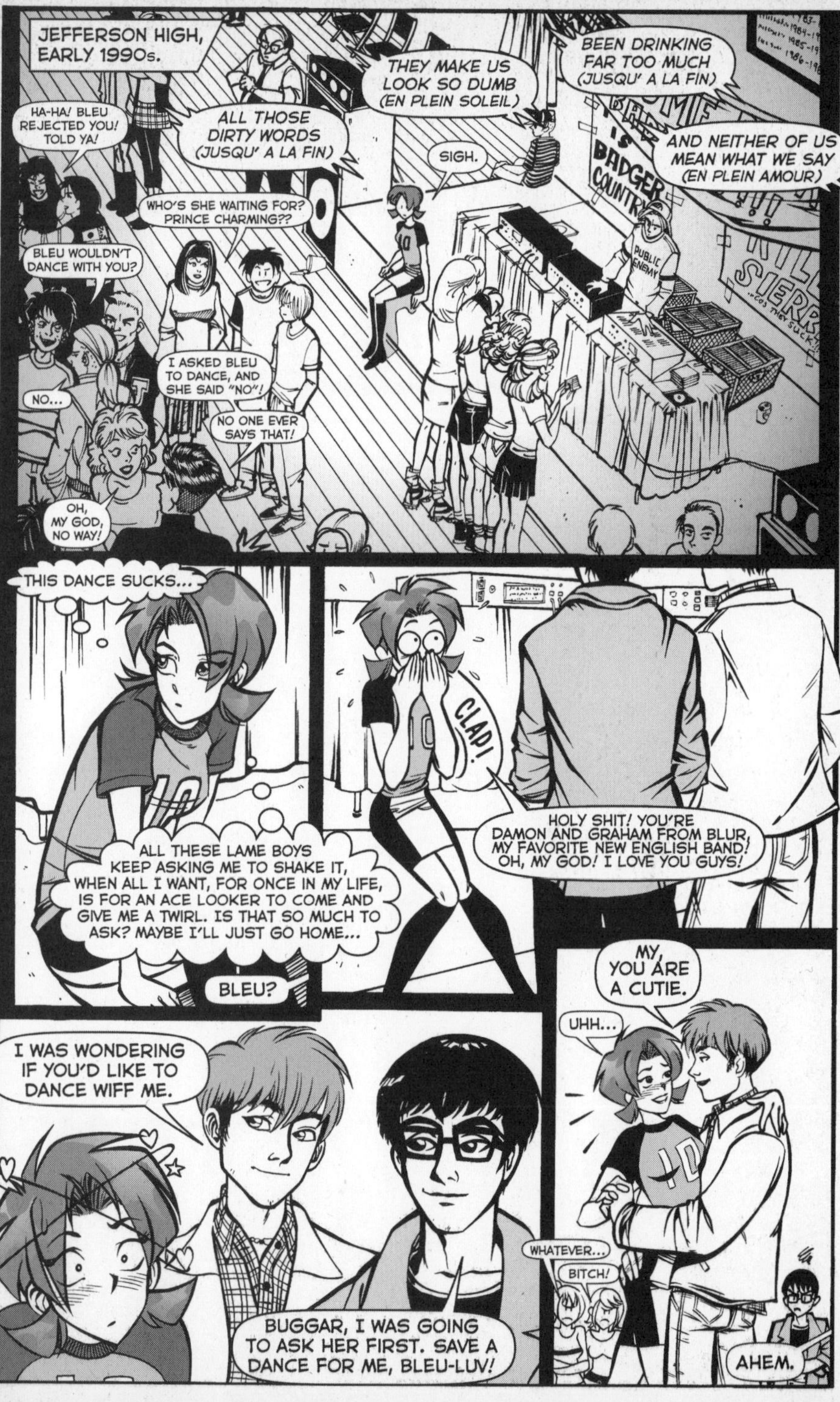
JEFFERSON HIGH, EARLY 1990s.
HA-HA! BLEU REJECTED YOU! TOLD YA!
ALL THOSE DIRTY WORDS (JUSQU' A LA FIN)
THEY MAKE US LOOK SO DUMB (EN PLEIN SOLEIL)
BEEN DRINKING FAR TOO MUCH (JUSQU' A LA FIN)
AND NEITHER OF US MEAN WHAT WE SAY (EN PLEIN AMOUR)
SIGH.
WHO'S SHE WAITING FOR? PRINCE CHARMING??
BLEU WOULDN'T DANCE WITH YOU?
BADGER COUNTRY
PUBLIC ENEMY
I ASKED BLEU TO DANCE, AND SHE SAID "NO"!
NO...
NO ONE EVER SAYS THAT!
OH, MY GOD, NO WAY!
THIS DANCE SUCKS...
ALL THESE LAME BOYS KEEP ASKING ME TO SHAKE IT, WHEN ALL I WANT, FOR ONCE IN MY LIFE, IS FOR AN ACE LOOKER TO COME AND GIVE ME A TWIRL. IS THAT SO MUCH TO ASK? MAYBE I'LL JUST GO HOME...
BLEU?
CLAP!
HOLY SHIT! YOU'RE DAMON AND GRAHAM FROM BLUR, MY FAVORITE NEW ENGLISH BAND! OH, MY GOD! I LOVE YOU GUYS!
I WAS WONDERING IF YOU'D LIKE TO DANCE WIFF ME.
BUGGAR, I WAS GOING TO ASK HER FIRST. SAVE A DANCE FOR ME, BLEU-LUV!
MY, YOU ARE A CUTIE.
UHH...
WHATEVER...
BITCH!
AHEM.

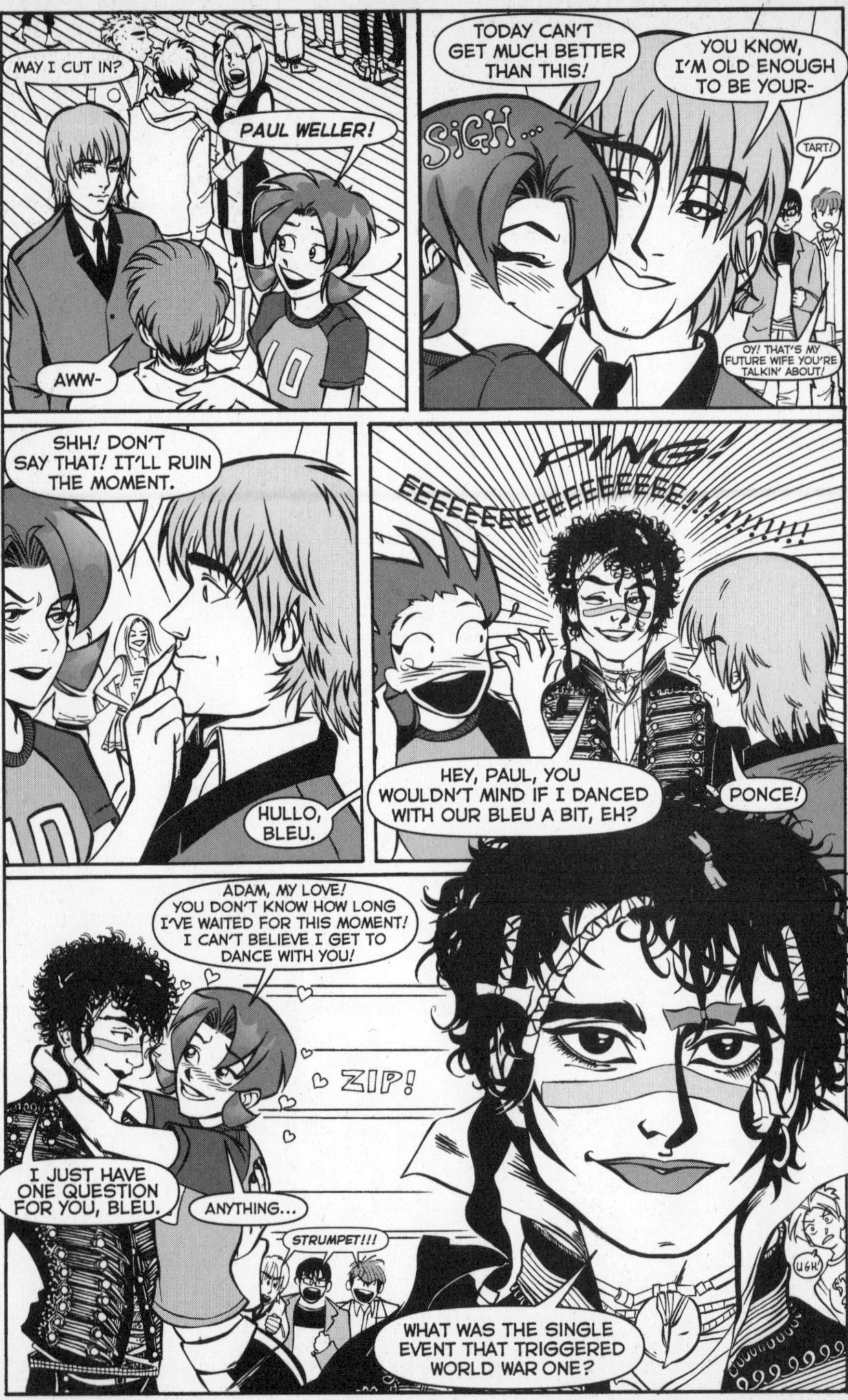
MAY I CUT IN?
PAUL WELLER!
AWW-
TODAY CAN'T GET MUCH BETTER THAN THIS!
SIGH...
YOU KNOW, I'M OLD ENOUGH TO BE YOUR-
TART!
OY! THAT'S MY FUTURE WIFE YOU'RE TALKIN' ABOUT!
SHH! DON'T SAY THAT! IT'LL RUIN THE MOMENT.
HULLO, BLEU.
PING!
EEEEEEEEEEEEEEEE!!!!!!!!!!
HEY, PAUL, YOU WOULDN'T MIND IF I DANCED WITH OUR BLEU A BIT, EH?
PONCE!
ADAM, MY LOVE! YOU DON'T KNOW HOW LONG I'VE WAITED FOR THIS MOMENT! I CAN'T BELIEVE I GET TO DANCE WITH YOU!
ZIP!
I JUST HAVE ONE QUESTION FOR YOU, BLEU.
ANYTHING...
STRUMPET!!!
UGH!
WHAT WAS THE SINGLE EVENT THAT TRIGGERED WORLD WAR ONE?

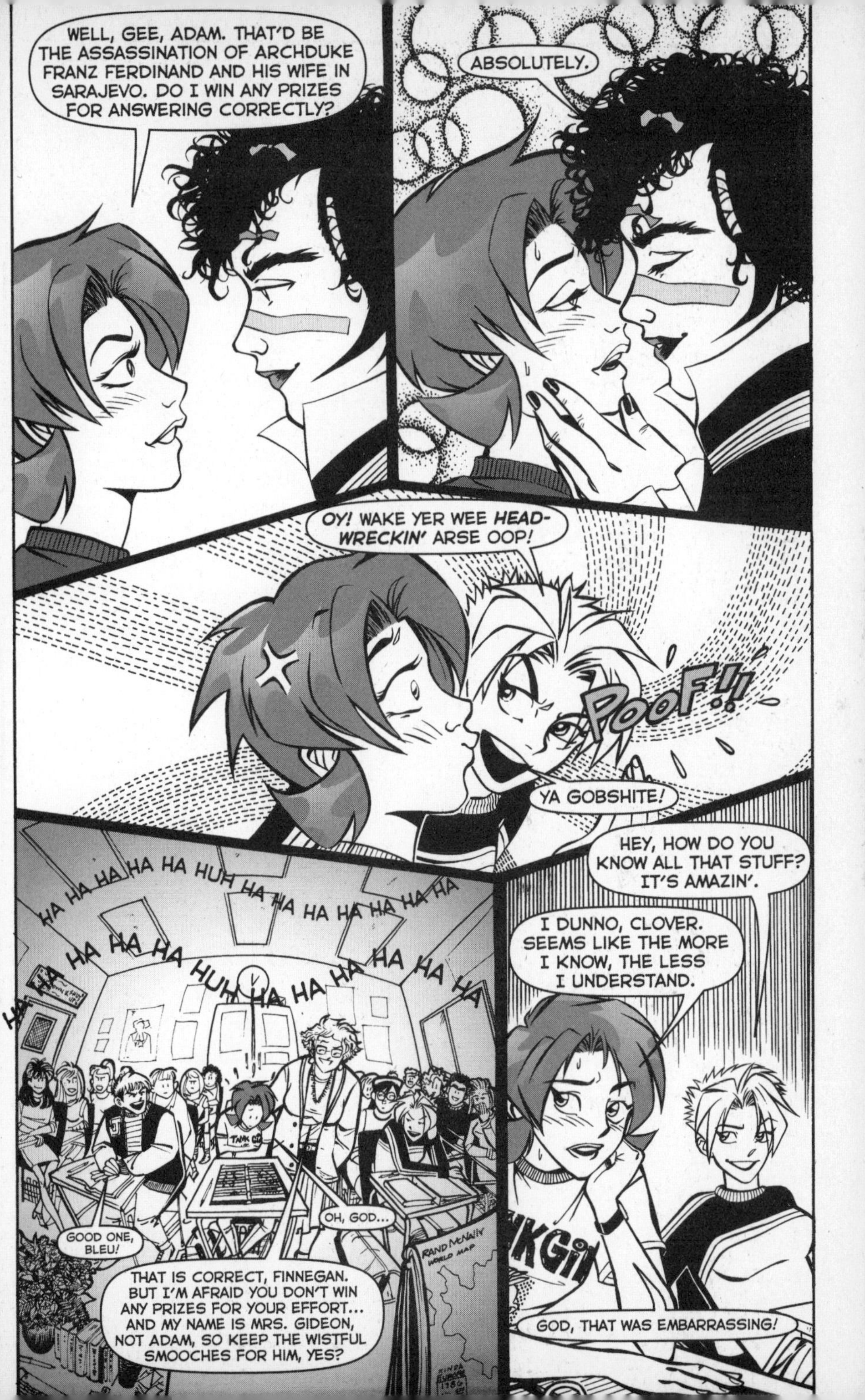
WELL, GEE, ADAM. THAT'D BE THE ASSASSINATION OF ARCHDUKE FRANZ FERDINAND AND HIS WIFE IN SARAJEVO. DO I WIN ANY PRIZES FOR ANSWERING CORRECTLY?
ABSOLUTELY.
OY! WAKE YER WEE HEAD-WRECKIN' ARSE OOP!
POOF!!
YA GOBSHITE!
HA HA HA HA HA HUH HA HA HA HA HA HA HA
HA HA HA HA HA HUH HA HA HA HA HA HA
HA HA
GOOD ONE, BLEU!
OH, GOD...
RAND McNALLY WORLD MAP
THAT IS CORRECT, FINNEGAN. BUT I'M AFRAID YOU DON'T WIN ANY PRIZES FOR YOUR EFFORT... AND MY NAME IS MRS. GIDEON, NOT ADAM, SO KEEP THE WISTFUL SMOOCHES FOR HIM, YES?
HEY, HOW DO YOU KNOW ALL THAT STUFF? IT'S AMAZIN'.
I DUNNO, CLOVER. SEEMS LIKE THE MORE I KNOW, THE LESS I UNDERSTAND.
GOD, THAT WAS EMBARRASSING!

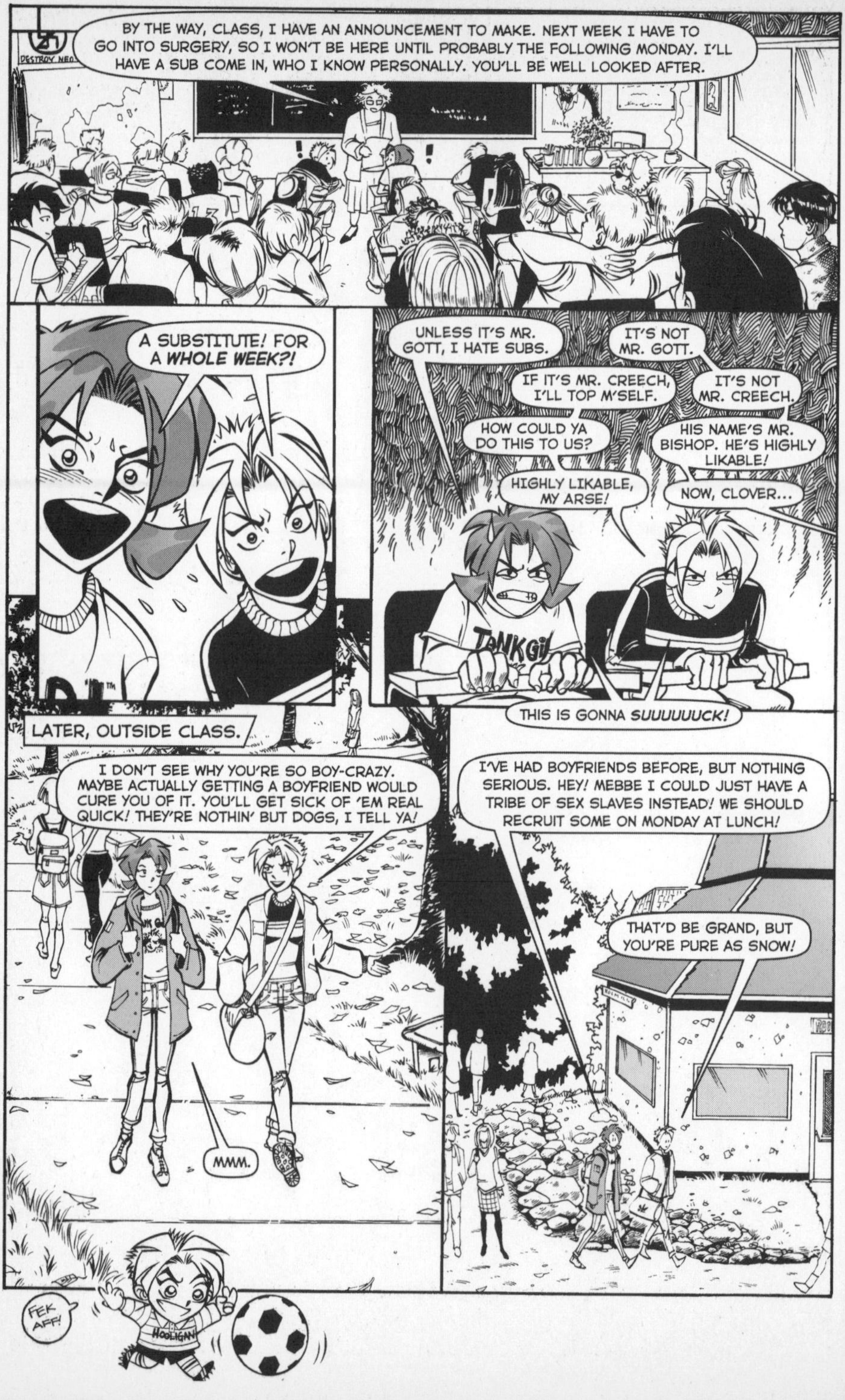

BY THE WAY, CLASS, I HAVE AN ANNOUNCEMENT TO MAKE. NEXT WEEK I HAVE TO GO INTO SURGERY, SO I WON'T BE HERE UNTIL PROBABLY THE FOLLOWING MONDAY. I'LL HAVE A SUB COME IN, WHO I KNOW PERSONALLY. YOU'LL BE WELL LOOKED AFTER.
A SUBSTITUTE! FOR A *WHOLE WEEK?!*
UNLESS IT'S MR. GOTT, I HATE SUBS.
IT'S NOT MR. GOTT.
IF IT'S MR. CREECH, I'LL TOP M'SELF.
IT'S NOT MR. CREECH.
HOW COULD YA DO THIS TO US?
HIS NAME'S MR. BISHOP. HE'S HIGHLY LIKABLE!
HIGHLY LIKABLE, MY ARSE!
NOW, CLOVER...
THIS IS GONNA *SUUUUUUCK!*
LATER, OUTSIDE CLASS.
I DON'T SEE WHY YOU'RE SO BOY-CRAZY. MAYBE ACTUALLY GETTING A BOYFRIEND WOULD CURE YOU OF IT. YOU'LL GET SICK OF 'EM REAL QUICK! THEY'RE NOTHIN' BUT DOGS, I TELL YA!
MMM.
I'VE HAD BOYFRIENDS BEFORE, BUT NOTHING SERIOUS. HEY! MEBBE I COULD JUST HAVE A TRIBE OF SEX SLAVES INSTEAD! WE SHOULD RECRUIT SOME ON MONDAY AT LUNCH!
THAT'D BE GRAND, BUT YOU'RE PURE AS SNOW!
FEK AFF!
HOOLIGAN

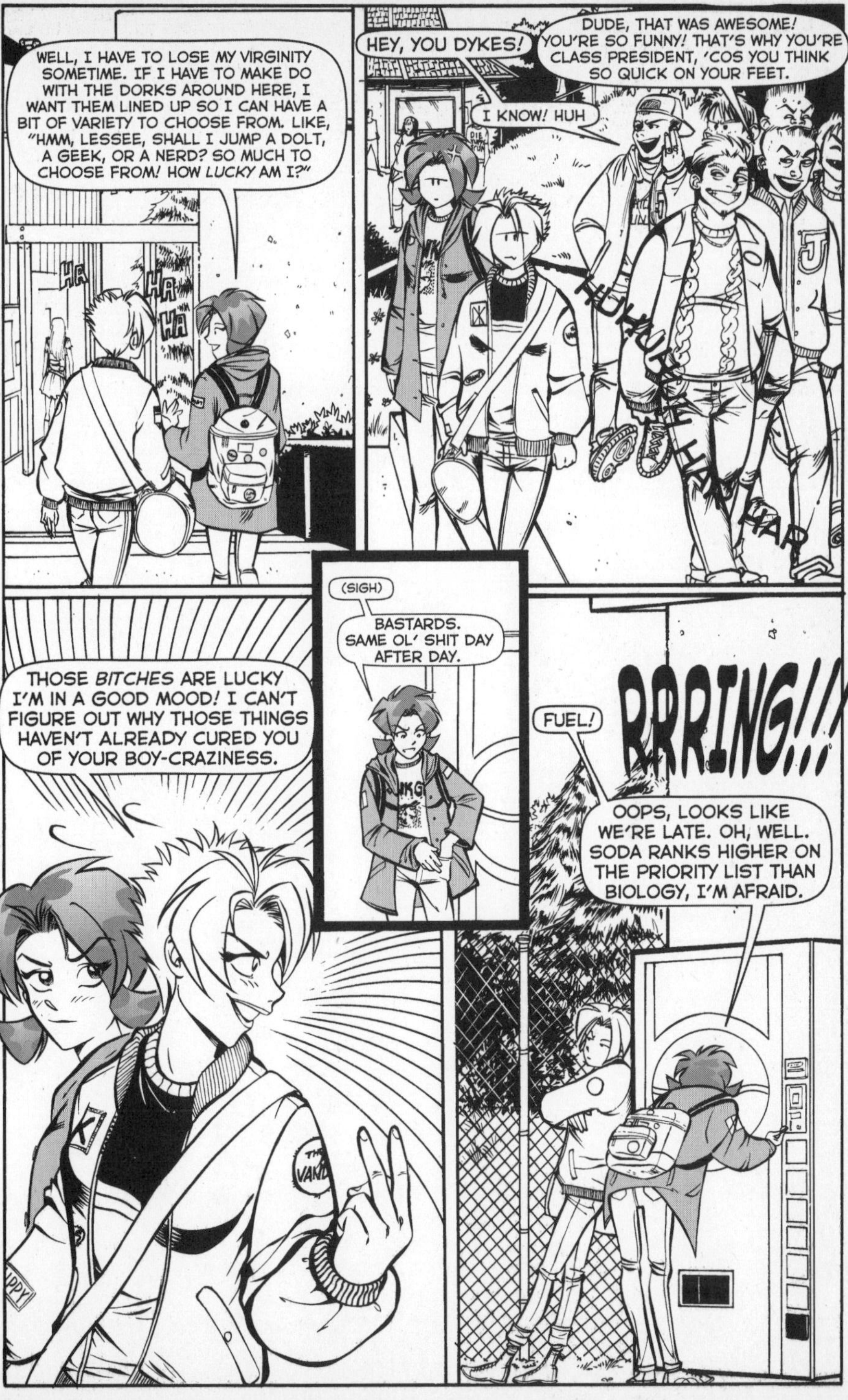

WELL, I HAVE TO LOSE MY VIRGINITY SOMETIME. IF I HAVE TO MAKE DO WITH THE DORKS AROUND HERE, I WANT THEM LINED UP SO I CAN HAVE A BIT OF VARIETY TO CHOOSE FROM. LIKE, "HMM, LESSEE, SHALL I JUMP A DOLT, A GEEK, OR A NERD? SO MUCH TO CHOOSE FROM! HOW *LUCKY* AM I?"
HA
HA
HA
HEY, YOU DYKES!
DUDE, THAT WAS AWESOME! YOU'RE SO FUNNY! THAT'S WHY YOU'RE CLASS PRESIDENT, 'COS YOU THINK SO QUICK ON YOUR FEET.
I KNOW! HUH
HUHUHUHUH HAR HAR
THOSE *BITCHES* ARE LUCKY I'M IN A GOOD MOOD! I CAN'T FIGURE OUT WHY THOSE THINGS HAVEN'T ALREADY CURED YOU OF YOUR BOY-CRAZINESS.
(SIGH)
BASTARDS. SAME OL' SHIT DAY AFTER DAY.
BRRING!!!
FUEL!
OOPS, LOOKS LIKE WE'RE LATE. OH, WELL. SODA RANKS HIGHER ON THE PRIORITY LIST THAN BIOLOGY, I'M AFRAID.

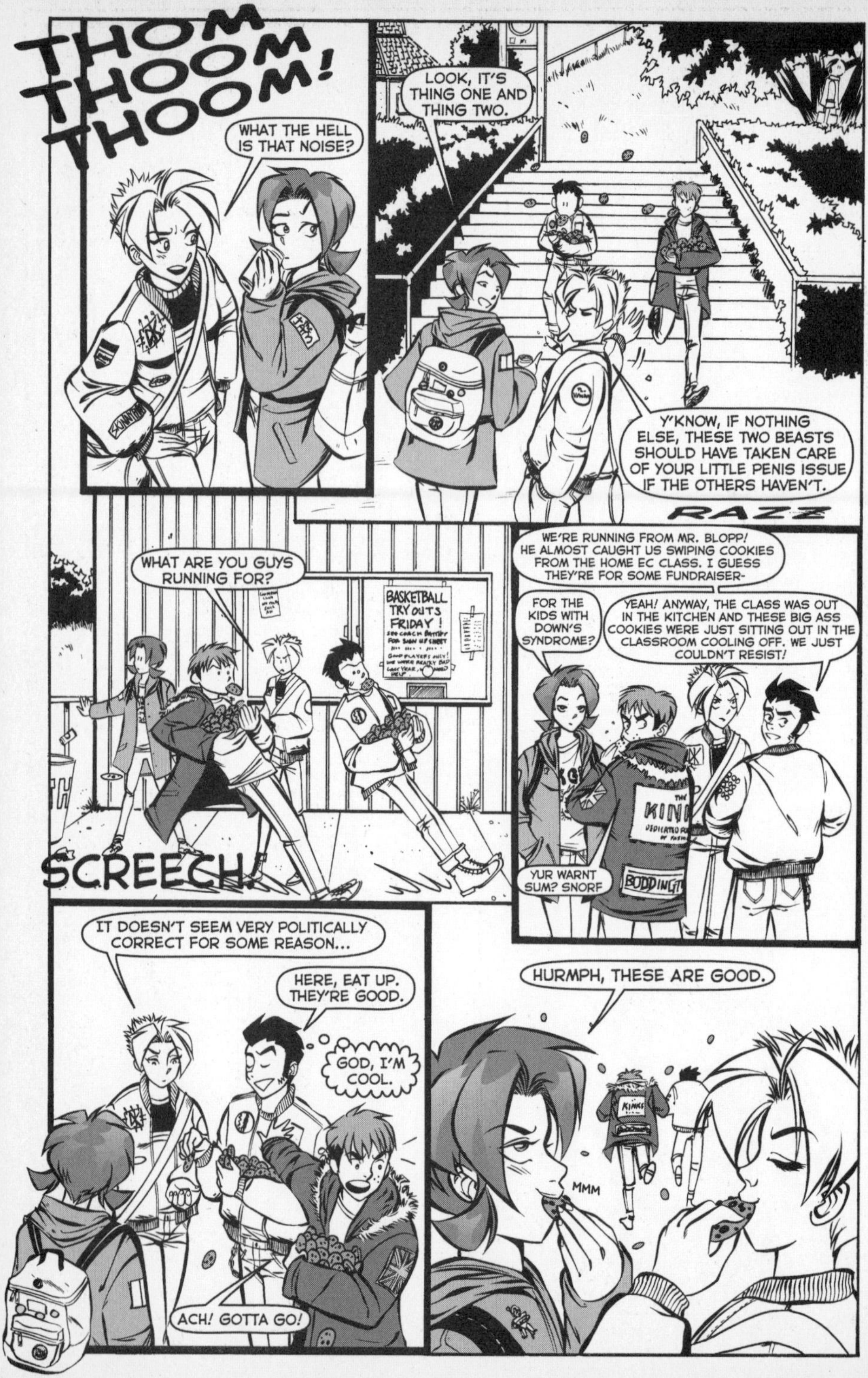
THOM THOOM THOOM!
WHAT THE HELL IS THAT NOISE?
LOOK, IT'S THING ONE AND THING TWO.
Y'KNOW, IF NOTHING ELSE, THESE TWO BEASTS SHOULD HAVE TAKEN CARE OF YOUR LITTLE PENIS ISSUE IF THE OTHERS HAVEN'T.
RAZZ
WHAT ARE YOU GUYS RUNNING FOR?
BASKETBALL TRY OUTS FRIDAY!
SCREECH!
WE'RE RUNNING FROM MR. BLOPP! HE ALMOST CAUGHT US SWIPING COOKIES FROM THE HOME EC CLASS. I GUESS THEY'RE FOR SOME FUNDRAISER-
FOR THE KIDS WITH DOWN'S SYNDROME?
YEAH! ANYWAY, THE CLASS WAS OUT IN THE KITCHEN AND THESE BIG ASS COOKIES WERE JUST SITTING OUT IN THE CLASSROOM COOLING OFF. WE JUST COULDN'T RESIST!
YUR WARNT SUM? SNORF
IT DOESN'T SEEM VERY POLITICALLY CORRECT FOR SOME REASON...
HERE, EAT UP. THEY'RE GOOD.
GOD, I'M COOL.
ACH! GOTTA GO!
HURMPH, THESE ARE GOOD.
MMM

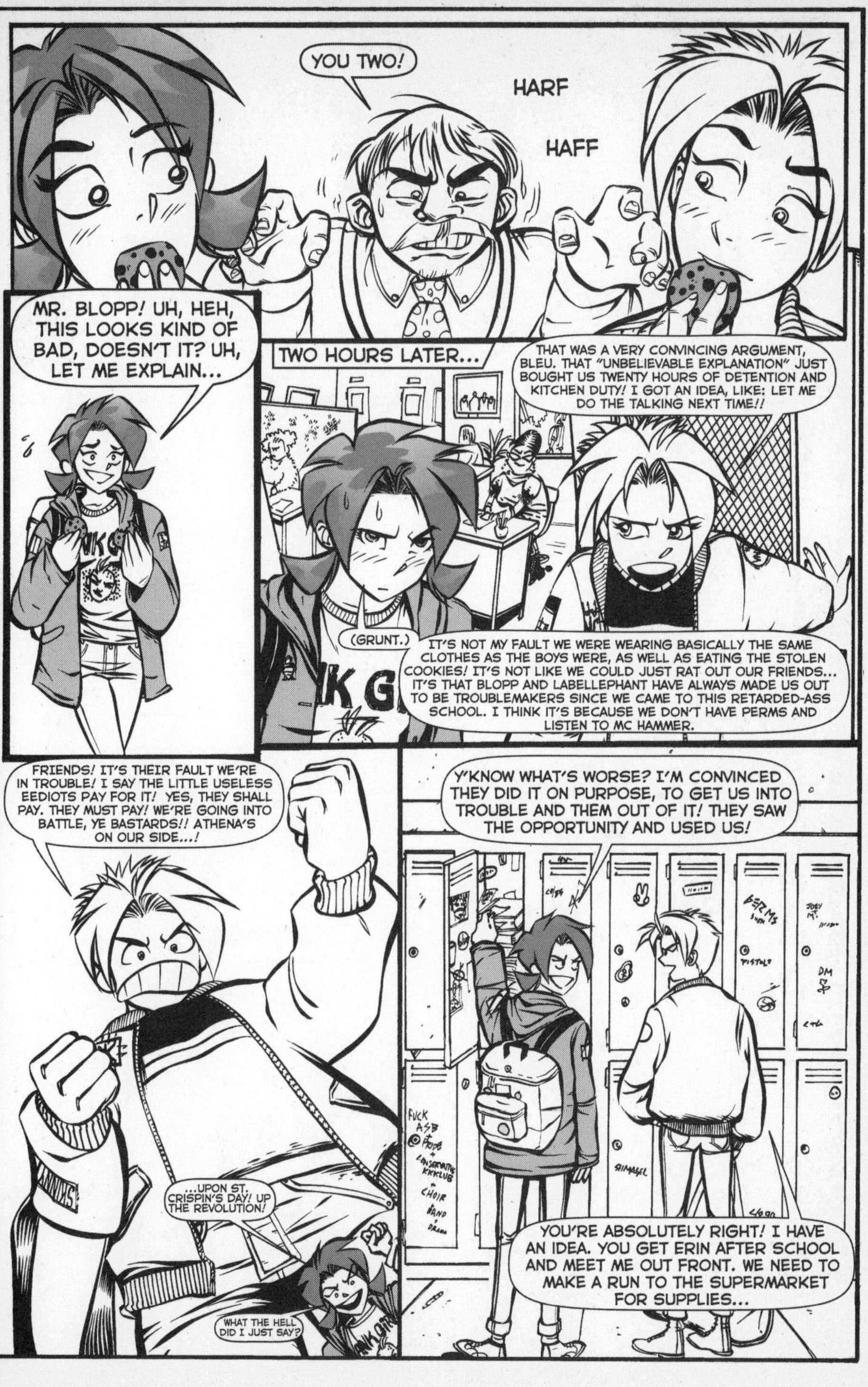
YOU TWO!
HARF
HAFF
MR. BLOPP! UH, HEH, THIS LOOKS KIND OF BAD, DOESN'T IT? UH, LET ME EXPLAIN...
TWO HOURS LATER...
THAT WAS A VERY CONVINCING ARGUMENT, BLEU. THAT "UNBELIEVABLE EXPLANATION" JUST BOUGHT US TWENTY HOURS OF DETENTION AND KITCHEN DUTY! I GOT AN IDEA, LIKE: LET ME DO THE TALKING NEXT TIME!!
(GRUNT.)
IT'S NOT MY FAULT WE WERE WEARING BASICALLY THE SAME CLOTHES AS THE BOYS WERE, AS WELL AS EATING THE STOLEN COOKIES! IT'S NOT LIKE WE COULD JUST RAT OUT OUR FRIENDS... IT'S THAT BLOPP AND LABELLEPHANT HAVE ALWAYS MADE US OUT TO BE TROUBLEMAKERS SINCE WE CAME TO THIS RETARDED-ASS SCHOOL. I THINK IT'S BECAUSE WE DON'T HAVE PERMS AND LISTEN TO MC HAMMER.
FRIENDS! IT'S THEIR FAULT WE'RE IN TROUBLE! I SAY THE LITTLE USELESS EEDIOTS PAY FOR IT! YES, THEY SHALL PAY. THEY MUST PAY! WE'RE GOING INTO BATTLE, YE BASTARDS!! ATHENA'S ON OUR SIDE...!
...UPON ST. CRISPIN'S DAY! UP THE REVOLUTION!
WHAT THE HELL DID I JUST SAY?
Y'KNOW WHAT'S WORSE? I'M CONVINCED THEY DID IT ON PURPOSE, TO GET US INTO TROUBLE AND THEM OUT OF IT! THEY SAW THE OPPORTUNITY AND USED US!
FUCK ASB
YOU'RE ABSOLUTELY RIGHT! I HAVE AN IDEA. YOU GET ERIN AFTER SCHOOL AND MEET ME OUT FRONT. WE NEED TO MAKE A RUN TO THE SUPERMARKET FOR SUPPLIES...

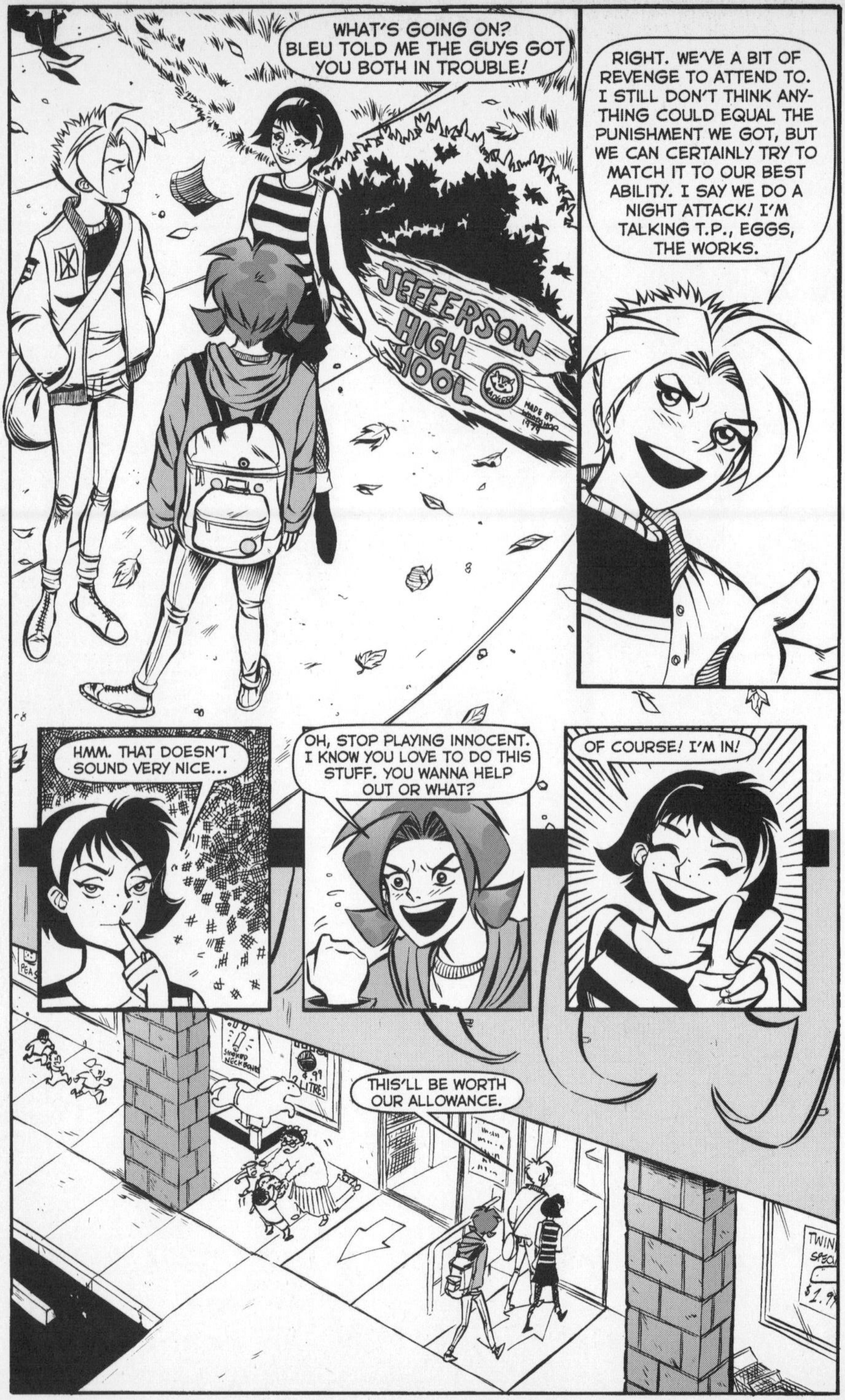
WHAT'S GOING ON? BLEU TOLD ME THE GUYS GOT YOU BOTH IN TROUBLE!
JEFFERSON
RIGHT. WE'VE A BIT OF REVENGE TO ATTEND TO. I STILL DON'T THINK ANYTHING COULD EQUAL THE PUNISHMENT WE GOT, BUT WE CAN CERTAINLY TRY TO MATCH IT TO OUR BEST ABILITY. I SAY WE DO A NIGHT ATTACK! I'M TALKING T.P., EGGS, THE WORKS.
HMM. THAT DOESN'T SOUND VERY NICE...
OH, STOP PLAYING INNOCENT. I KNOW YOU LOVE TO DO THIS STUFF. YOU WANNA HELP OUT OR WHAT?
OF COURSE! I'M IN!
THIS'LL BE WORTH OUR ALLOWANCE.

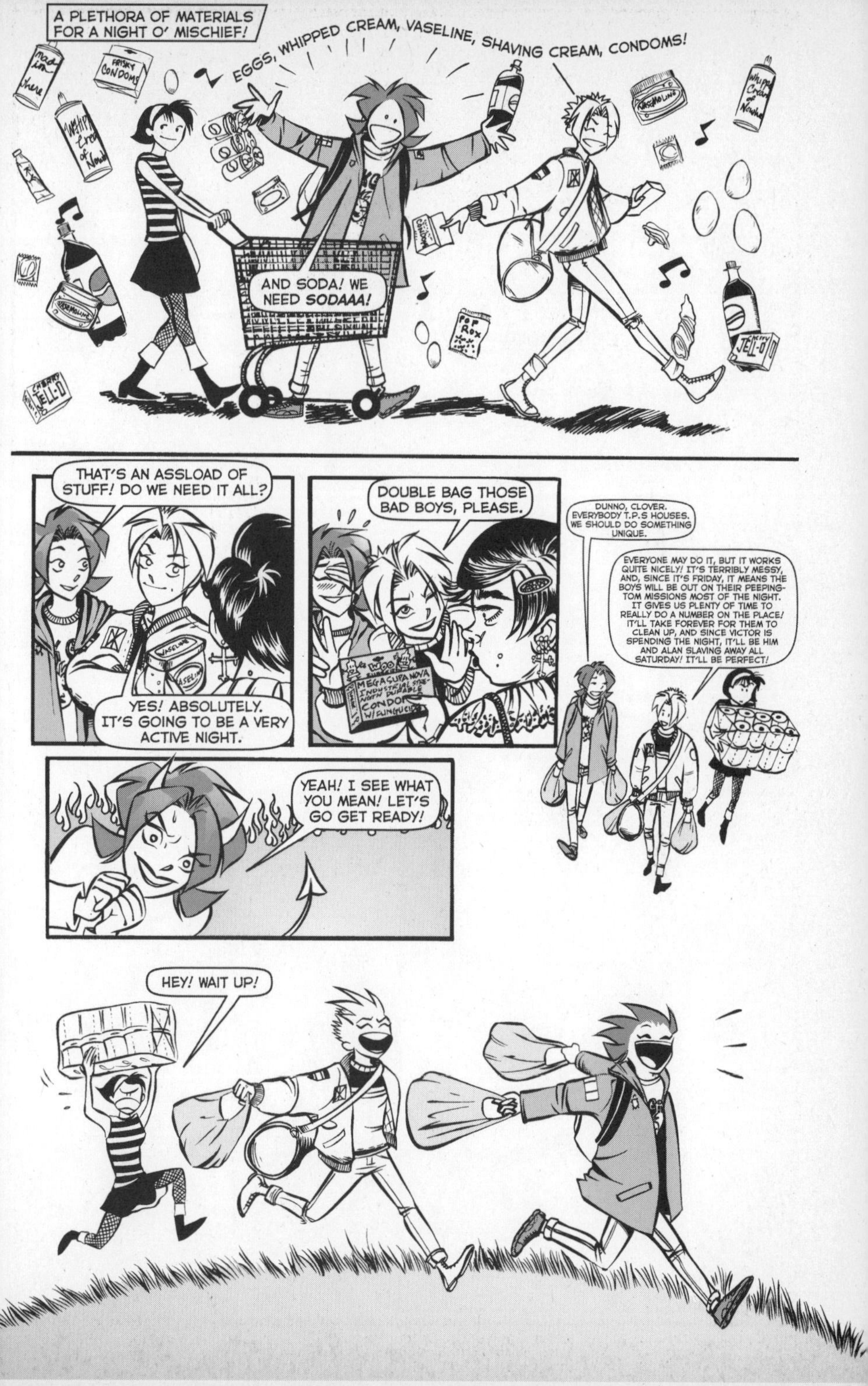
A PLETHORA OF MATERIALS FOR A NIGHT O' MISCHIEF!
EGGS, WHIPPED CREAM, VASELINE, SHAVING CREAM, CONDOMS!
AND SODA! WE NEED SODAAA!
THAT'S AN ASSLOAD OF STUFF! DO WE NEED IT ALL?
YES! ABSOLUTELY. IT'S GOING TO BE A VERY ACTIVE NIGHT.
DOUBLE BAG THOSE BAD BOYS, PLEASE.
YEAH! I SEE WHAT YOU MEAN! LET'S GO GET READY!
DUNNO, CLOVER. EVERYBODY T.P.S HOUSES. WE SHOULD DO SOMETHING UNIQUE.
EVERYONE MAY DO IT, BUT IT WORKS QUITE NICELY! IT'S TERRIBLY MESSY, AND, SINCE IT'S FRIDAY, IT MEANS THE BOYS WILL BE OUT ON THEIR PEEPING-TOM MISSIONS MOST OF THE NIGHT. IT GIVES US PLENTY OF TIME TO REALLY DO A NUMBER ON THE PLACE! IT'LL TAKE FOREVER FOR THEM TO CLEAN UP, AND SINCE VICTOR IS SPENDING THE NIGHT, IT'LL BE HIM AND ALAN SLAVING AWAY ALL SATURDAY! IT'LL BE PERFECT!
HEY! WAIT UP!

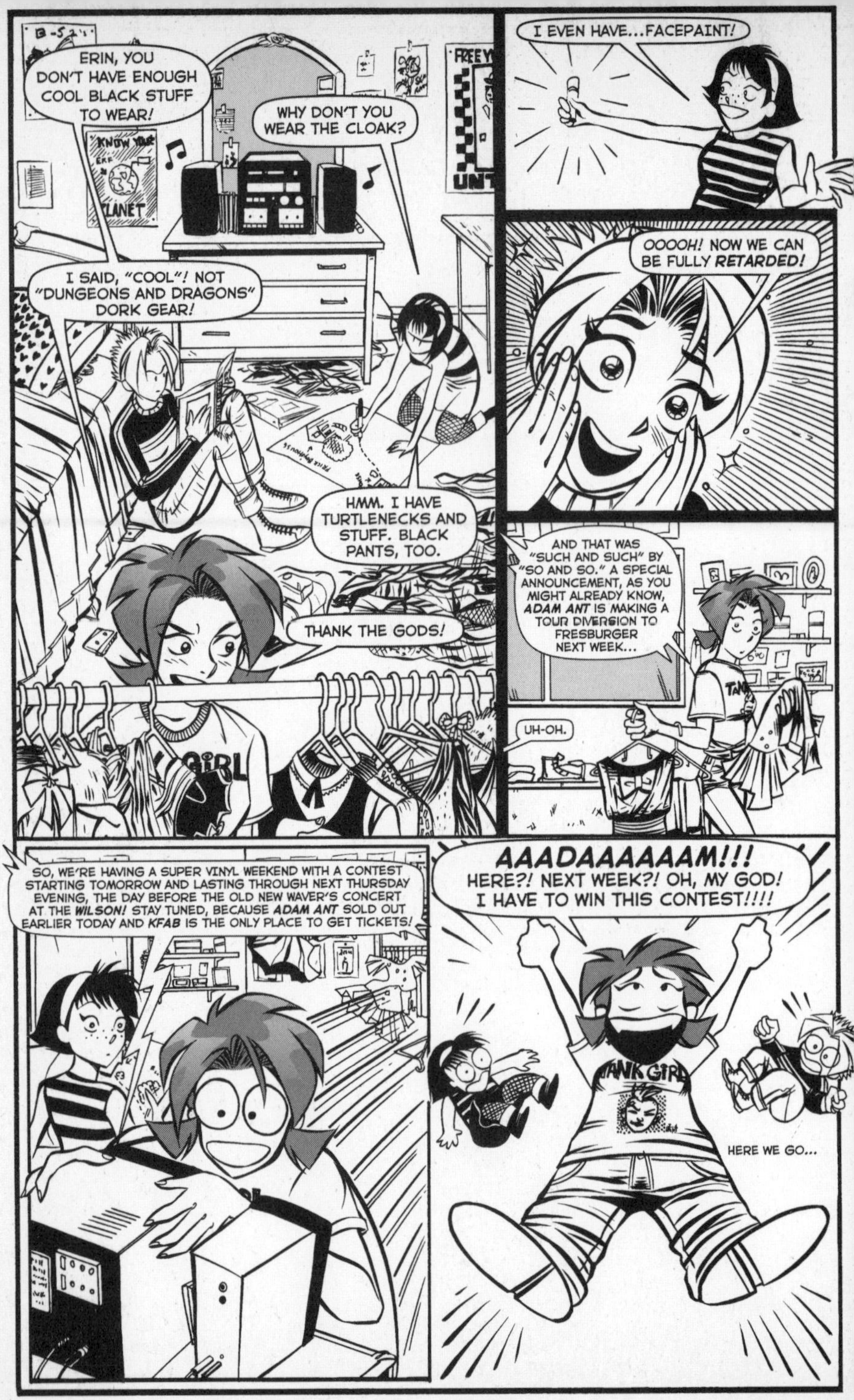
ERIN, YOU DON'T HAVE ENOUGH COOL BLACK STUFF TO WEAR!
WHY DON'T YOU WEAR THE CLOAK?
I SAID, "COOL"! NOT "DUNGEONS AND DRAGONS" DORK GEAR!
HMM. I HAVE TURTLENECKS AND STUFF. BLACK PANTS, TOO.
THANK THE GODS!
I EVEN HAVE...FACEPAINT!
OOOOH! NOW WE CAN BE FULLY RETARDED!
AND THAT WAS "SUCH AND SUCH" BY "SO AND SO." A SPECIAL ANNOUNCEMENT, AS YOU MIGHT ALREADY KNOW, ADAM ANT IS MAKING A TOUR DIVERSION TO FRESBURGER NEXT WEEK...
UH-OH.
SO, WE'RE HAVING A SUPER VINYL WEEKEND WITH A CONTEST STARTING TOMORROW AND LASTING THROUGH NEXT THURSDAY EVENING, THE DAY BEFORE THE OLD NEW WAVER'S CONCERT AT THE WILSON! STAY TUNED, BECAUSE ADAM ANT SOLD OUT EARLIER TODAY AND KFAB IS THE ONLY PLACE TO GET TICKETS!
AAADAAAAAAM!!! HERE?! NEXT WEEK?! OH, MY GOD! I HAVE TO WIN THIS CONTEST!!!!
HERE WE GO...

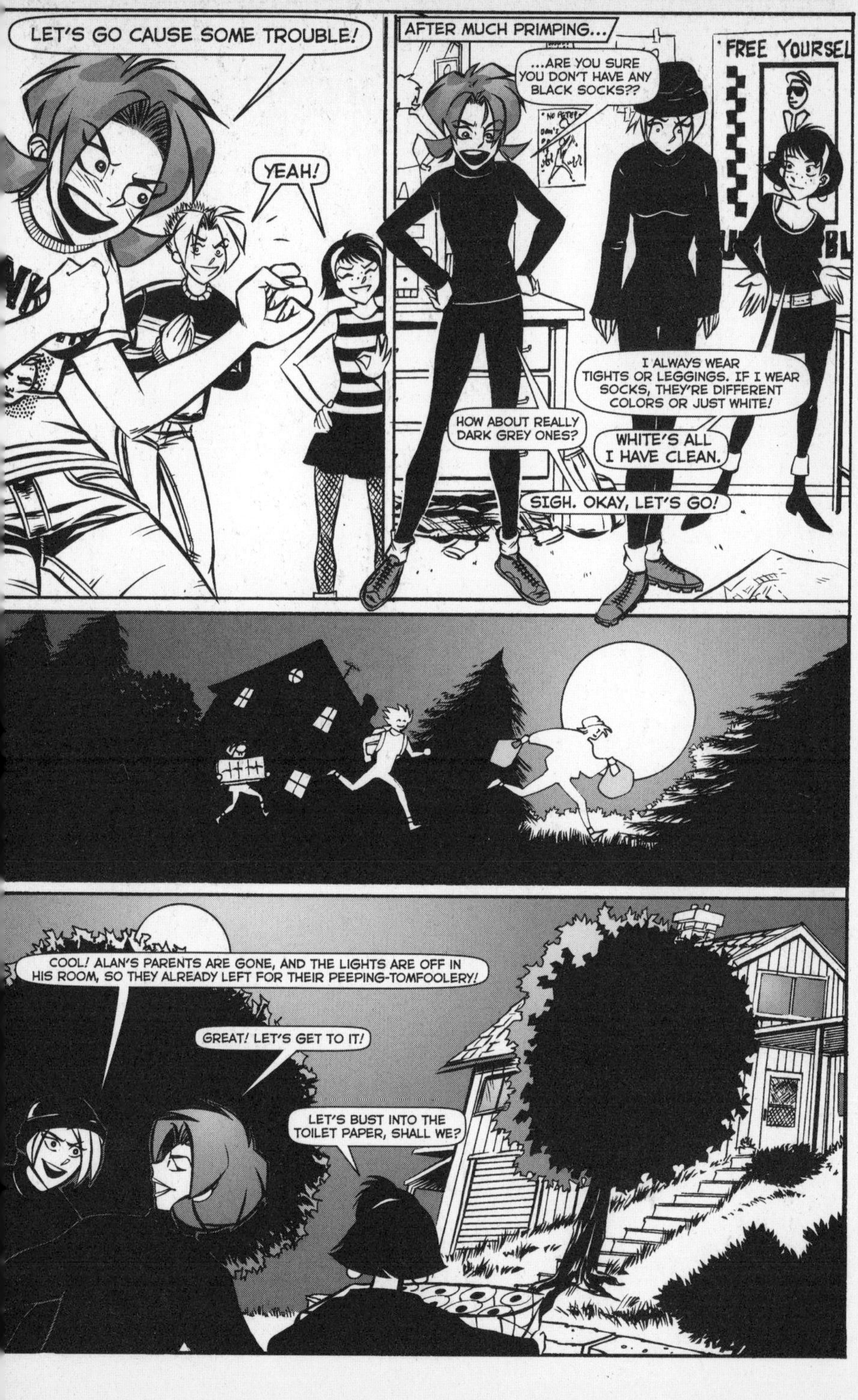
LET'S GO CAUSE SOME TROUBLE!
YEAH!
AFTER MUCH PRIMPING...
...ARE YOU SURE YOU DON'T HAVE ANY BLACK SOCKS??
FREE YOURSEL
HOW ABOUT REALLY DARK GREY ONES?
I ALWAYS WEAR TIGHTS OR LEGGINGS. IF I WEAR SOCKS, THEY'RE DIFFERENT COLORS OR JUST WHITE!
WHITE'S ALL I HAVE CLEAN.
SIGH. OKAY, LET'S GO!
COOL! ALAN'S PARENTS ARE GONE, AND THE LIGHTS ARE OFF IN HIS ROOM, SO THEY ALREADY LEFT FOR THEIR PEEPING-TOMFOOLERY!
GREAT! LET'S GET TO IT!
LET'S BUST INTO THE TOILET PAPER, SHALL WE?

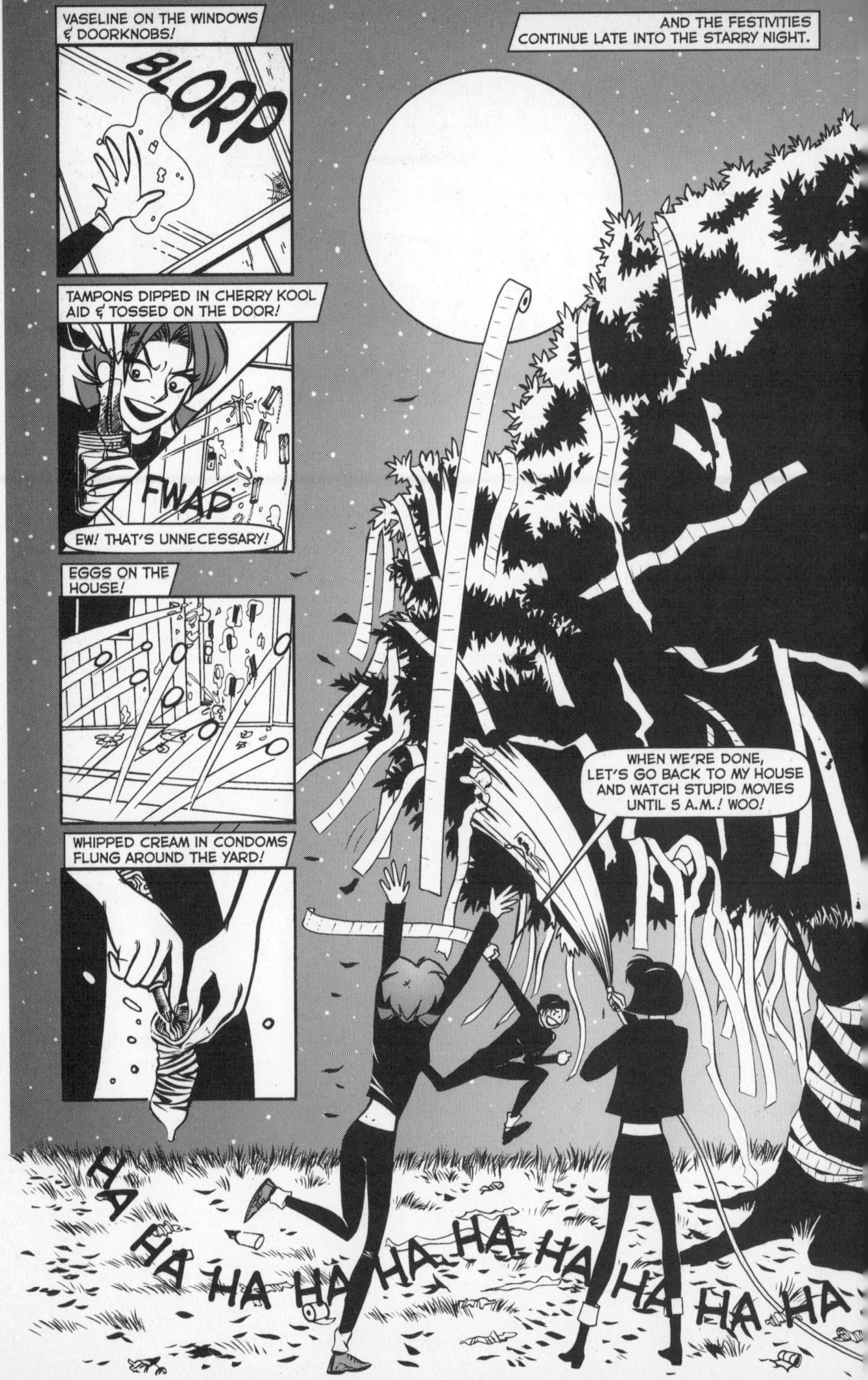
VASELINE ON THE WINDOWS & DOORKNOBS!
BLORP
TAMPONS DIPPED IN CHERRY KOOL AID & TOSSED ON THE DOOR!
FWAP
EW! THAT'S UNNECESSARY!
EGGS ON THE HOUSE!
WHIPPED CREAM IN CONDOMS FLUNG AROUND THE YARD!
AND THE FESTIVITIES CONTINUE LATE INTO THE STARRY NIGHT.
WHEN WE'RE DONE, LET'S GO BACK TO MY HOUSE AND WATCH STUPID MOVIES UNTIL 5 A.M.! WOO!
HA HA HA HA HA HA HA HA HA HA

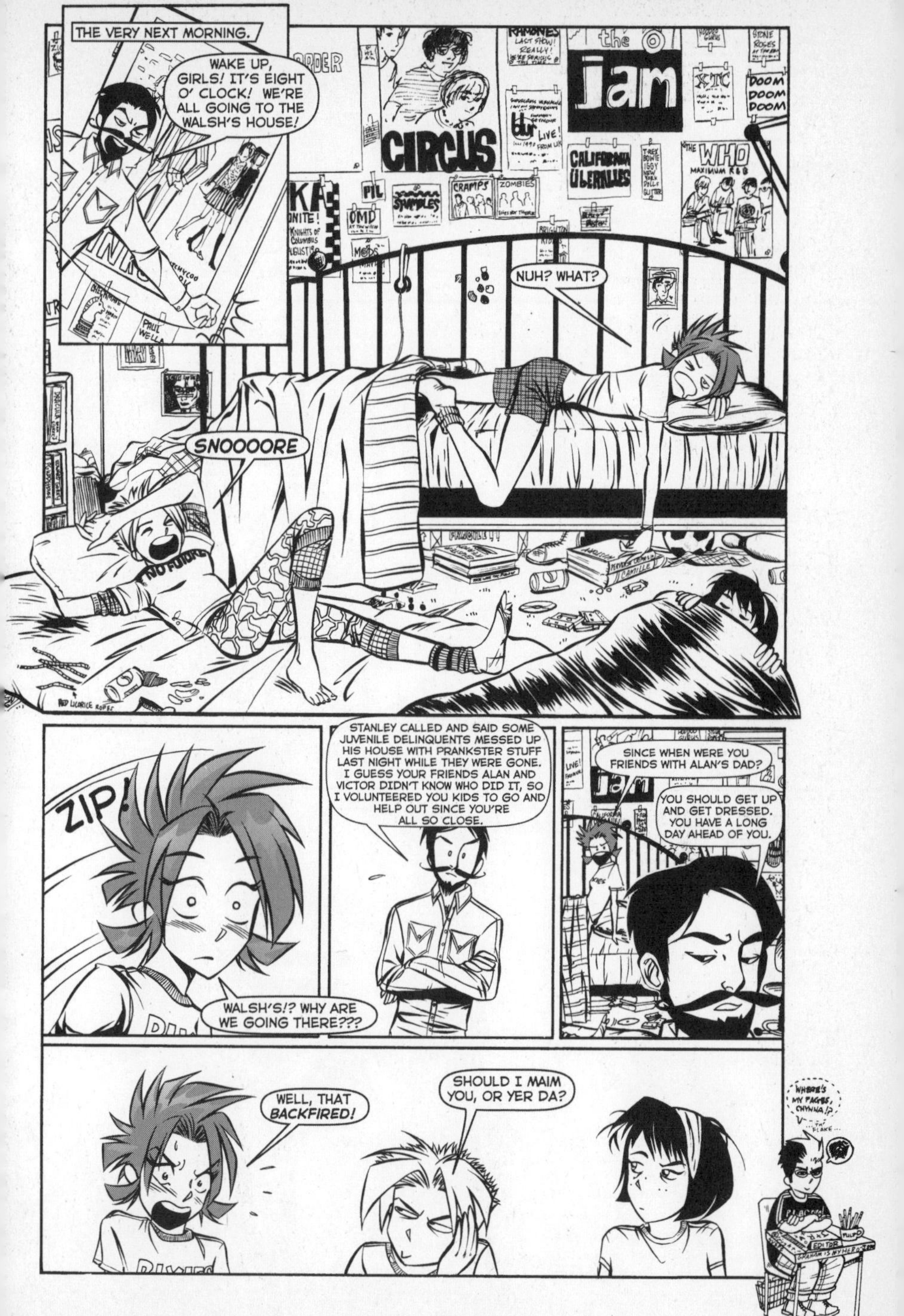
THE VERY NEXT MORNING.
WAKE UP, GIRLS! IT'S EIGHT O' CLOCK! WE'RE ALL GOING TO THE WALSH'S HOUSE!
NUH? WHAT?
SNOOOORE
ZIP!
WALSH'S!? WHY ARE WE GOING THERE???
STANLEY CALLED AND SAID SOME JUVENILE DELINQUENTS MESSED UP HIS HOUSE WITH PRANKSTER STUFF LAST NIGHT WHILE THEY WERE GONE. I GUESS YOUR FRIENDS ALAN AND VICTOR DIDN'T KNOW WHO DID IT, SO I VOLUNTEERED YOU KIDS TO GO AND HELP OUT SINCE YOU'RE ALL SO CLOSE.
SINCE WHEN WERE YOU FRIENDS WITH ALAN'S DAD?
YOU SHOULD GET UP AND GET DRESSED. YOU HAVE A LONG DAY AHEAD OF YOU.
WELL, THAT *BACKFIRED!*
SHOULD I MAIM YOU, OR YER DA?
WHERE'S MY PAGES, CHYNNA!?
...TH' FLAKE...

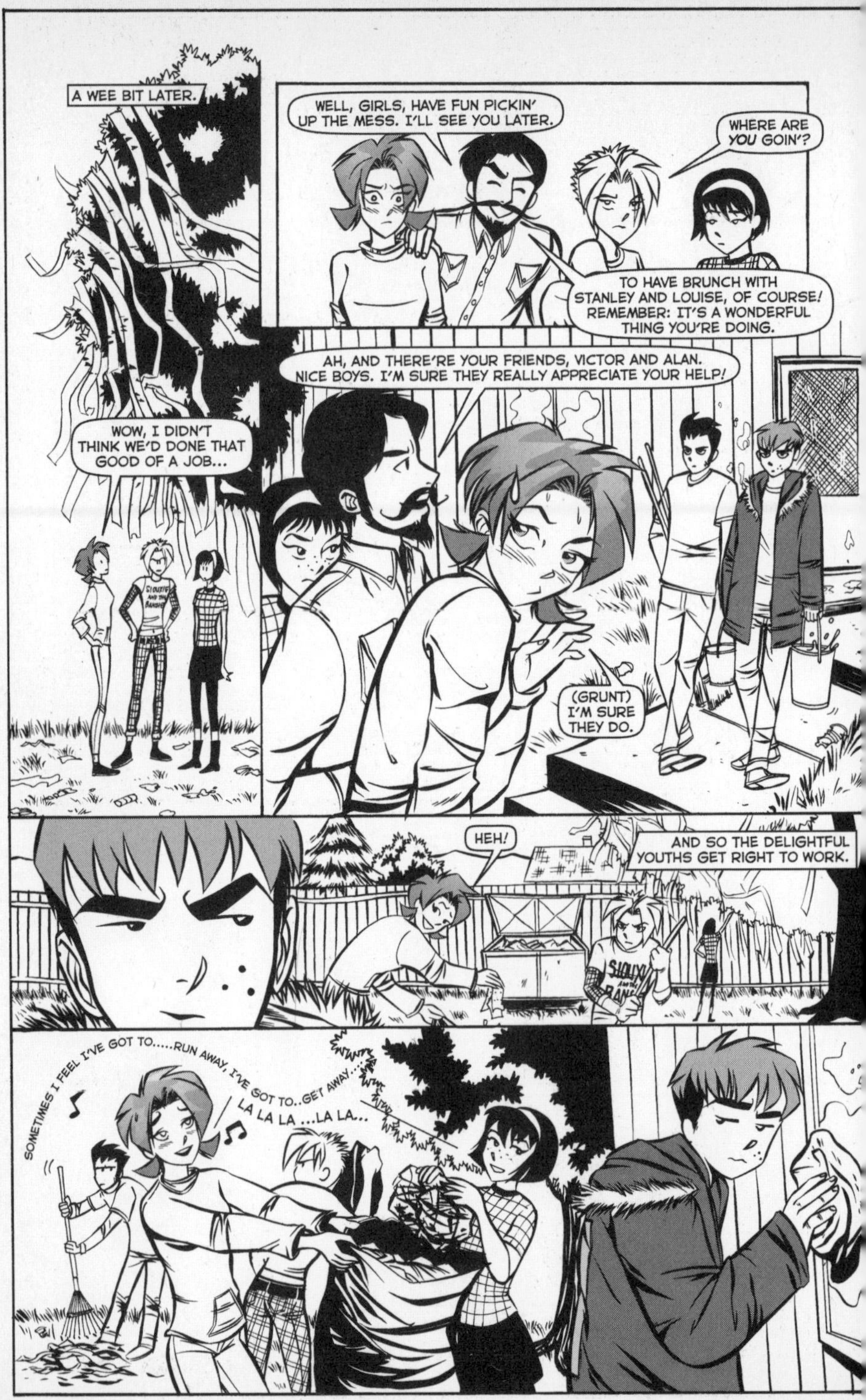
A WEE BIT LATER.
WELL, GIRLS, HAVE FUN PICKIN' UP THE MESS. I'LL SEE YOU LATER.
WHERE ARE YOU GOIN'?
TO HAVE BRUNCH WITH STANLEY AND LOUISE, OF COURSE! REMEMBER: IT'S A WONDERFUL THING YOU'RE DOING.
WOW, I DIDN'T THINK WE'D DONE THAT GOOD OF A JOB...
AH, AND THERE'RE YOUR FRIENDS, VICTOR AND ALAN. NICE BOYS. I'M SURE THEY REALLY APPRECIATE YOUR HELP!
(GRUNT) I'M SURE THEY DO.
HEH!
AND SO THE DELIGHTFUL YOUTHS GET RIGHT TO WORK.
SOMETIMES I FEEL I'VE GOT TO.....RUN AWAY, I'VE GOT TO..GET AWAY...
LA LA LA ...LA LA...

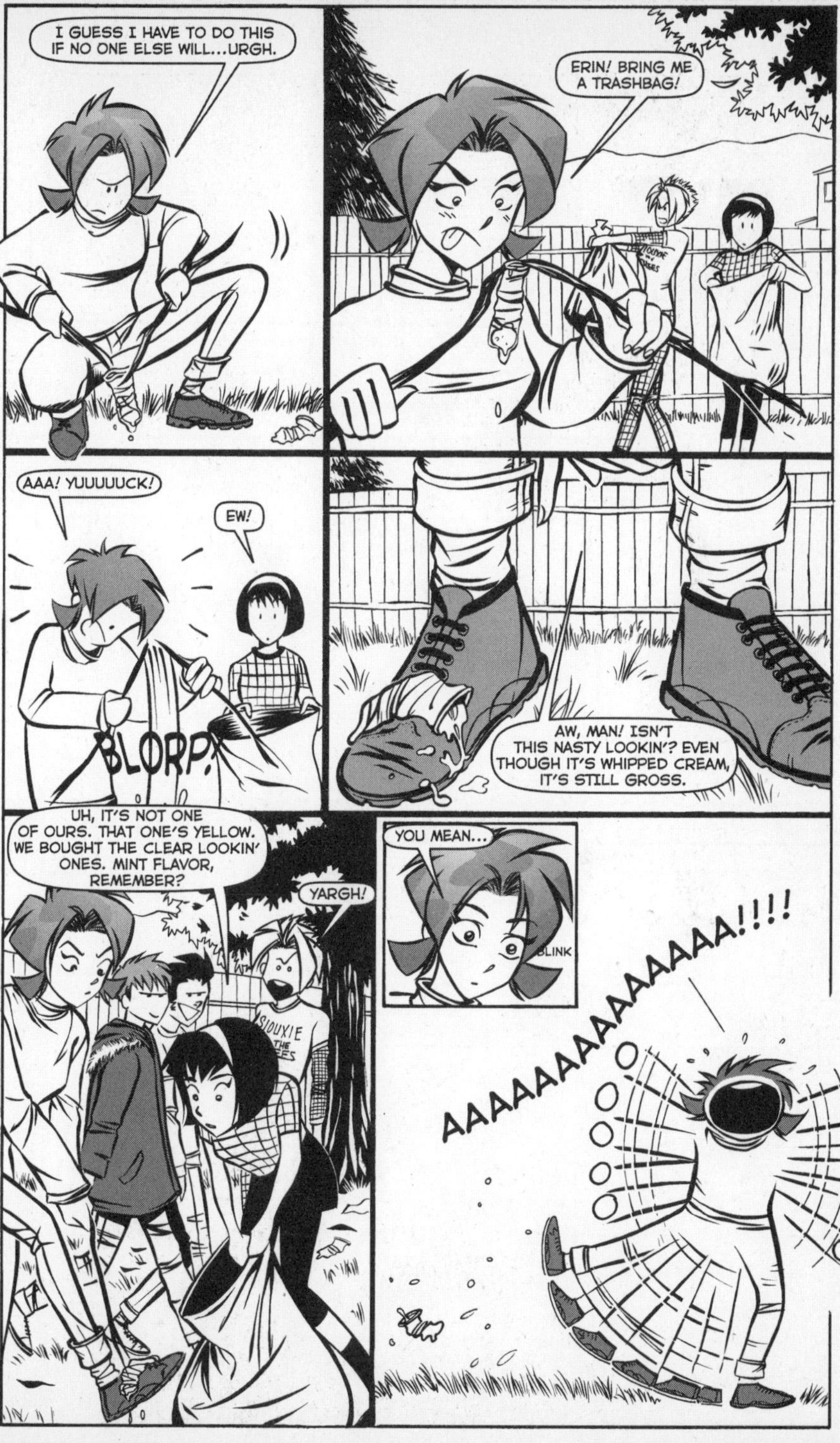
I GUESS I HAVE TO DO THIS IF NO ONE ELSE WILL...URGH.
ERIN! BRING ME A TRASHBAG!
AAA! YUUUUUCK!
EW!
BLORP!
AW, MAN! ISN'T THIS NASTY LOOKIN'? EVEN THOUGH IT'S WHIPPED CREAM, IT'S STILL GROSS.
UH, IT'S NOT ONE OF OURS. THAT ONE'S YELLOW. WE BOUGHT THE CLEAR LOOKIN' ONES. MINT FLAVOR, REMEMBER?
YARGH!
SIOUXIE THE
YOU MEAN...
BLINK
AAAAAAAAAAAAAAAAAA!!!!

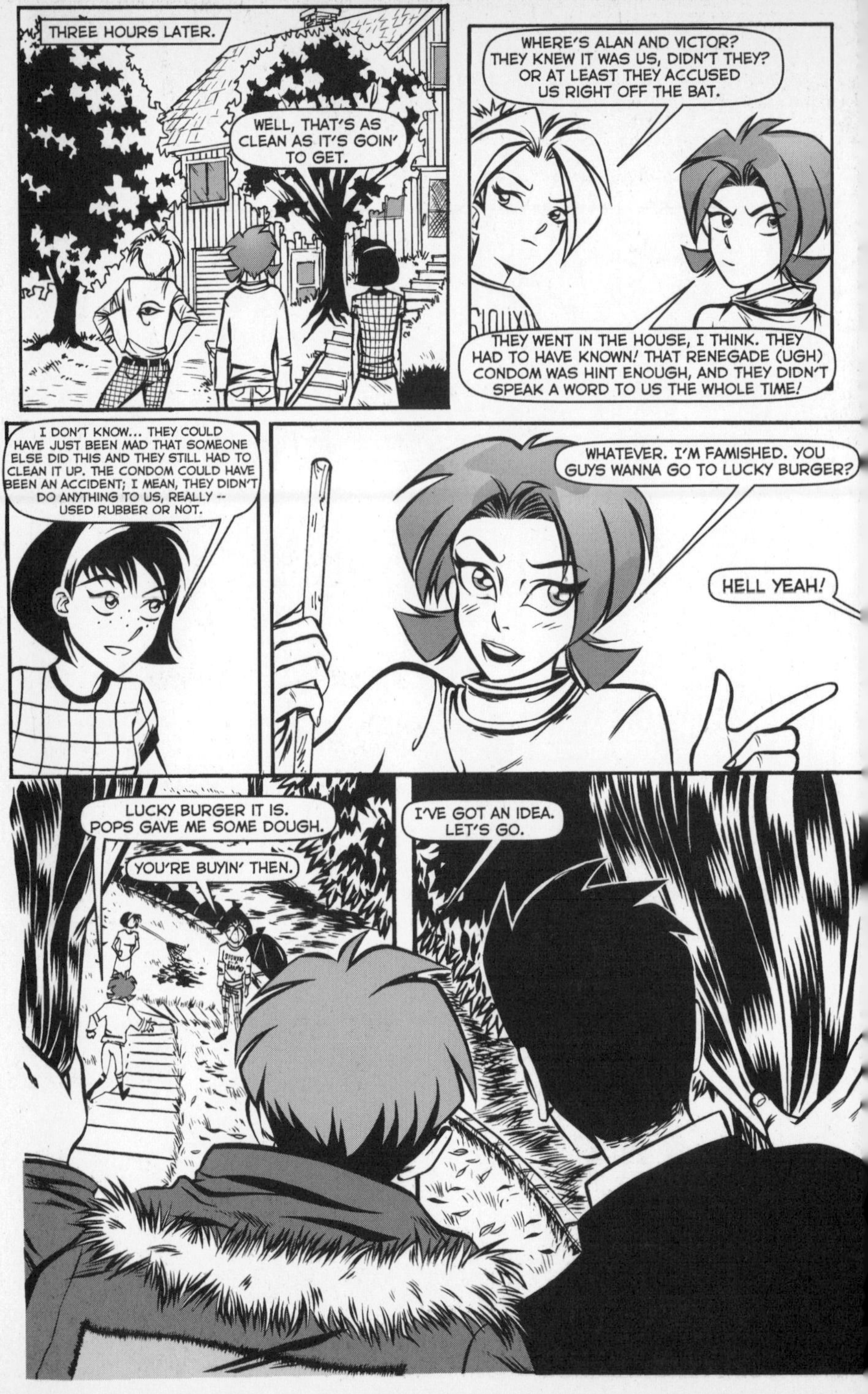
THREE HOURS LATER.
WELL, THAT'S AS CLEAN AS IT'S GOIN' TO GET.
WHERE'S ALAN AND VICTOR? THEY KNEW IT WAS US, DIDN'T THEY? OR AT LEAST THEY ACCUSED US RIGHT OFF THE BAT.
THEY WENT IN THE HOUSE, I THINK. THEY HAD TO HAVE KNOWN! THAT RENEGADE (UGH) CONDOM WAS HINT ENOUGH, AND THEY DIDN'T SPEAK A WORD TO US THE WHOLE TIME!
I DON'T KNOW... THEY COULD HAVE JUST BEEN MAD THAT SOMEONE ELSE DID THIS AND THEY STILL HAD TO CLEAN IT UP. THE CONDOM COULD HAVE BEEN AN ACCIDENT; I MEAN, THEY DIDN'T DO ANYTHING TO US, REALLY -- USED RUBBER OR NOT.
WHATEVER. I'M FAMISHED. YOU GUYS WANNA GO TO LUCKY BURGER?
HELL YEAH!
LUCKY BURGER IT IS. POPS GAVE ME SOME DOUGH.
YOU'RE BUYIN' THEN.
I'VE GOT AN IDEA. LET'S GO.

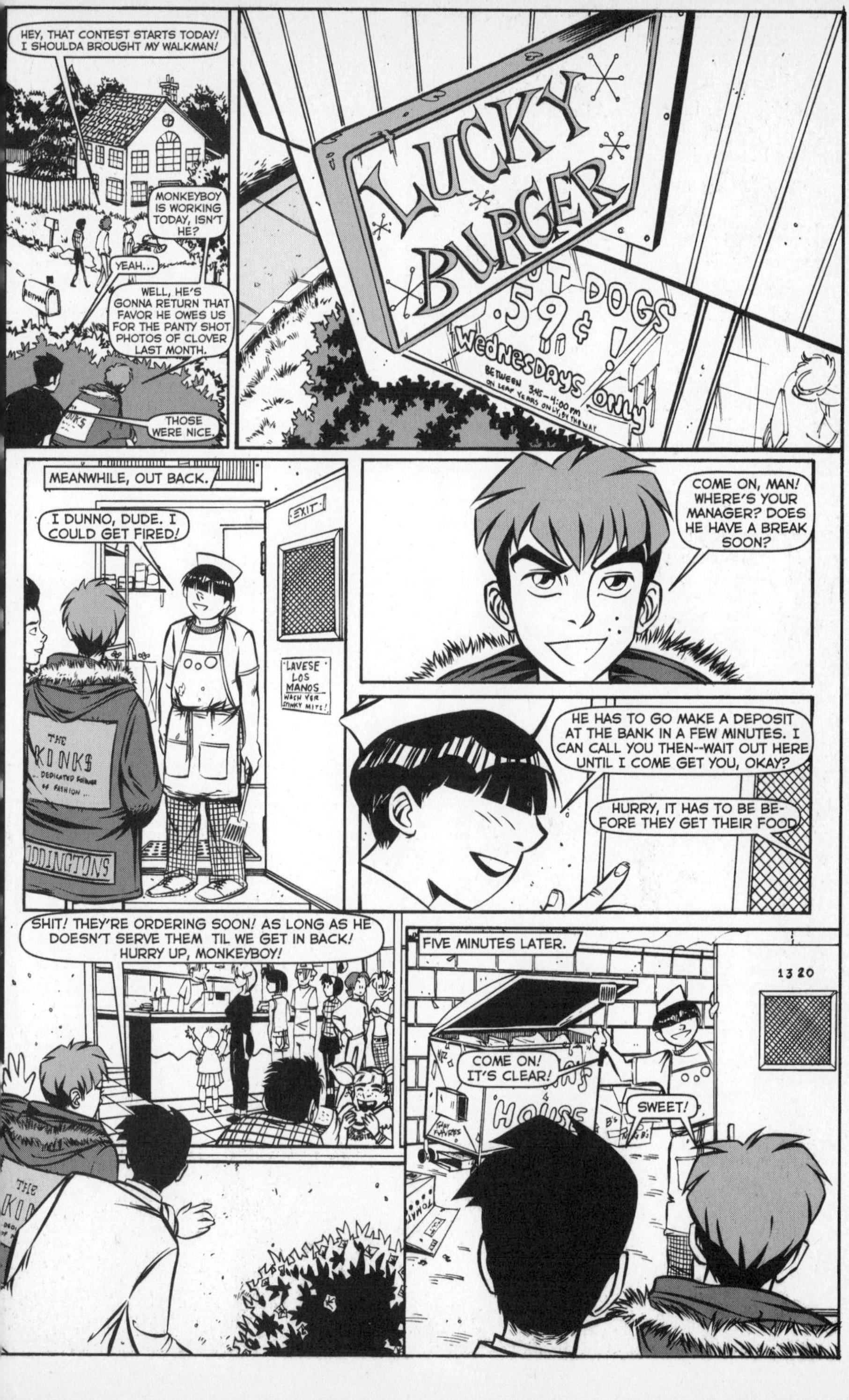
HEY, THAT CONTEST STARTS TODAY! I SHOULDA BROUGHT MY WALKMAN!
MONKEYBOY IS WORKING TODAY, ISN'T HE?
YEAH...
WELL, HE'S GONNA RETURN THAT FAVOR HE OWES US FOR THE PANTY SHOT PHOTOS OF CLOVER LAST MONTH.
THOSE WERE NICE.
LUCKY BURGER
HOT DOGS .59¢! WEDNESDAYS ONLY
BETWEEN 3:45–4:00 PM ON LEAP YEARS ONLY, BY THE WAY
MEANWHILE, OUT BACK.
I DUNNO, DUDE. I COULD GET FIRED!
EXIT
LAVESE LOS MANOS
WASH YER STINKY MITS!
THE KONKS
COME ON, MAN! WHERE'S YOUR MANAGER? DOES HE HAVE A BREAK SOON?
HE HAS TO GO MAKE A DEPOSIT AT THE BANK IN A FEW MINUTES. I CAN CALL YOU THEN--WAIT OUT HERE UNTIL I COME GET YOU, OKAY?
HURRY, IT HAS TO BE BEFORE THEY GET THEIR FOOD.
SHIT! THEY'RE ORDERING SOON! AS LONG AS HE DOESN'T SERVE THEM TIL WE GET IN BACK! HURRY UP, MONKEYBOY!
FIVE MINUTES LATER.
1320
COME ON! IT'S CLEAR!
SWEET!

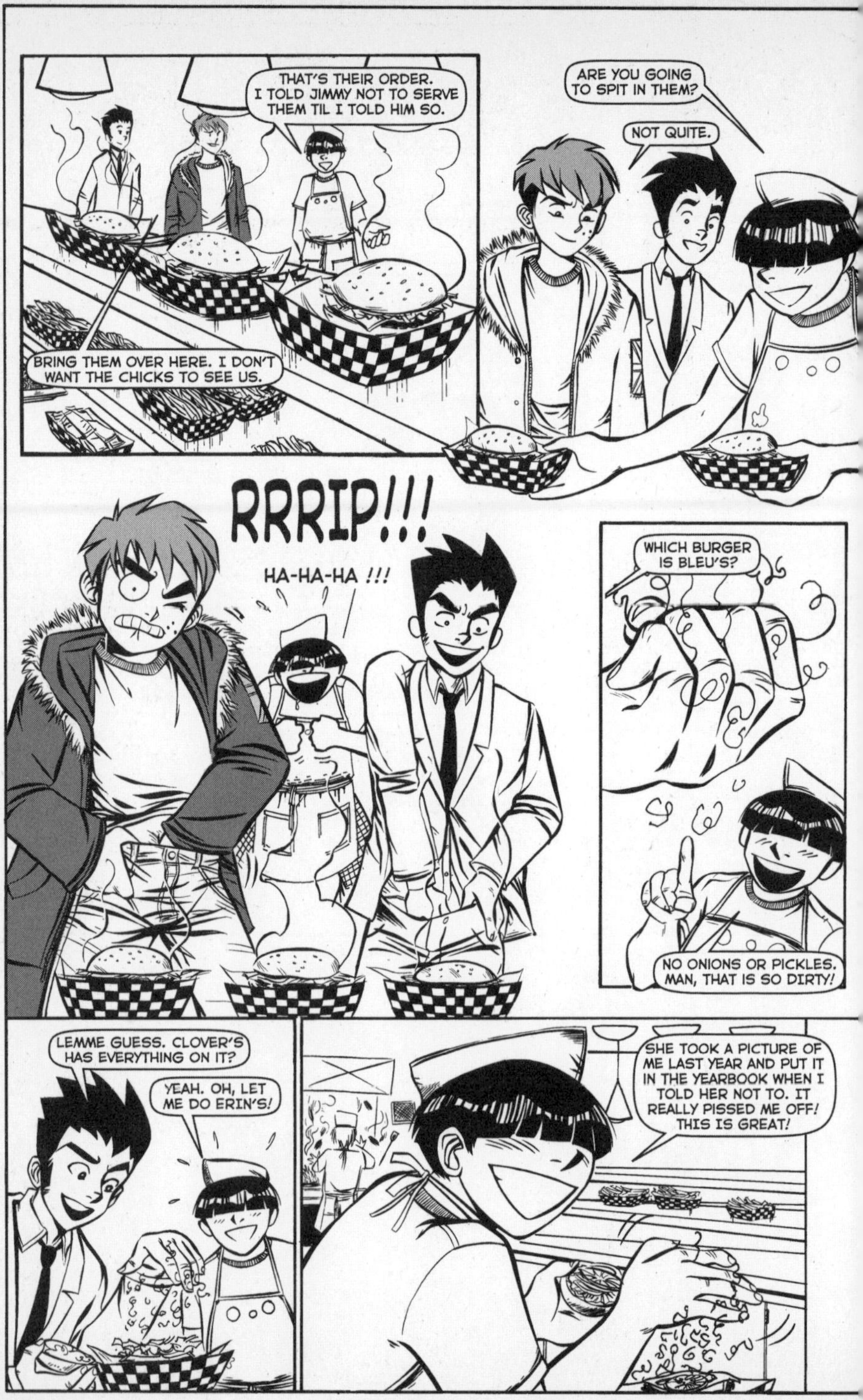

THAT'S THEIR ORDER. I TOLD JIMMY NOT TO SERVE THEM TIL I TOLD HIM SO.
BRING THEM OVER HERE. I DON'T WANT THE CHICKS TO SEE US.
ARE YOU GOING TO SPIT IN THEM?
NOT QUITE.
RRRIP!!!
HA-HA-HA !!!
WHICH BURGER IS BLEU'S?
NO ONIONS OR PICKLES. MAN, THAT IS SO DIRTY!
LEMME GUESS. CLOVER'S HAS EVERYTHING ON IT?
YEAH. OH, LET ME DO ERIN'S!
SHE TOOK A PICTURE OF ME LAST YEAR AND PUT IT IN THE YEARBOOK WHEN I TOLD HER NOT TO. IT REALLY PISSED ME OFF! THIS IS GREAT!

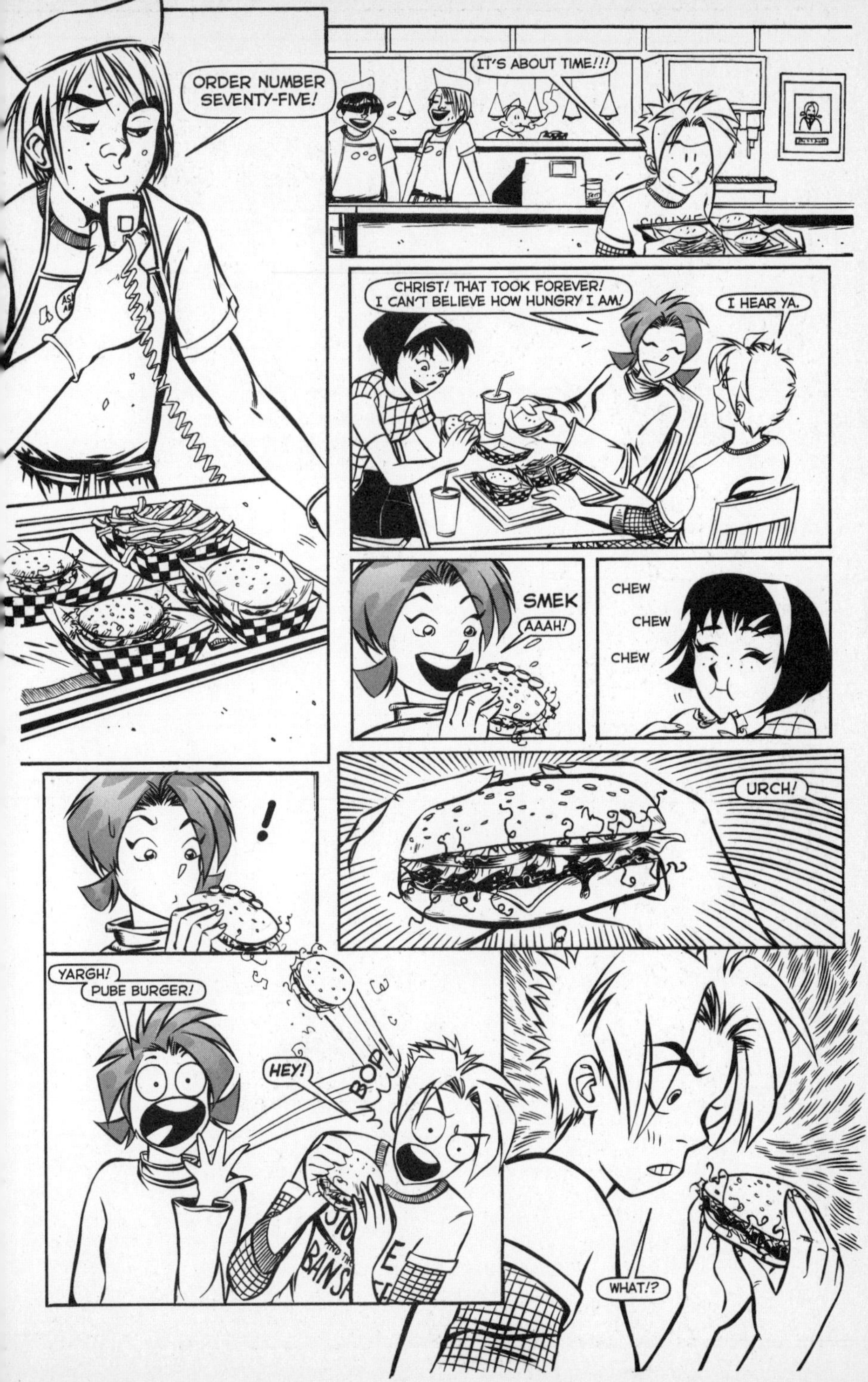
ORDER NUMBER SEVENTY-FIVE!
IT'S ABOUT TIME!!!
CHRIST! THAT TOOK FOREVER! I CAN'T BELIEVE HOW HUNGRY I AM!
I HEAR YA.
SMEK
AAAH!
CHEW
CHEW
CHEW
!
URCH!
YARGH!
PUBE BURGER!
BOP!
HEY!
WHAT!?

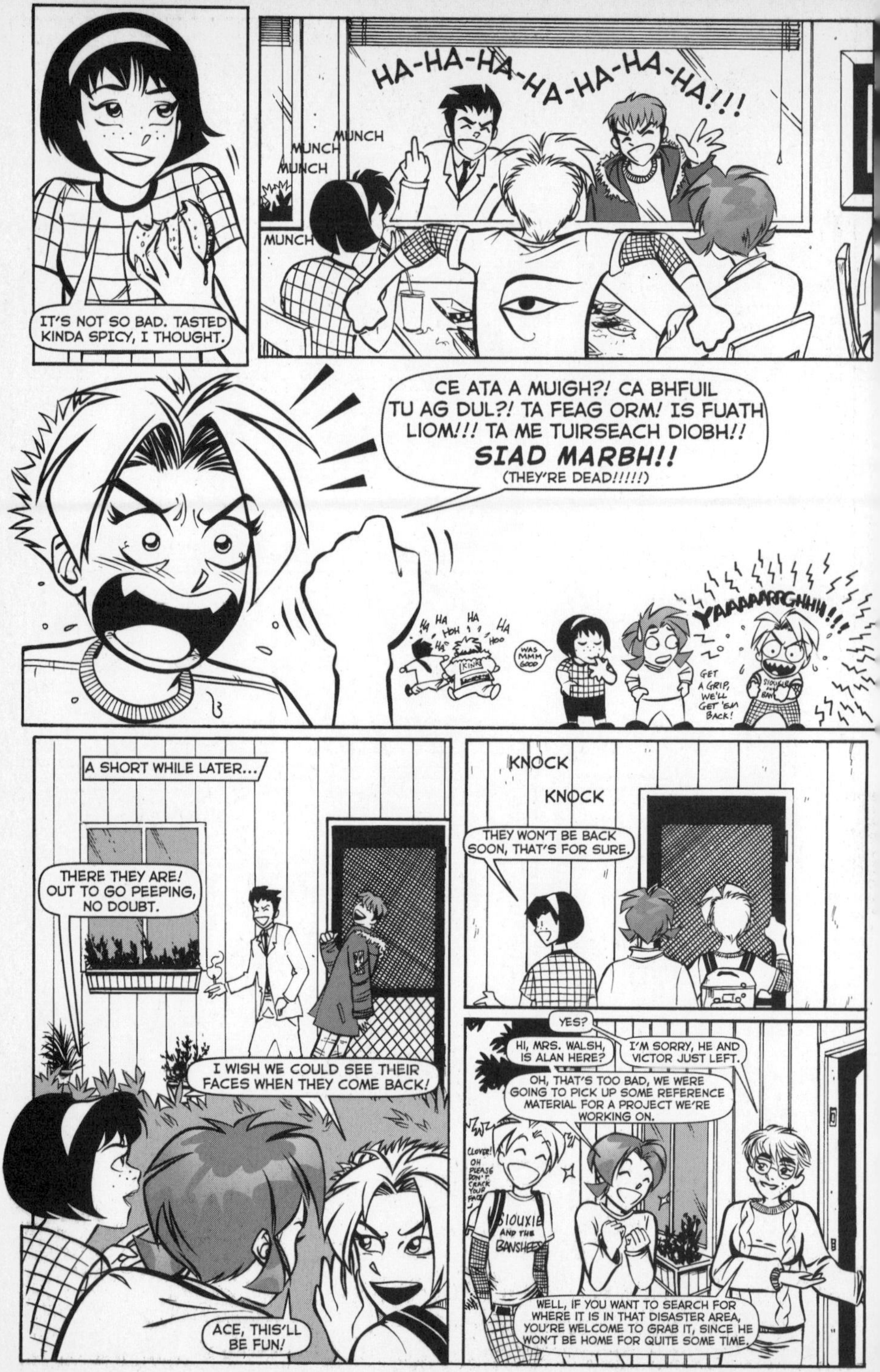
IT'S NOT SO BAD. TASTED KINDA SPICY, I THOUGHT.
HA-HA-HA-HA-HA-HA-HA!!!
MUNCH
MUNCH
MUNCH
MUNCH
CE ATA A MUIGH?! CA BHFUIL TU AG DUL?! TA FEAG ORM! IS FUATH LIOM!!! TA ME TUIRSEACH DIOBH!! SIAD MARBH!!
(THEY'RE DEAD!!!!!)
HA HA HOH HA HA HA HOO
WAS MMM GOOD
YAAAARRGHHH!!!
GET A GRIP, WE'LL GET 'EM BACK!
A SHORT WHILE LATER...
THERE THEY ARE! OUT TO GO PEEPING, NO DOUBT.
I WISH WE COULD SEE THEIR FACES WHEN THEY COME BACK!
ACE, THIS'LL BE FUN!
KNOCK
KNOCK
THEY WON'T BE BACK SOON, THAT'S FOR SURE.
YES?
HI, MRS. WALSH, IS ALAN HERE?
I'M SORRY, HE AND VICTOR JUST LEFT.
OH, THAT'S TOO BAD, WE WERE GOING TO PICK UP SOME REFERENCE MATERIAL FOR A PROJECT WE'RE WORKING ON.
CLOVER! OH PLEASE DON'T CRACK YOUR FACE
SIOUXIE AND THE BANSHEES
WELL, IF YOU WANT TO SEARCH FOR WHERE IT IS IN THAT DISASTER AREA, YOU'RE WELCOME TO GRAB IT, SINCE HE WON'T BE HOME FOR QUITE SOME TIME.

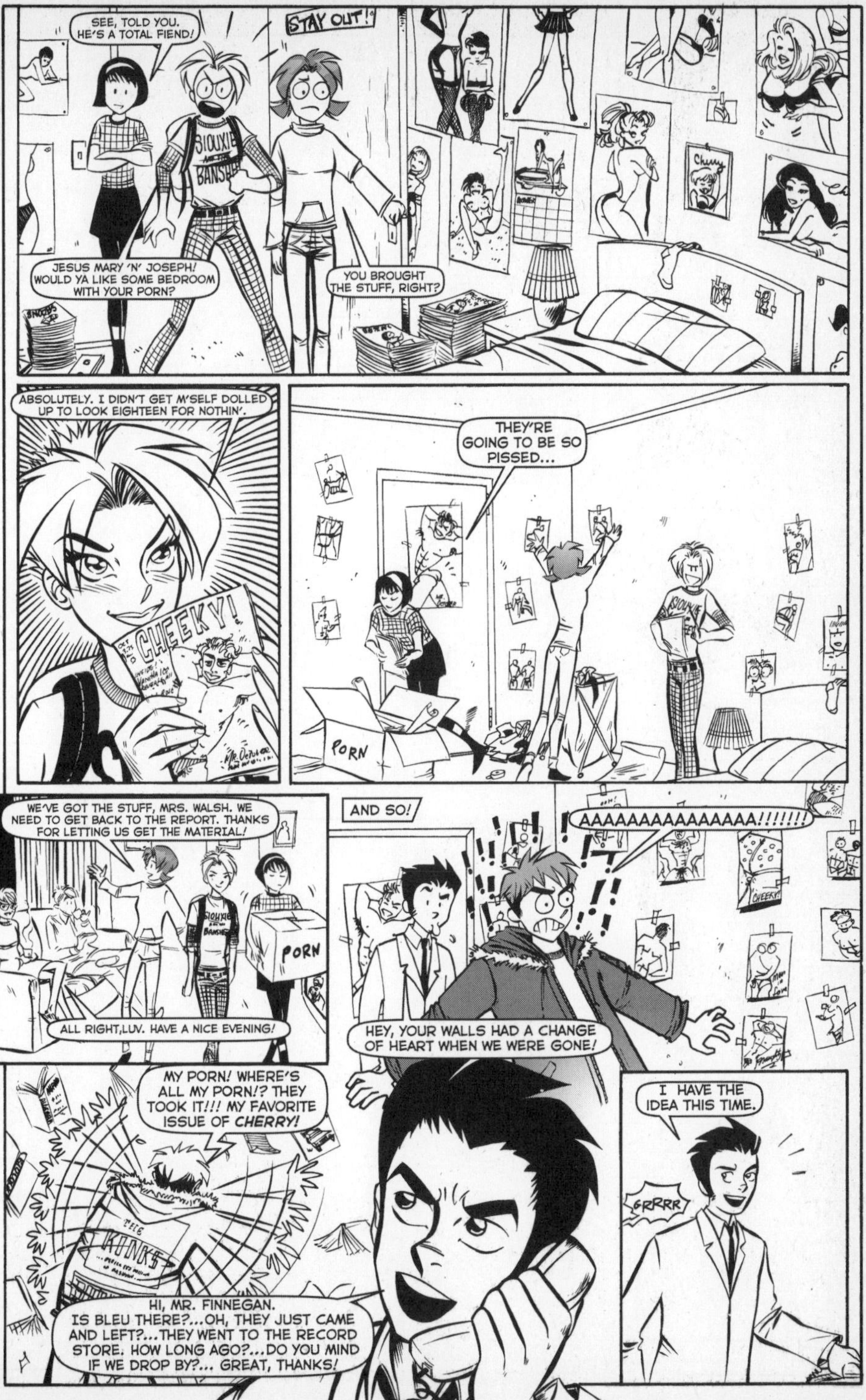
STAY OUT!
SEE, TOLD YOU. HE'S A TOTAL FIEND!
JESUS MARY 'N' JOSEPH! WOULD YA LIKE SOME BEDROOM WITH YOUR PORN?
YOU BROUGHT THE STUFF, RIGHT?
ABSOLUTELY. I DIDN'T GET M'SELF DOLLED UP TO LOOK EIGHTEEN FOR NOTHIN'.
CHEEKY!
THEY'RE GOING TO BE SO PISSED...
PORN
WE'VE GOT THE STUFF, MRS. WALSH. WE NEED TO GET BACK TO THE REPORT. THANKS FOR LETTING US GET THE MATERIAL!
PORN
ALL RIGHT,LUV. HAVE A NICE EVENING!
AND SO!
AAAAAAAAAAAAAAA!!!!!!!
HEY, YOUR WALLS HAD A CHANGE OF HEART WHEN WE WERE GONE!
CHEEKY!
MY PORN! WHERE'S ALL MY PORN!? THEY TOOK IT!!! MY FAVORITE ISSUE OF CHERRY!
THE KINKS
HI, MR. FINNEGAN. IS BLEU THERE?...OH, THEY JUST CAME AND LEFT?...THEY WENT TO THE RECORD STORE. HOW LONG AGO?...DO YOU MIND IF WE DROP BY?... GREAT, THANKS!
I HAVE THE IDEA THIS TIME.
GRRRR

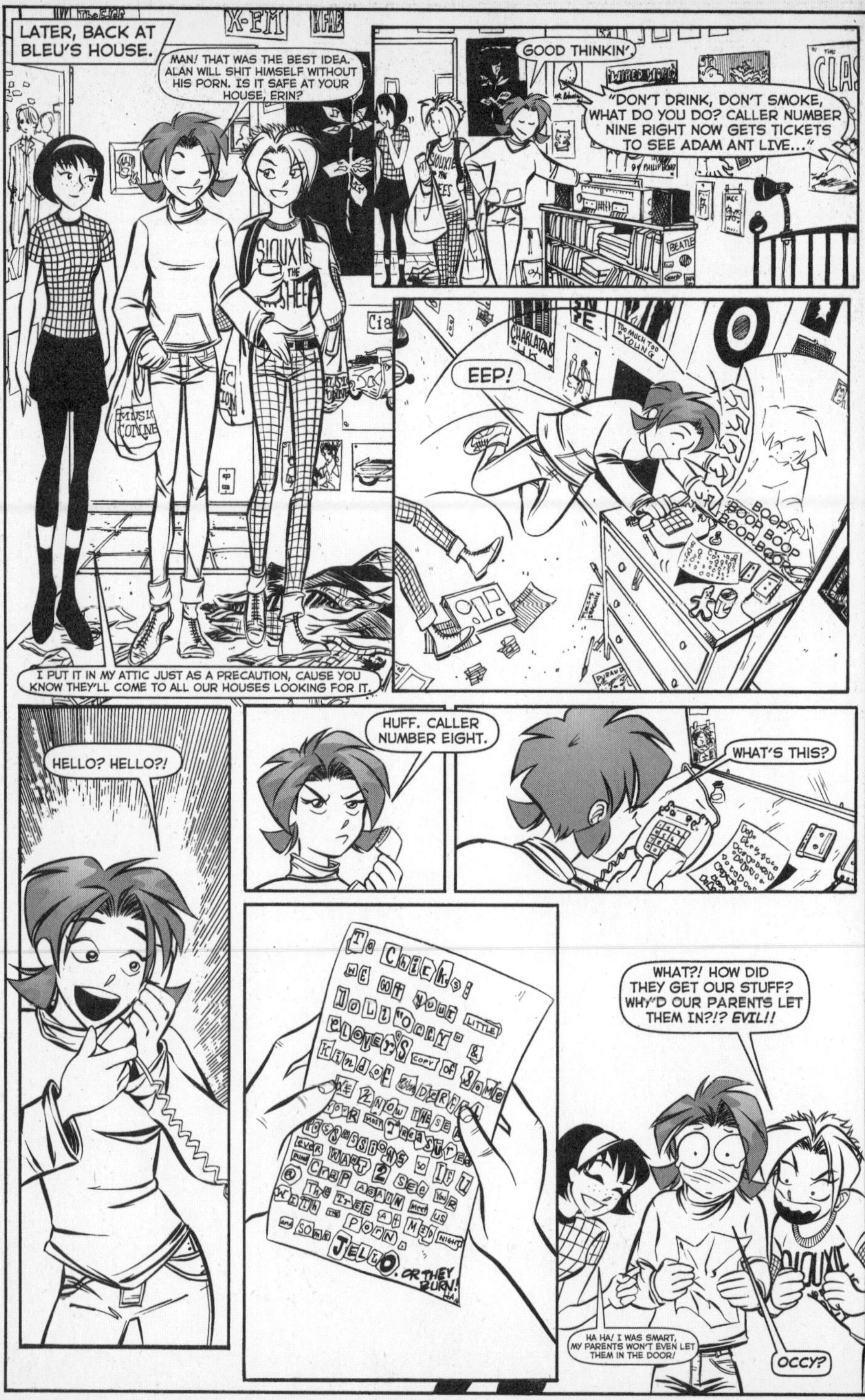
LATER, BACK AT BLEU'S HOUSE.
MAN! THAT WAS THE BEST IDEA. ALAN WILL SHIT HIMSELF WITHOUT HIS PORN. IS IT SAFE AT YOUR HOUSE, ERIN?
I PUT IT IN MY ATTIC JUST AS A PRECAUTION, CAUSE YOU KNOW THEY'LL COME TO ALL OUR HOUSES LOOKING FOR IT.
GOOD THINKIN'.
"DON'T DRINK, DON'T SMOKE, WHAT DO YOU DO? CALLER NUMBER NINE RIGHT NOW GETS TICKETS TO SEE ADAM ANT LIVE..."
EEP!
BOOP! BOOP BOOP BOOP BOOP
HELLO? HELLO?!
HUFF. CALLER NUMBER EIGHT.
WHAT'S THIS?
To Chicks! We got your little Doll "Occy" & eLover's copy of Some Kind of Wonderful. We 2 know these R your most Treasured Possessions so If U ever want 2 see your pure Crap again meet us @ The Tree at midnight with the Porn. and some Jello. OR THEY BURN! HA
WHAT?! HOW DID THEY GET OUR STUFF? WHY'D OUR PARENTS LET THEM IN?!? EVIL!!
HA HA! I WAS SMART, MY PARENTS WON'T EVEN LET THEM IN THE DOOR!
OCCY?

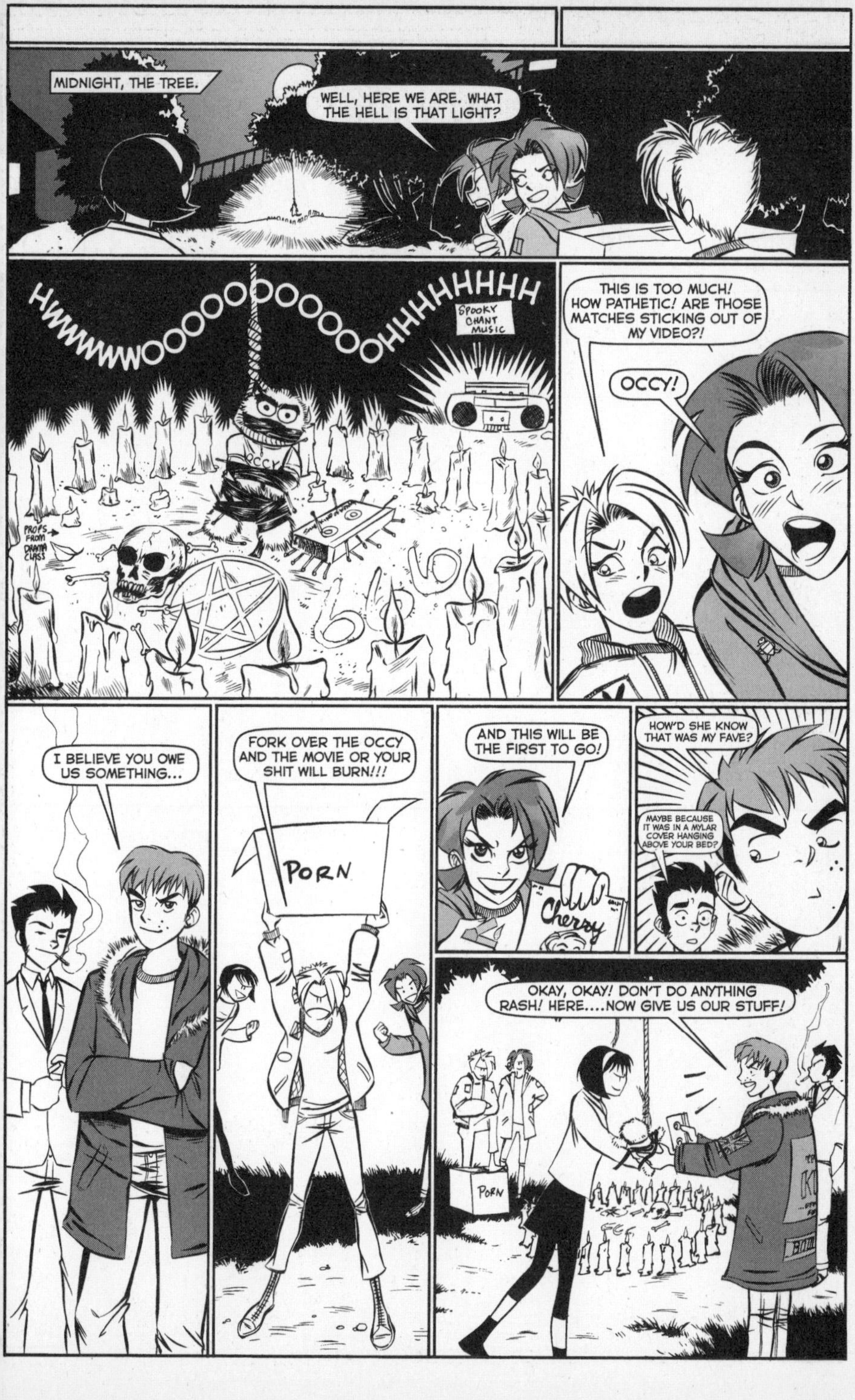

MIDNIGHT, THE TREE.
WELL, HERE WE ARE. WHAT THE HELL IS THAT LIGHT?
HWWWWWOOOOOOOOOOOOOHHHHHHHH
SPOOKY CHANT MUSIC
OCCY
PROPS FROM DRAMA CLASS
666
THIS IS TOO MUCH! HOW PATHETIC! ARE THOSE MATCHES STICKING OUT OF MY VIDEO?!
OCCY!
I BELIEVE YOU OWE US SOMETHING...
FORK OVER THE OCCY AND THE MOVIE OR YOUR SHIT WILL BURN!!!
PORN
AND THIS WILL BE THE FIRST TO GO!
Cherry
HOW'D SHE KNOW THAT WAS MY FAVE?
MAYBE BECAUSE IT WAS IN A MYLAR COVER HANGING ABOVE YOUR BED?
OKAY, OKAY! DON'T DO ANYTHING RASH! HERE....NOW GIVE US OUR STUFF!
PORN

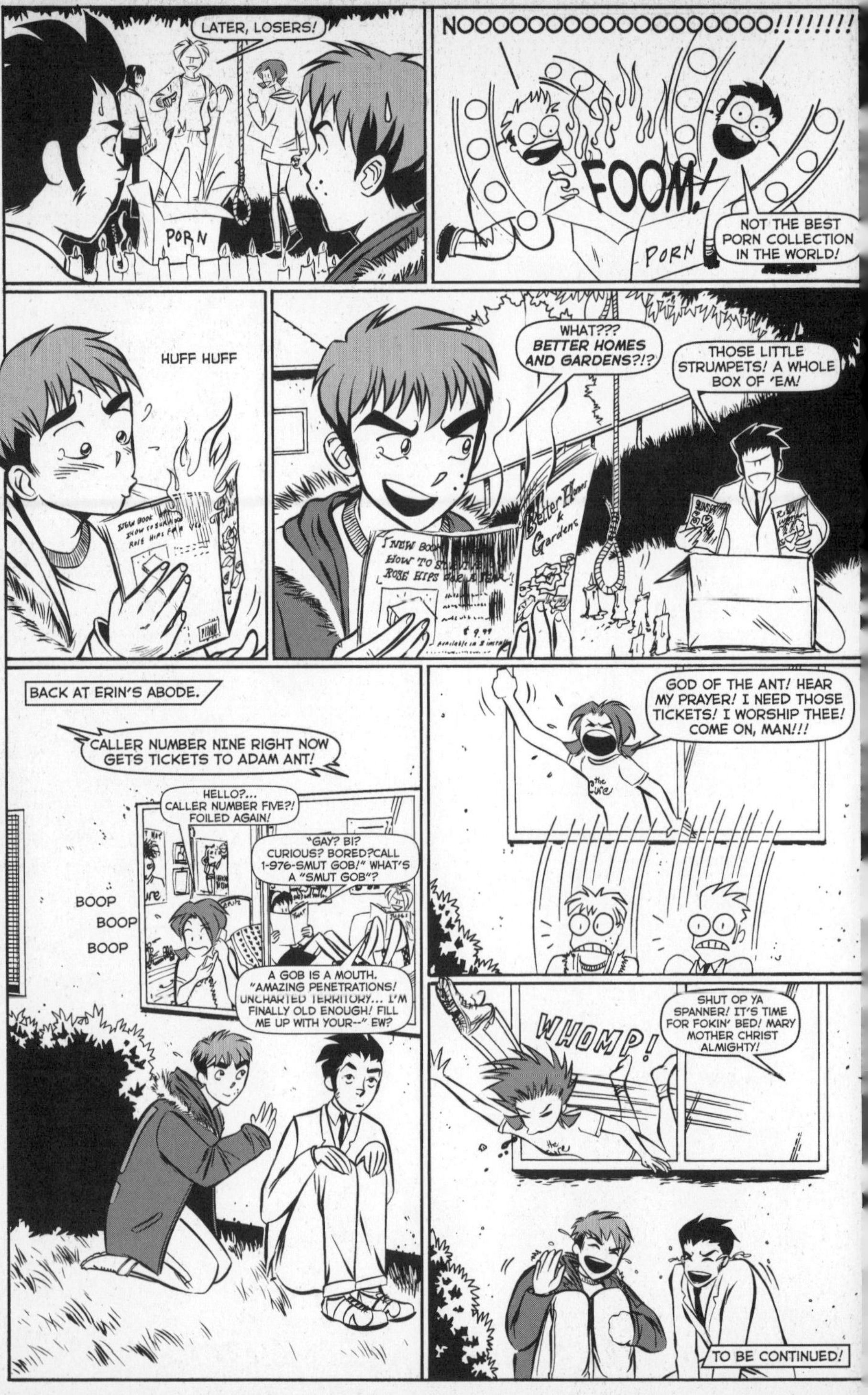
LATER, LOSERS!
PORN
NOOOOOOOOOOOOOOOOOOOO!!!!!!!!
FOOM!
PORN
NOT THE BEST PORN COLLECTION IN THE WORLD!
HUFF HUFF
WHAT??? BETTER HOMES AND GARDENS?!?
THOSE LITTLE STRUMPETS! A WHOLE BOX OF 'EM!
NEW BOOK HOW TO SURVIVE ROSE HIPS FOR A YEAR!
Better Homes & Gardens
BACK AT ERIN'S ABODE.
CALLER NUMBER NINE RIGHT NOW GETS TICKETS TO ADAM ANT!
HELLO?... CALLER NUMBER FIVE?! FOILED AGAIN!
"GAY? BI? CURIOUS? BORED? CALL 1-976-SMUT GOB!" WHAT'S A "SMUT GOB"?
BOOP
BOOP
BOOP
A GOB IS A MOUTH. "AMAZING PENETRATIONS! UNCHARTED TERRITORY... I'M FINALLY OLD ENOUGH! FILL ME UP WITH YOUR--" EW?
GOD OF THE ANT! HEAR MY PRAYER! I NEED THOSE TICKETS! I WORSHIP THEE! COME ON, MAN!!!
WHOMP!
SHUT OP YA SPANNER! IT'S TIME FOR FOKIN' BED! MARY MOTHER CHRIST ALMIGHTY!
TO BE CONTINUED!

# chapter two:
# "SUBSTITUTE"

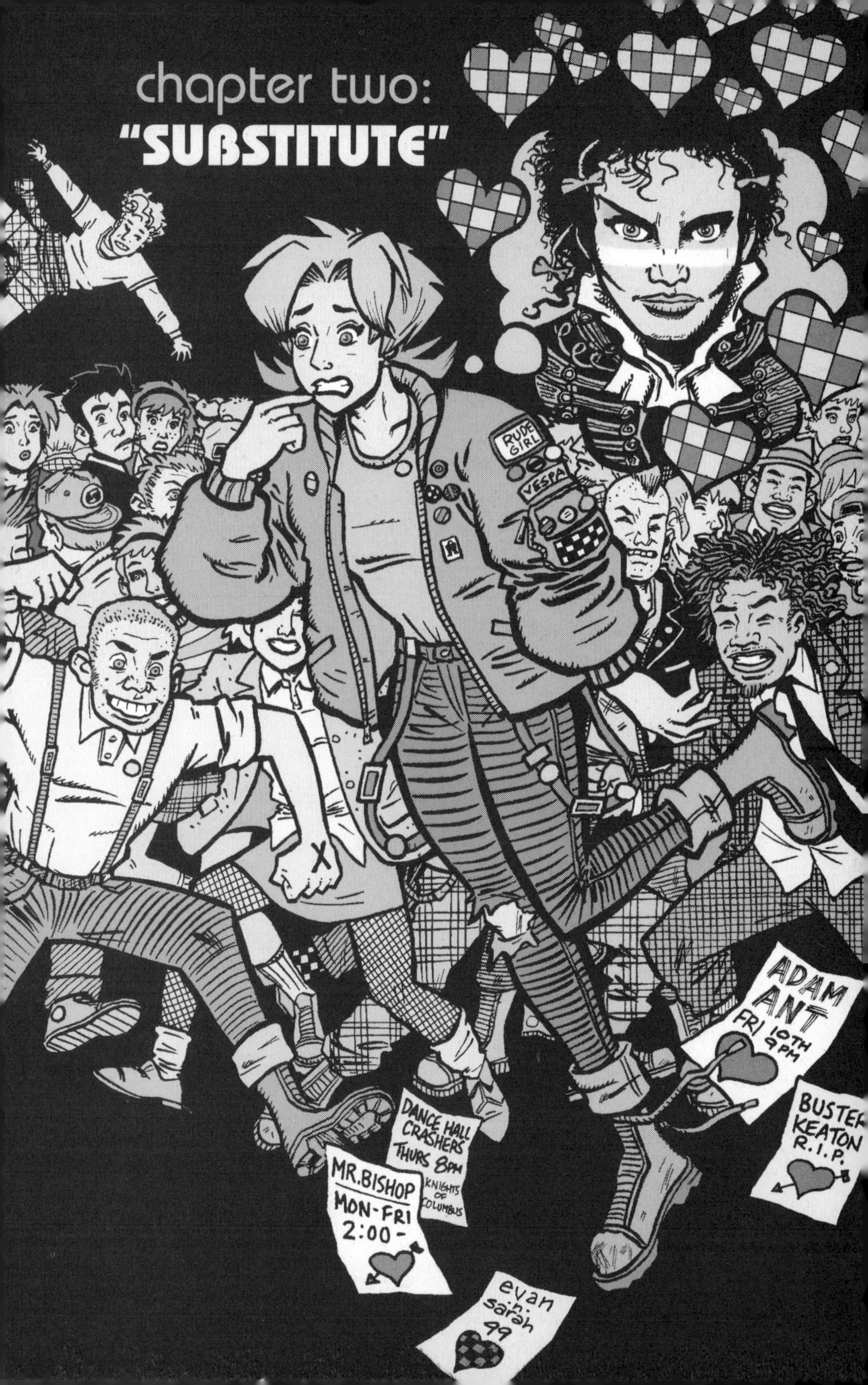

RUDE GIRL
VESPA
ADAM ANT FRI 10TH 9PM
BUSTER KEATON R.I.P.
DANCE HALL CRASHERS THURS 8PM KNIGHTS OF COLUMBUS
MR. BISHOP MON-FRI 2:00-
evan -n- sarah 99

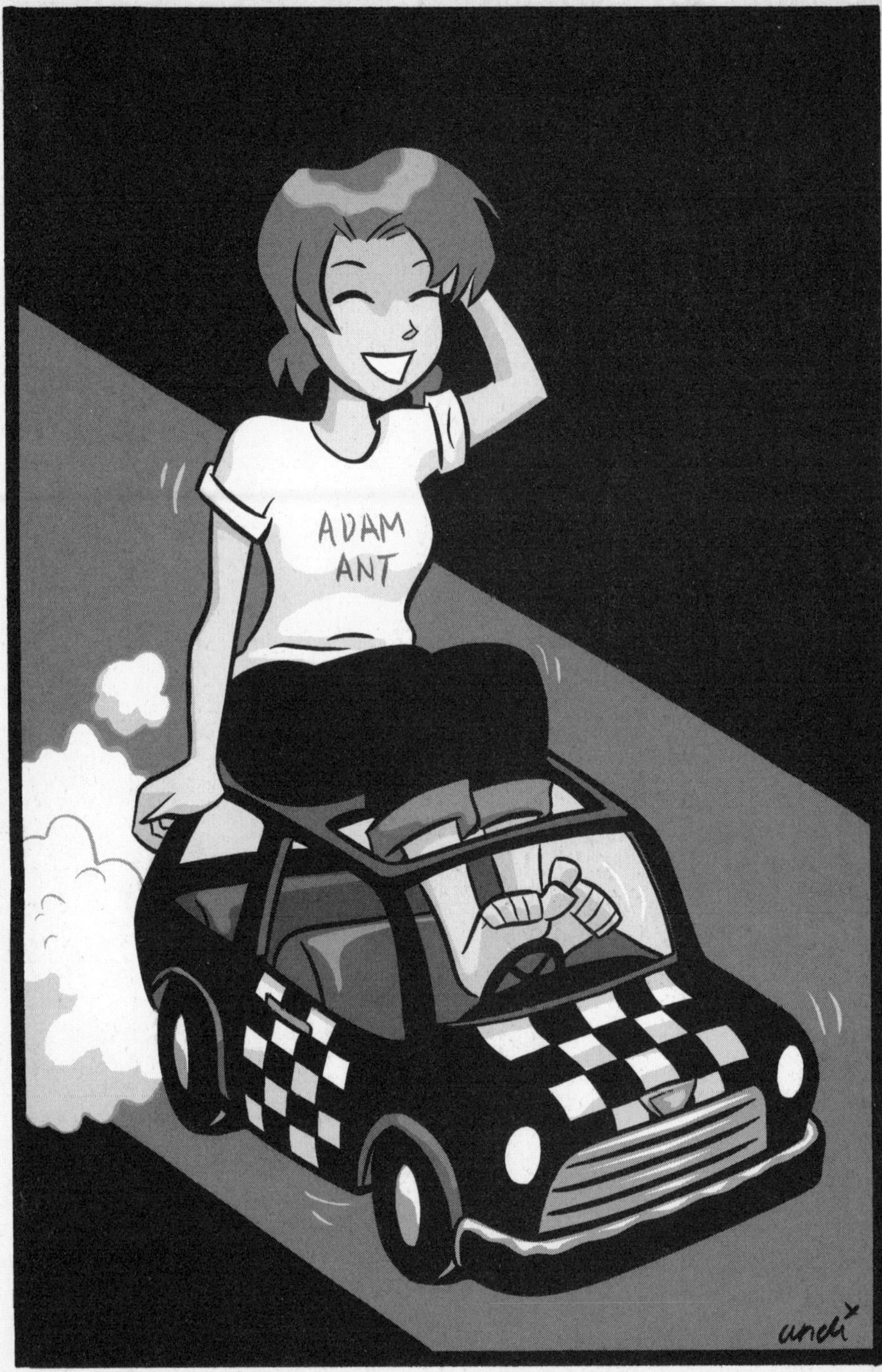
ADAM
ANT
andi

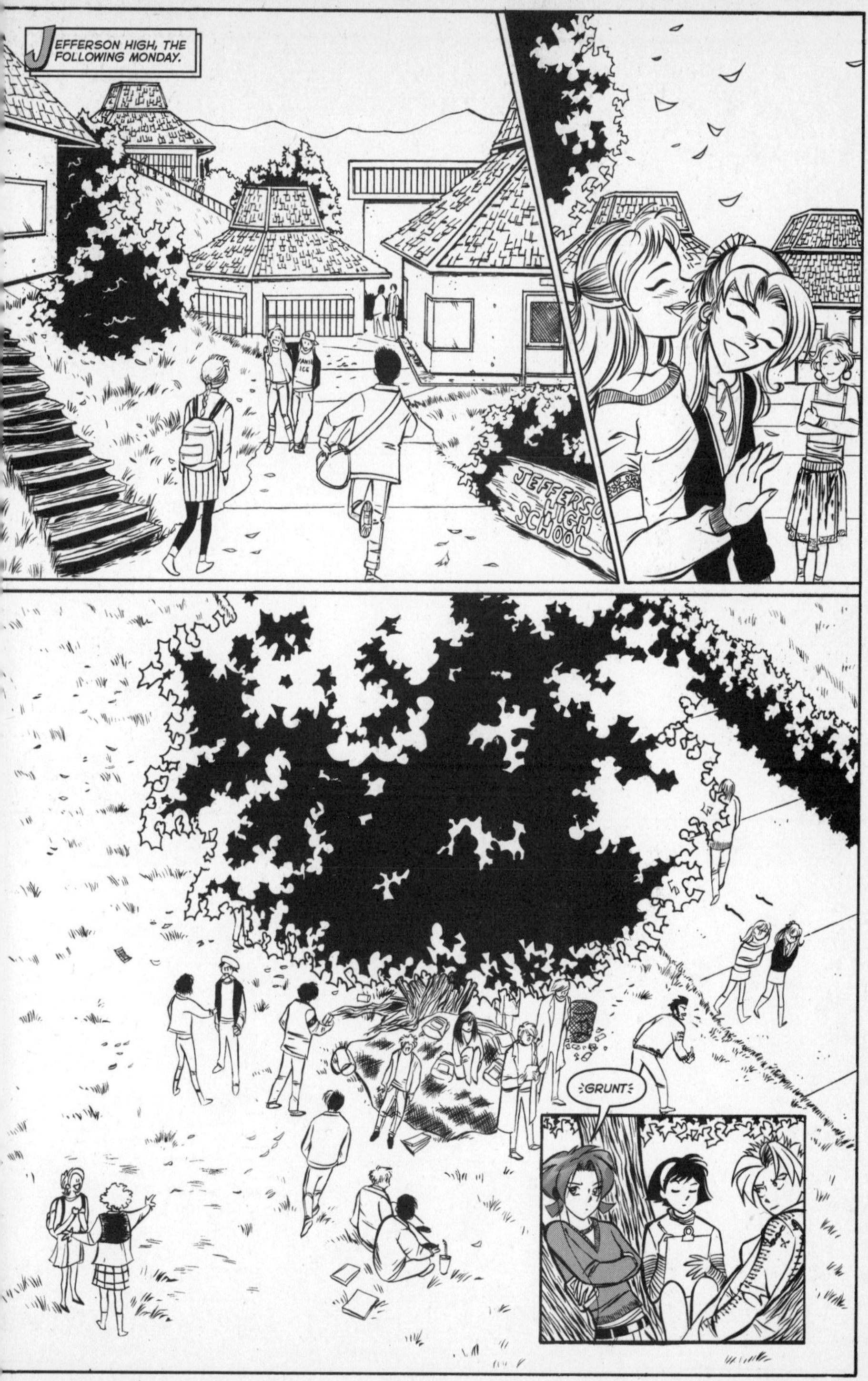
JEFFERSON HIGH, THE FOLLOWING MONDAY.
JEFFERSON HIGH SCHOOL
GRUNT

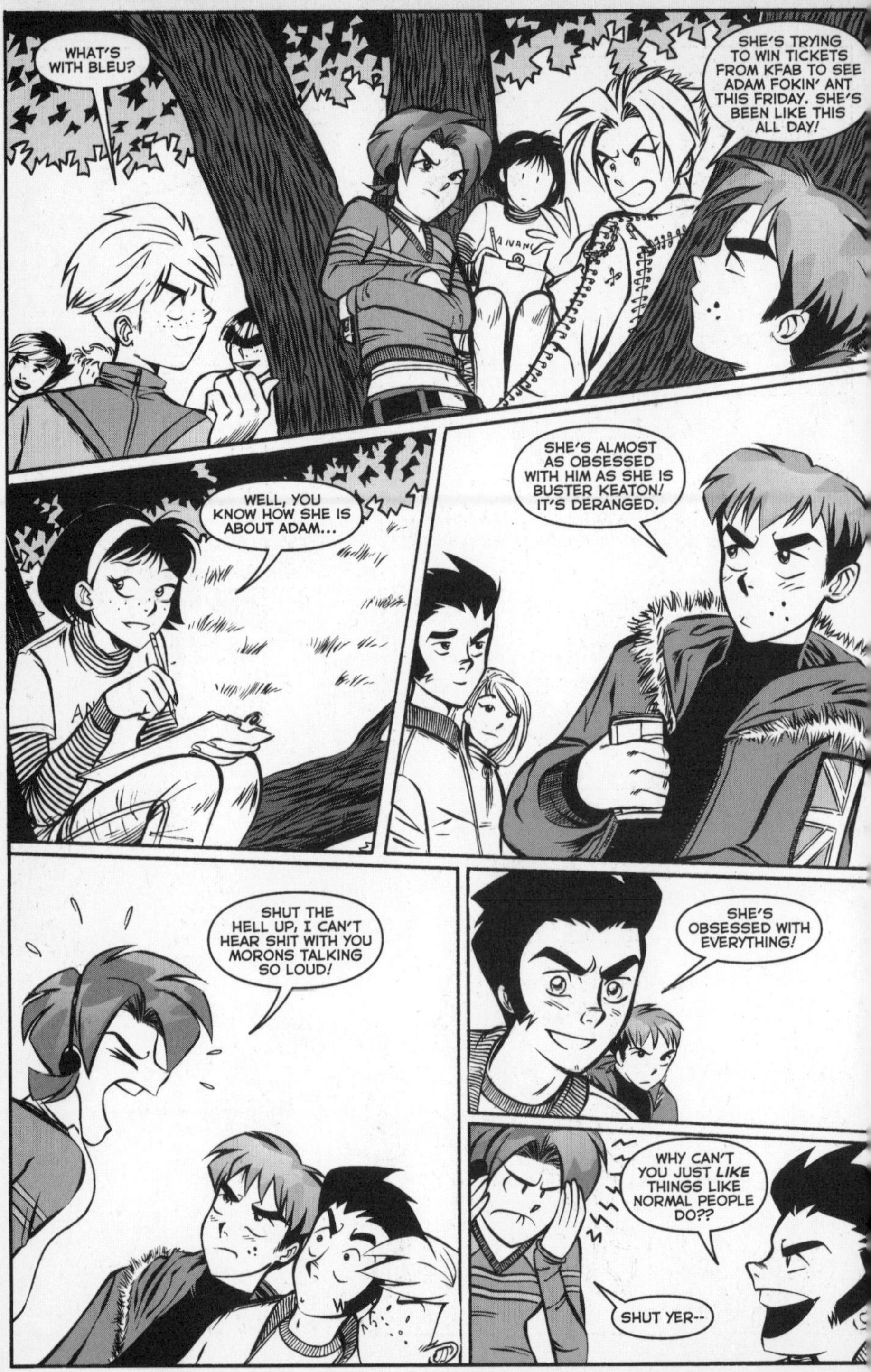
WHAT'S WITH BLEU?
SHE'S TRYING TO WIN TICKETS FROM KFAB TO SEE ADAM FOKIN' ANT THIS FRIDAY. SHE'S BEEN LIKE THIS ALL DAY!
WELL, YOU KNOW HOW SHE IS ABOUT ADAM...
SHE'S ALMOST AS OBSESSED WITH HIM AS SHE IS BUSTER KEATON! IT'S DERANGED.
SHUT THE HELL UP, I CAN'T HEAR SHIT WITH YOU MORONS TALKING SO LOUD!
SHE'S OBSESSED WITH EVERYTHING!
WHY CAN'T YOU JUST LIKE THINGS LIKE NORMAL PEOPLE DO??
SHUT YER--

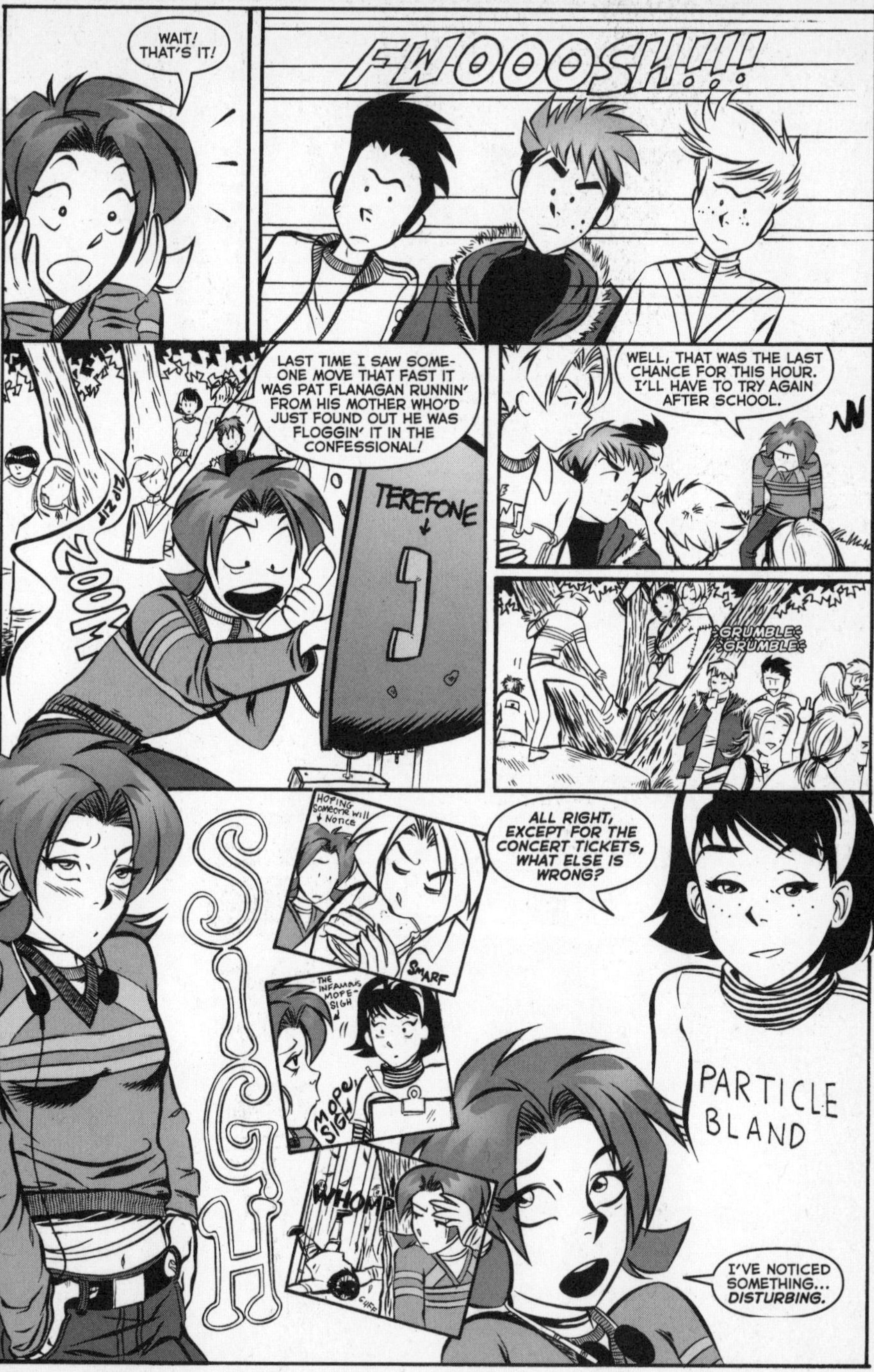
WAIT! THAT'S IT!
FWOOOSH!!!
LAST TIME I SAW SOME-ONE MOVE THAT FAST IT WAS PAT FLANAGAN RUNNIN' FROM HIS MOTHER WHO'D JUST FOUND OUT HE WAS FLOGGIN' IT IN THE CONFESSIONAL!
ZIP ZIP
ZOOM
TEREFONE
WELL, THAT WAS THE LAST CHANCE FOR THIS HOUR. I'LL HAVE TO TRY AGAIN AFTER SCHOOL.
GRUMBLE GRUMBLE
SIGH
HOPING Someone will Notice
SMARF
ALL RIGHT, EXCEPT FOR THE CONCERT TICKETS, WHAT ELSE IS WRONG?
THE INFAMOUS MOPE-SIGH
MOPE SIGH
WHOMP
CHFF
PARTICLE BLAND
I'VE NOTICED SOMETHING... DISTURBING.

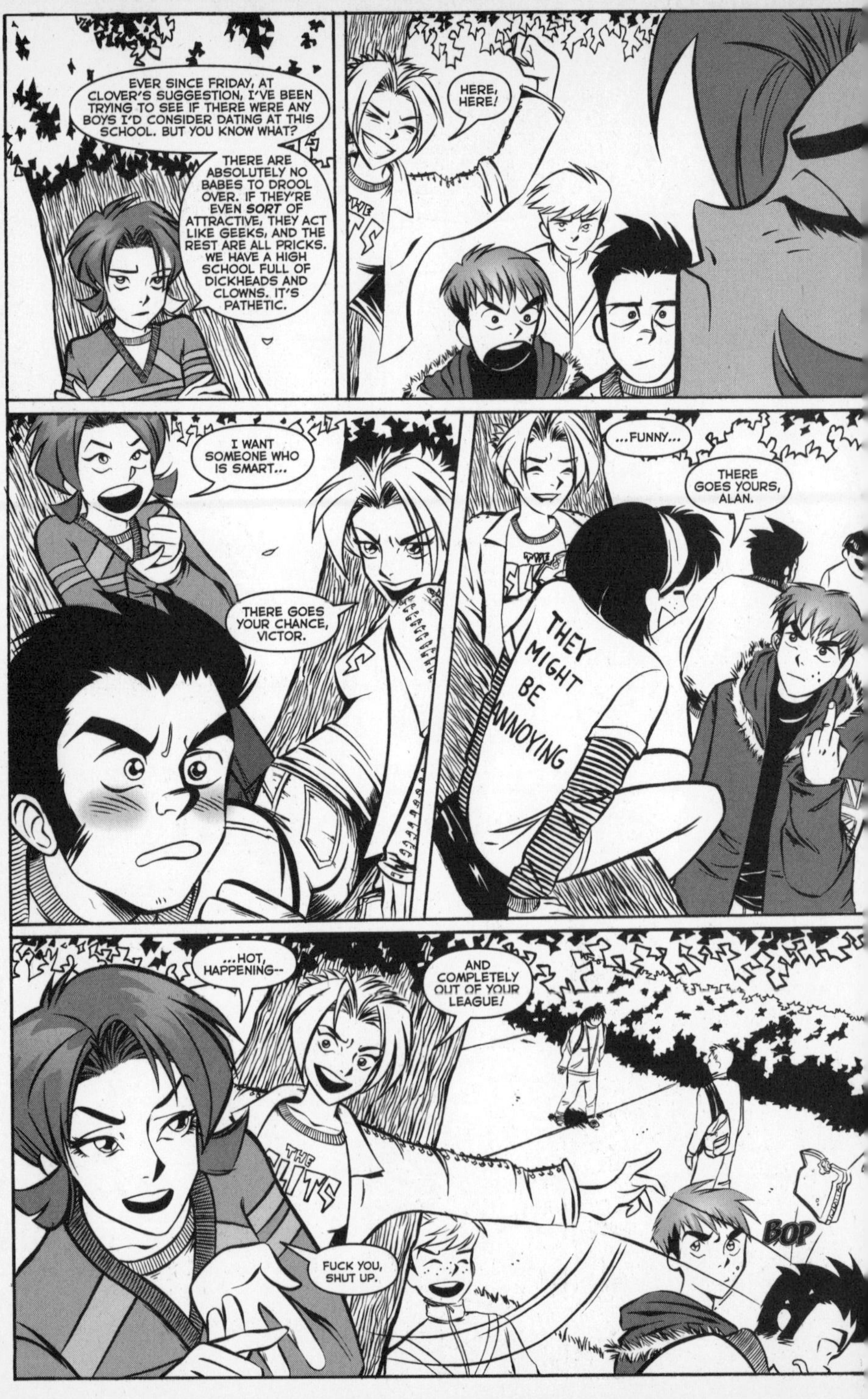
EVER SINCE FRIDAY, AT CLOVER'S SUGGESTION, I'VE BEEN TRYING TO SEE IF THERE WERE ANY BOYS I'D CONSIDER DATING AT THIS SCHOOL. BUT YOU KNOW WHAT?
THERE ARE ABSOLUTELY NO BABES TO DROOL OVER. IF THEY'RE EVEN *SORT* OF ATTRACTIVE, THEY ACT LIKE GEEKS, AND THE REST ARE ALL PRICKS. WE HAVE A HIGH SCHOOL FULL OF DICKHEADS AND CLOWNS. IT'S PATHETIC.
HERE, HERE!
I WANT SOMEONE WHO IS SMART...
THERE GOES YOUR CHANCE, VICTOR.
...FUNNY...
THERE GOES YOURS, ALAN.
THEY MIGHT BE ANNOYING
...HOT, HAPPENING--
AND COMPLETELY OUT OF YOUR LEAGUE!
FUCK YOU, SHUT UP.
BOP

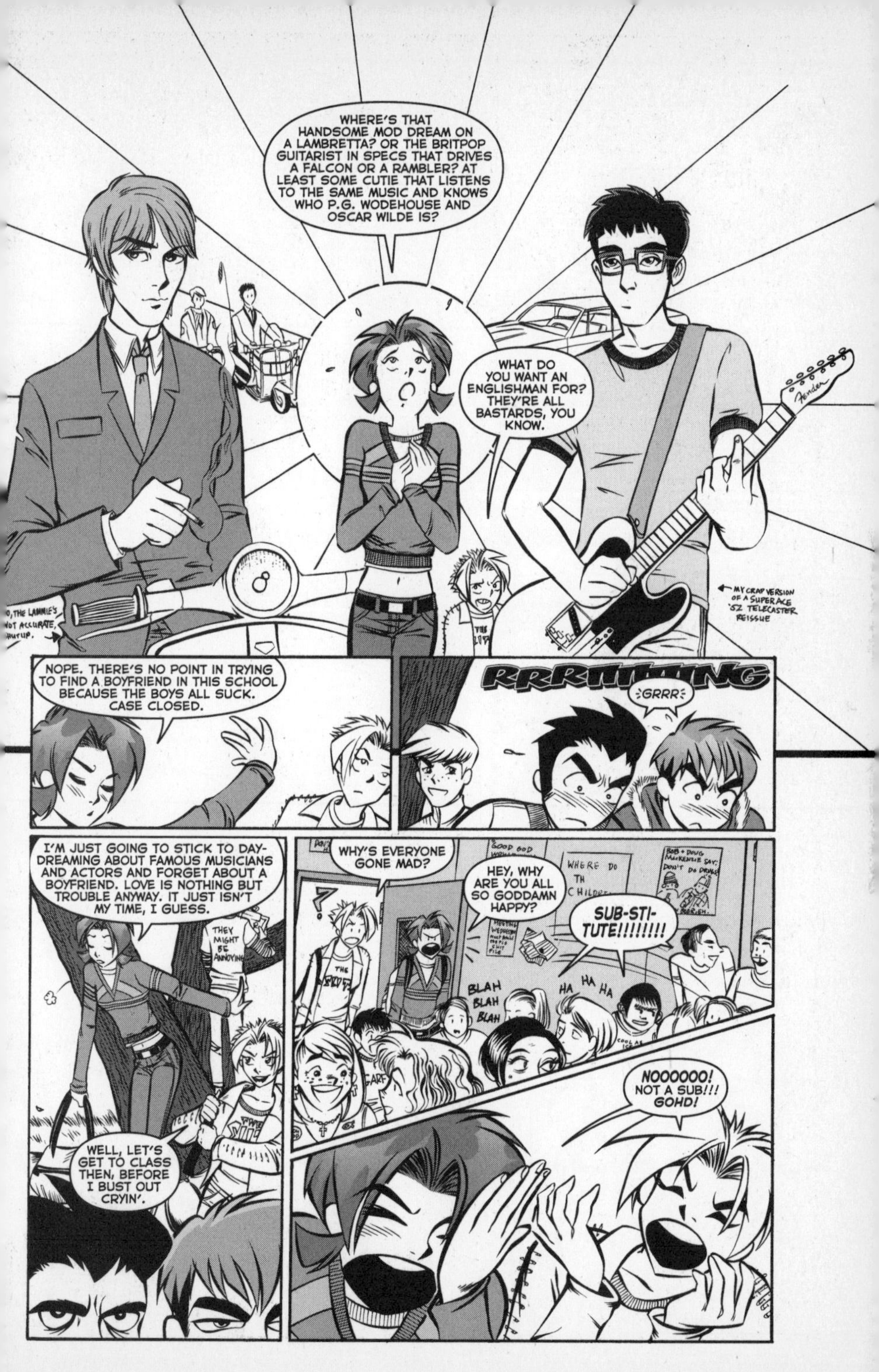
WHERE'S THAT HANDSOME MOD DREAM ON A LAMBRETTA? OR THE BRITPOP GUITARIST IN SPECS THAT DRIVES A FALCON OR A RAMBLER? AT LEAST SOME CUTIE THAT LISTENS TO THE SAME MUSIC AND KNOWS WHO P.G. WODEHOUSE AND OSCAR WILDE IS?
WHAT DO YOU WANT AN ENGLISHMAN FOR? THEY'RE ALL BASTARDS, YOU KNOW.
MY CRAP VERSION OF A SUPERACE '52 TELECASTER REISSUE
NOPE. THERE'S NO POINT IN TRYING TO FIND A BOYFRIEND IN THIS SCHOOL BECAUSE THE BOYS ALL SUCK. CASE CLOSED.
RRRIIIIING
GRRR
I'M JUST GOING TO STICK TO DAY-DREAMING ABOUT FAMOUS MUSICIANS AND ACTORS AND FORGET ABOUT A BOYFRIEND. LOVE IS NOTHING BUT TROUBLE ANYWAY. IT JUST ISN'T MY TIME, I GUESS.
THEY MIGHT BE ANNOYING
WELL, LET'S GET TO CLASS THEN, BEFORE I BUST OUT CRYIN'.
WHY'S EVERYONE GONE MAD?
HEY, WHY ARE YOU ALL SO GODDAMN HAPPY?
SUB-STI-TUTE!!!!!!!!
BLAH BLAH BLAH
HA HA HA
NOOOOOO! NOT A SUB!!! GOHD!

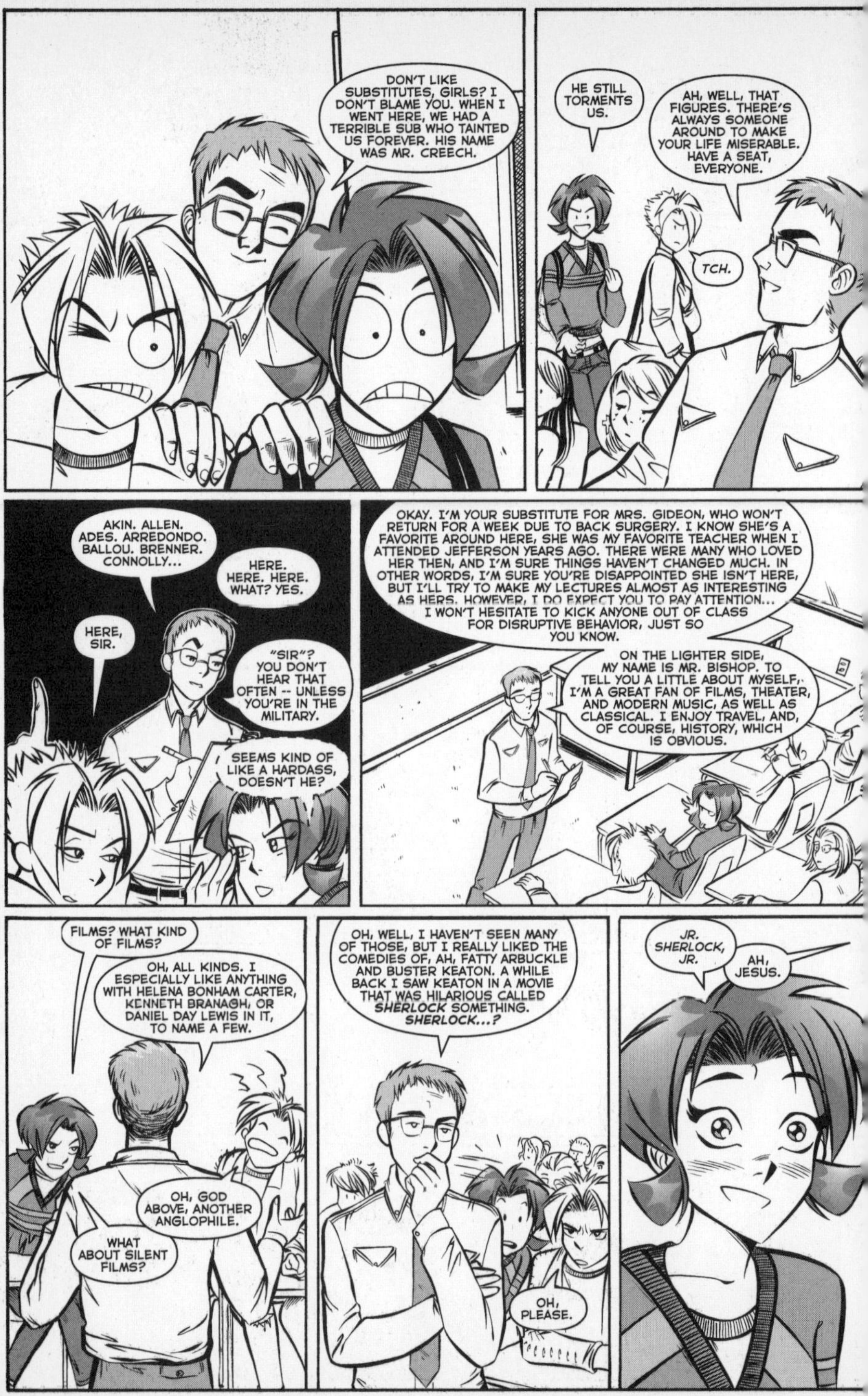

DON'T LIKE SUBSTITUTES, GIRLS? I DON'T BLAME YOU. WHEN I WENT HERE, WE HAD A TERRIBLE SUB WHO TAINTED US FOREVER. HIS NAME WAS MR. CREECH.
HE STILL TORMENTS US.
AH, WELL, THAT FIGURES. THERE'S ALWAYS SOMEONE AROUND TO MAKE YOUR LIFE MISERABLE. HAVE A SEAT, EVERYONE.
TCH.
AKIN. ALLEN. ADES. ARREDONDO. BALLOU. BRENNER. CONNOLLY...
HERE. HERE. HERE. WHAT? YES.
HERE, SIR.
"SIR"? YOU DON'T HEAR THAT OFTEN -- UNLESS YOU'RE IN THE MILITARY.
SEEMS KIND OF LIKE A HARDASS, DOESN'T HE?
OKAY. I'M YOUR SUBSTITUTE FOR MRS. GIDEON, WHO WON'T RETURN FOR A WEEK DUE TO BACK SURGERY. I KNOW SHE'S A FAVORITE AROUND HERE, SHE WAS MY FAVORITE TEACHER WHEN I ATTENDED JEFFERSON YEARS AGO. THERE WERE MANY WHO LOVED HER THEN, AND I'M SURE THINGS HAVEN'T CHANGED MUCH. IN OTHER WORDS, I'M SURE YOU'RE DISAPPOINTED SHE ISN'T HERE, BUT I'LL TRY TO MAKE MY LECTURES ALMOST AS INTERESTING AS HERS. HOWEVER, I DO EXPECT YOU TO PAY ATTENTION... I WON'T HESITATE TO KICK ANYONE OUT OF CLASS FOR DISRUPTIVE BEHAVIOR, JUST SO YOU KNOW.
ON THE LIGHTER SIDE, MY NAME IS MR. BISHOP. TO TELL YOU A LITTLE ABOUT MYSELF, I'M A GREAT FAN OF FILMS, THEATER, AND MODERN MUSIC, AS WELL AS CLASSICAL. I ENJOY TRAVEL, AND, OF COURSE, HISTORY, WHICH IS OBVIOUS.
FILMS? WHAT KIND OF FILMS?
OH, ALL KINDS. I ESPECIALLY LIKE ANYTHING WITH HELENA BONHAM CARTER, KENNETH BRANAGH, OR DANIEL DAY LEWIS IN IT, TO NAME A FEW.
OH, GOD ABOVE, ANOTHER ANGLOPHILE.
WHAT ABOUT SILENT FILMS?
OH, WELL, I HAVEN'T SEEN MANY OF THOSE, BUT I REALLY LIKED THE COMEDIES OF, AH, FATTY ARBUCKLE AND BUSTER KEATON. A WHILE BACK I SAW KEATON IN A MOVIE THAT WAS HILARIOUS CALLED SHERLOCK SOMETHING. SHERLOCK...?
OH, PLEASE.
JR. SHERLOCK, JR.
AH, JESUS.

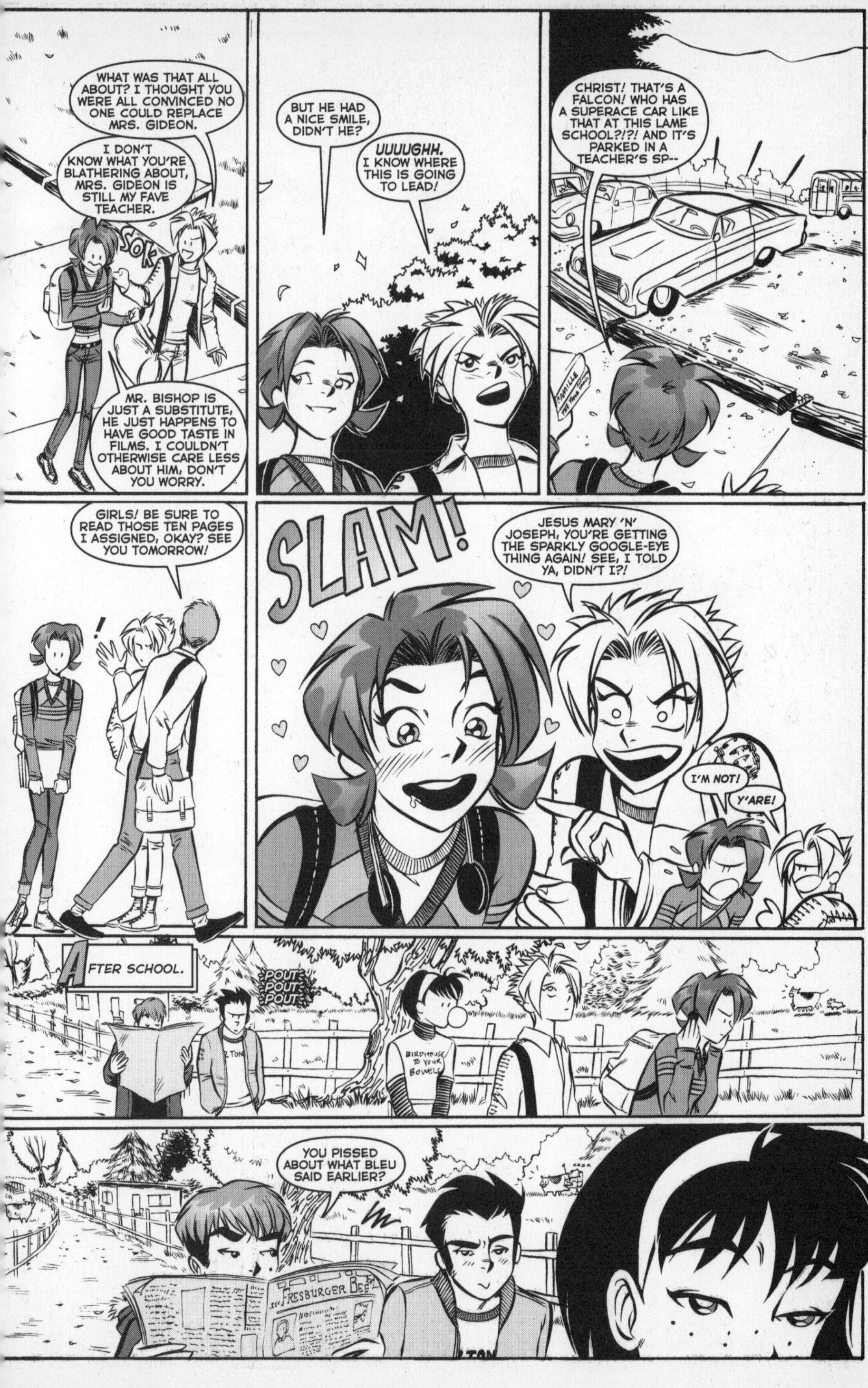
WHAT WAS THAT ALL ABOUT? I THOUGHT YOU WERE ALL CONVINCED NO ONE COULD REPLACE MRS. GIDEON.
I DON'T KNOW WHAT YOU'RE BLATHERING ABOUT, MRS. GIDEON IS STILL MY FAVE TEACHER.
SOK
MR. BISHOP IS JUST A SUBSTITUTE, HE JUST HAPPENS TO HAVE GOOD TASTE IN FILMS. I COULDN'T OTHERWISE CARE LESS ABOUT HIM, DON'T YOU WORRY.
BUT HE HAD A NICE SMILE, DIDN'T HE?
UUUUGHH. I KNOW WHERE THIS IS GOING TO LEAD!
CHRIST! THAT'S A FALCON! WHO HAS A SUPERACE CAR LIKE THAT AT THIS LAME SCHOOL?!?! AND IT'S PARKED IN A TEACHER'S SP--
GIRLS! BE SURE TO READ THOSE TEN PAGES I ASSIGNED, OKAY? SEE YOU TOMORROW!
!
SLAM!
JESUS MARY 'N' JOSEPH, YOU'RE GETTING THE SPARKLY GOOGLE-EYE THING AGAIN! SEE, I TOLD YA, DIDN'T I?!
I'M NOT!
Y'ARE!
AFTER SCHOOL.
POUT POUT POUT
BIRDHOUSE TO YOUR BOWELS
YOU PISSED ABOUT WHAT BLEU SAID EARLIER?
FRESBURGER BEE

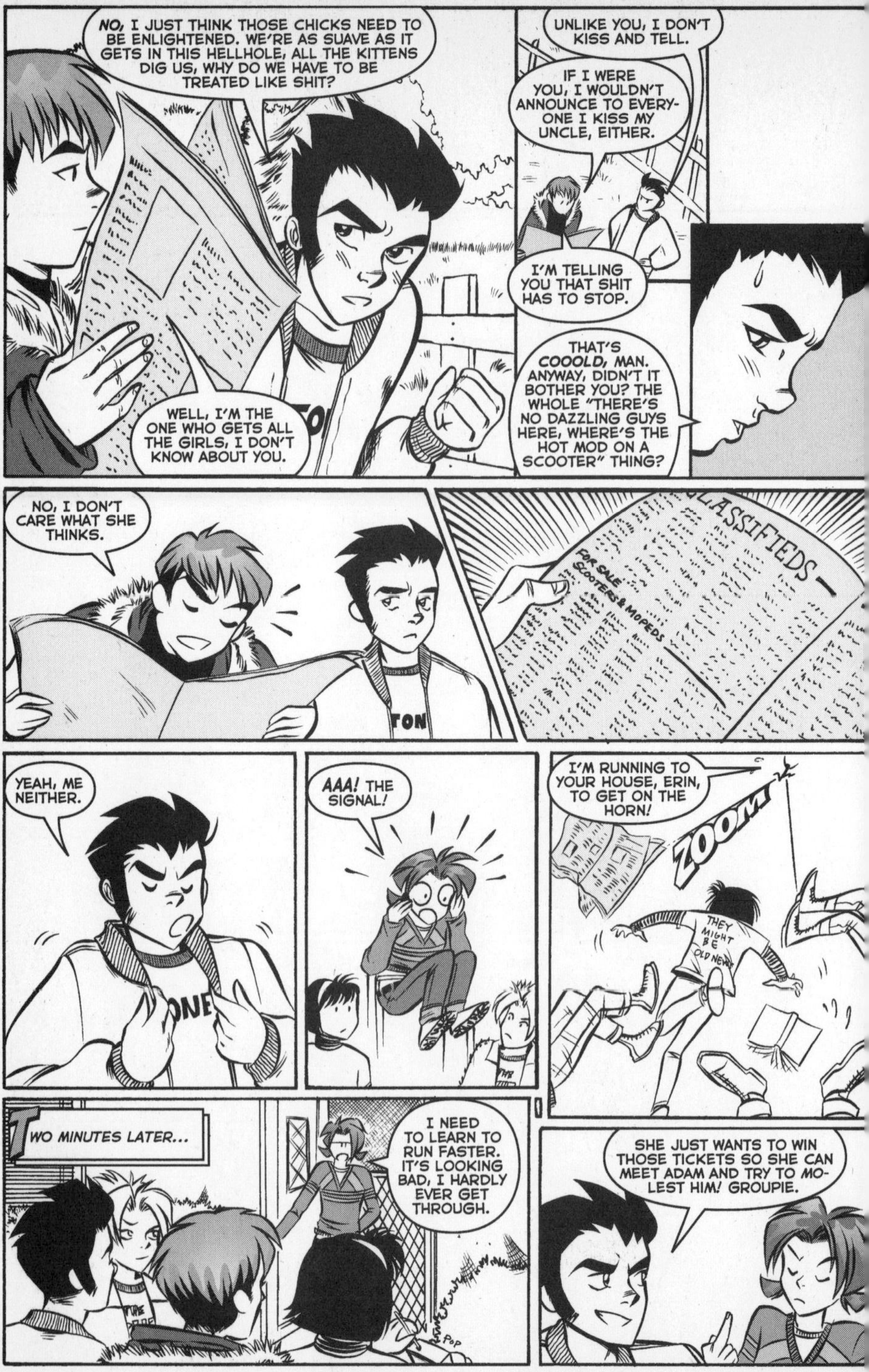
NO, I JUST THINK THOSE CHICKS NEED TO BE ENLIGHTENED. WE'RE AS SUAVE AS IT GETS IN THIS HELLHOLE, ALL THE KITTENS DIG US, WHY DO WE HAVE TO BE TREATED LIKE SHIT?
WELL, I'M THE ONE WHO GETS ALL THE GIRLS, I DON'T KNOW ABOUT YOU.
UNLIKE YOU, I DON'T KISS AND TELL.
IF I WERE YOU, I WOULDN'T ANNOUNCE TO EVERYONE I KISS MY UNCLE, EITHER.
I'M TELLING YOU THAT SHIT HAS TO STOP.
THAT'S COOOLD, MAN. ANYWAY, DIDN'T IT BOTHER YOU? THE WHOLE "THERE'S NO DAZZLING GUYS HERE, WHERE'S THE HOT MOD ON A SCOOTER" THING?
NO, I DON'T CARE WHAT SHE THINKS.
CLASSIFIEDS
FOR SALE SCOOTERS & MOPEDS
YEAH, ME NEITHER.
AAA! THE SIGNAL!
I'M RUNNING TO YOUR HOUSE, ERIN, TO GET ON THE HORN!
ZOOM!
THEY MIGHT BE OLD NEWS
TWO MINUTES LATER...
I NEED TO LEARN TO RUN FASTER. IT'S LOOKING BAD, I HARDLY EVER GET THROUGH.
POP
SHE JUST WANTS TO WIN THOSE TICKETS SO SHE CAN MEET ADAM AND TRY TO MOLEST HIM! GROUPIE.

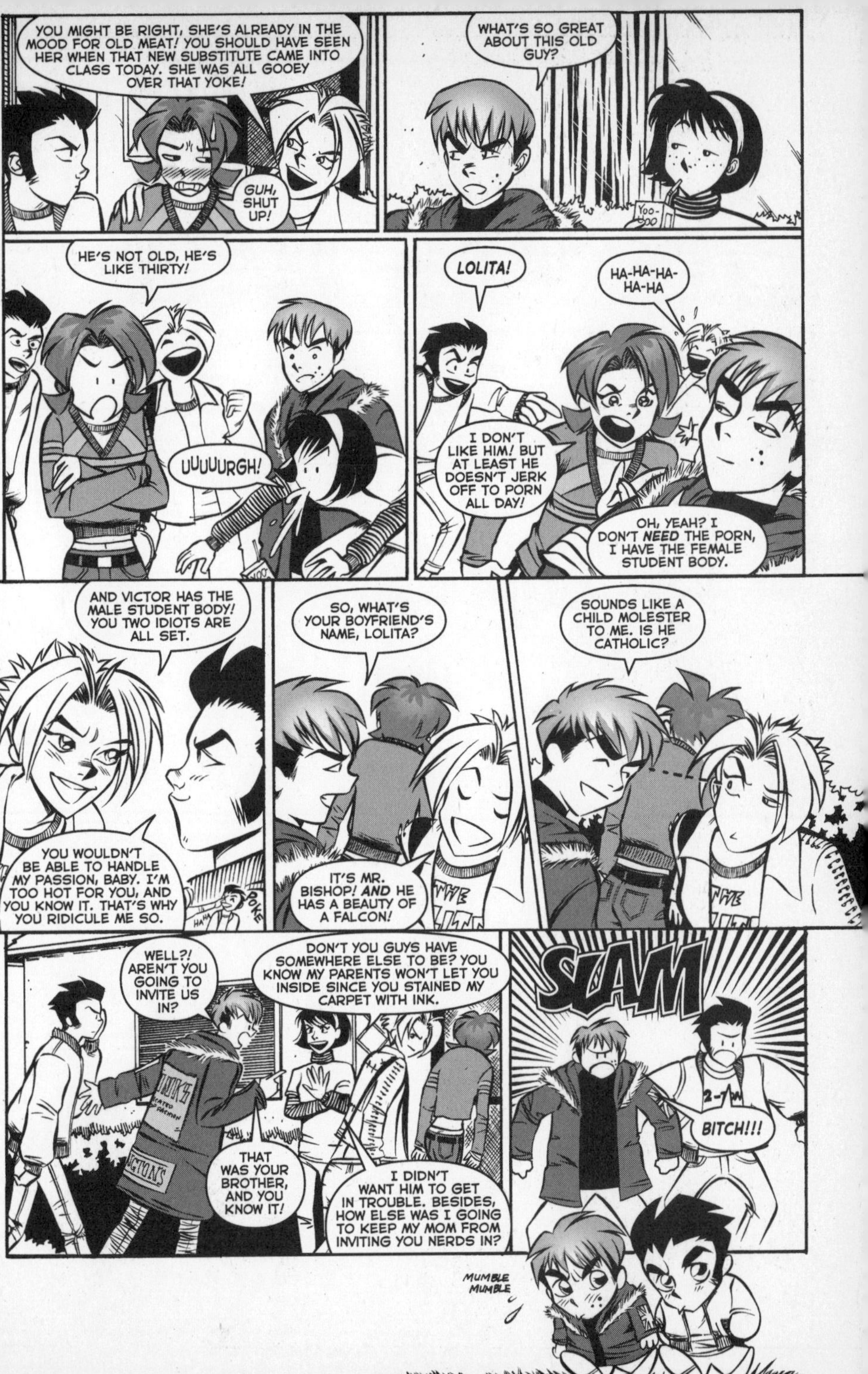
YOU MIGHT BE RIGHT, SHE'S ALREADY IN THE MOOD FOR OLD MEAT! YOU SHOULD HAVE SEEN HER WHEN THAT NEW SUBSTITUTE CAME INTO CLASS TODAY. SHE WAS ALL GOOEY OVER THAT YOKE!
GUH, SHUT UP!
WHAT'S SO GREAT ABOUT THIS OLD GUY?
YOO-HOO
HE'S NOT OLD, HE'S LIKE THIRTY!
UUUUURGH!
LOLITA!
HA-HA-HA-HA-HA
I DON'T LIKE HIM! BUT AT LEAST HE DOESN'T JERK OFF TO PORN ALL DAY!
OH, YEAH? I DON'T NEED THE PORN, I HAVE THE FEMALE STUDENT BODY.
AND VICTOR HAS THE MALE STUDENT BODY! YOU TWO IDIOTS ARE ALL SET.
YOU WOULDN'T BE ABLE TO HANDLE MY PASSION, BABY. I'M TOO HOT FOR YOU, AND YOU KNOW IT. THAT'S WHY YOU RIDICULE ME SO.
HA HA
POKE
SO, WHAT'S YOUR BOYFRIEND'S NAME, LOLITA?
IT'S MR. BISHOP! AND HE HAS A BEAUTY OF A FALCON!
SOUNDS LIKE A CHILD MOLESTER TO ME. IS HE CATHOLIC?
WELL?! AREN'T YOU GOING TO INVITE US IN?
DON'T YOU GUYS HAVE SOMEWHERE ELSE TO BE? YOU KNOW MY PARENTS WON'T LET YOU INSIDE SINCE YOU STAINED MY CARPET WITH INK.
THAT WAS YOUR BROTHER, AND YOU KNOW IT!
I DIDN'T WANT HIM TO GET IN TROUBLE. BESIDES, HOW ELSE WAS I GOING TO KEEP MY MOM FROM INVITING YOU NERDS IN?
SLAM
BITCH!!!
MUMBLE MUMBLE

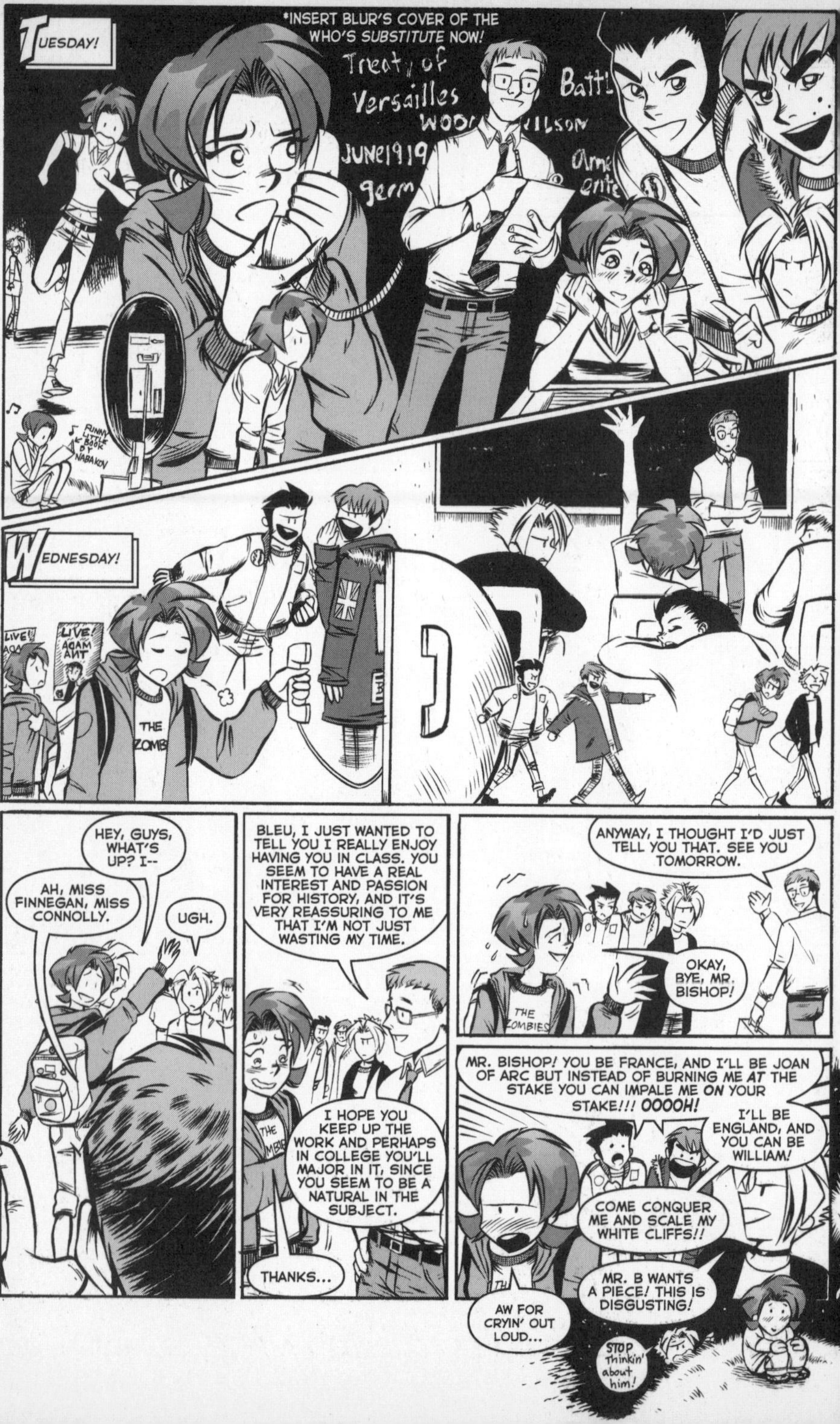
TUESDAY!
*INSERT BLUR'S COVER OF THE WHO'S SUBSTITUTE NOW!
Treaty of Versailles
Woodrow Wilson
JUNE 1919
germ
FUNNY LITTLE BOOK BY NABAKOV
WEDNESDAY!
LIVE! ADAM ANT
THE ZOMB
HEY, GUYS, WHAT'S UP? I--
AH, MISS FINNEGAN, MISS CONNOLLY.
UGH.
BLEU, I JUST WANTED TO TELL YOU I REALLY ENJOY HAVING YOU IN CLASS. YOU SEEM TO HAVE A REAL INTEREST AND PASSION FOR HISTORY, AND IT'S VERY REASSURING TO ME THAT I'M NOT JUST WASTING MY TIME.
I HOPE YOU KEEP UP THE WORK AND PERHAPS IN COLLEGE YOU'LL MAJOR IN IT, SINCE YOU SEEM TO BE A NATURAL IN THE SUBJECT.
THANKS...
ANYWAY, I THOUGHT I'D JUST TELL YOU THAT. SEE YOU TOMORROW.
OKAY, BYE, MR. BISHOP!
THE ZOMBIES
MR. BISHOP! YOU BE FRANCE, AND I'LL BE JOAN OF ARC BUT INSTEAD OF BURNING ME AT THE STAKE YOU CAN IMPALE ME ON YOUR STAKE!!! OOOOH!
I'LL BE ENGLAND, AND YOU CAN BE WILLIAM!
COME CONQUER ME AND SCALE MY WHITE CLIFFS!!
MR. B WANTS A PIECE! THIS IS DISGUSTING!
AW FOR CRYIN' OUT LOUD...
STOP Thinkin' about him!

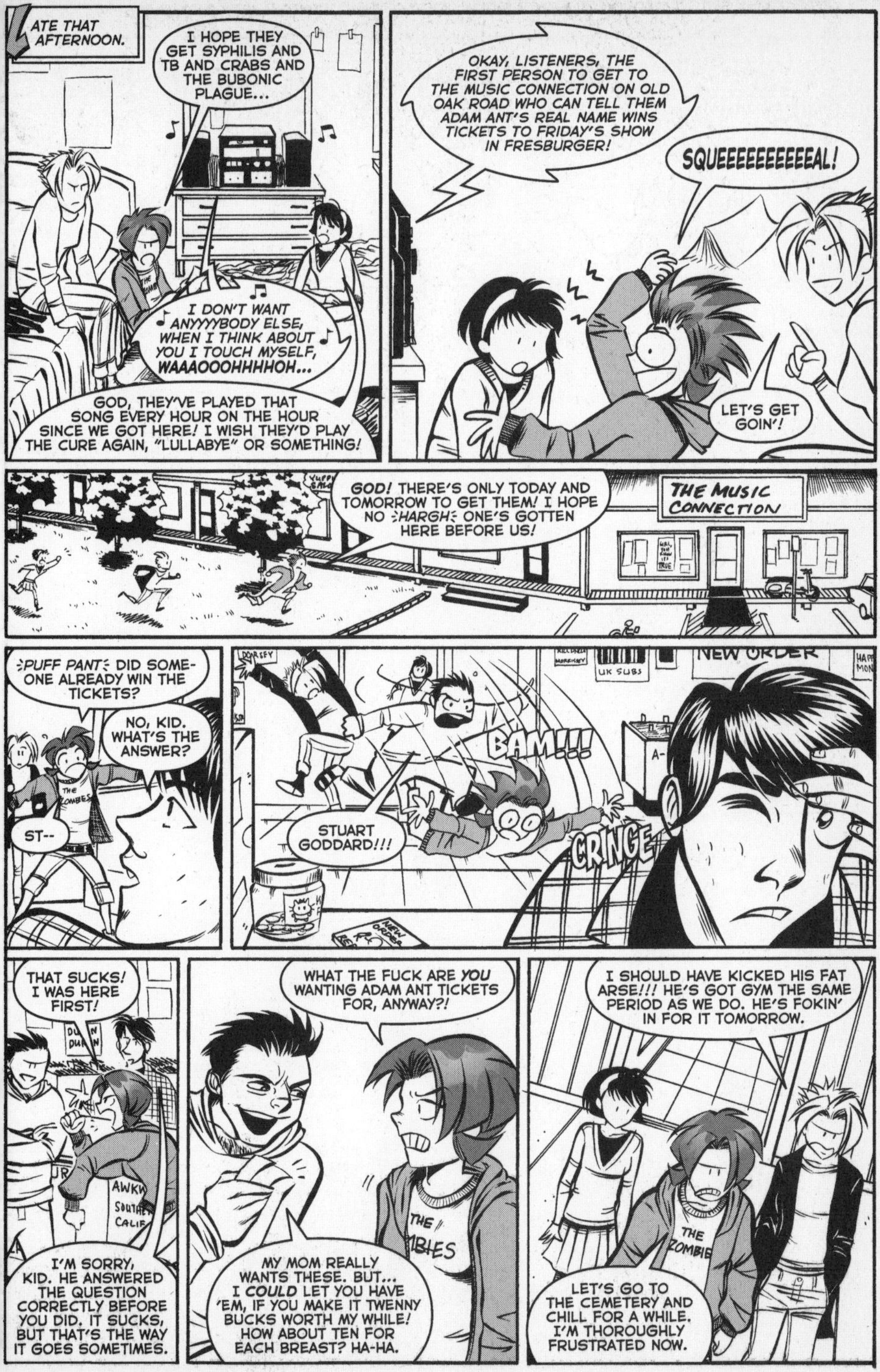
LATE THAT AFTERNOON.
I HOPE THEY GET SYPHILIS AND TB AND CRABS AND THE BUBONIC PLAGUE...
I DON'T WANT ANYYYYBODY ELSE, WHEN I THINK ABOUT YOU I TOUCH MYSELF, WAAAOOOHHHHOH...
GOD, THEY'VE PLAYED THAT SONG EVERY HOUR ON THE HOUR SINCE WE GOT HERE! I WISH THEY'D PLAY THE CURE AGAIN, "LULLABYE" OR SOMETHING!
OKAY, LISTENERS, THE FIRST PERSON TO GET TO THE MUSIC CONNECTION ON OLD OAK ROAD WHO CAN TELL THEM ADAM ANT'S REAL NAME WINS TICKETS TO FRIDAY'S SHOW IN FRESBURGER!
SQUEEEEEEEEEEAL!
LET'S GET GOIN'!
GOD! THERE'S ONLY TODAY AND TOMORROW TO GET THEM! I HOPE NO :HARGH: ONE'S GOTTEN HERE BEFORE US!
THE MUSIC CONNECTION
:PUFF PANT: DID SOME-ONE ALREADY WIN THE TICKETS?
NO, KID. WHAT'S THE ANSWER?
ST--
NEW ORDER
UK SUBS
BAM!!!
STUART GODDARD!!!
CRINGE
THAT SUCKS! I WAS HERE FIRST!
I'M SORRY, KID. HE ANSWERED THE QUESTION CORRECTLY BEFORE YOU DID. IT SUCKS, BUT THAT'S THE WAY IT GOES SOMETIMES.
WHAT THE FUCK ARE YOU WANTING ADAM ANT TICKETS FOR, ANYWAY?!
MY MOM REALLY WANTS THESE. BUT... I COULD LET YOU HAVE 'EM, IF YOU MAKE IT TWENNY BUCKS WORTH MY WHILE! HOW ABOUT TEN FOR EACH BREAST? HA-HA.
I SHOULD HAVE KICKED HIS FAT ARSE!!! HE'S GOT GYM THE SAME PERIOD AS WE DO. HE'S FOKIN' IN FOR IT TOMORROW.
LET'S GO TO THE CEMETERY AND CHILL FOR A WHILE. I'M THOROUGHLY FRUSTRATED NOW.

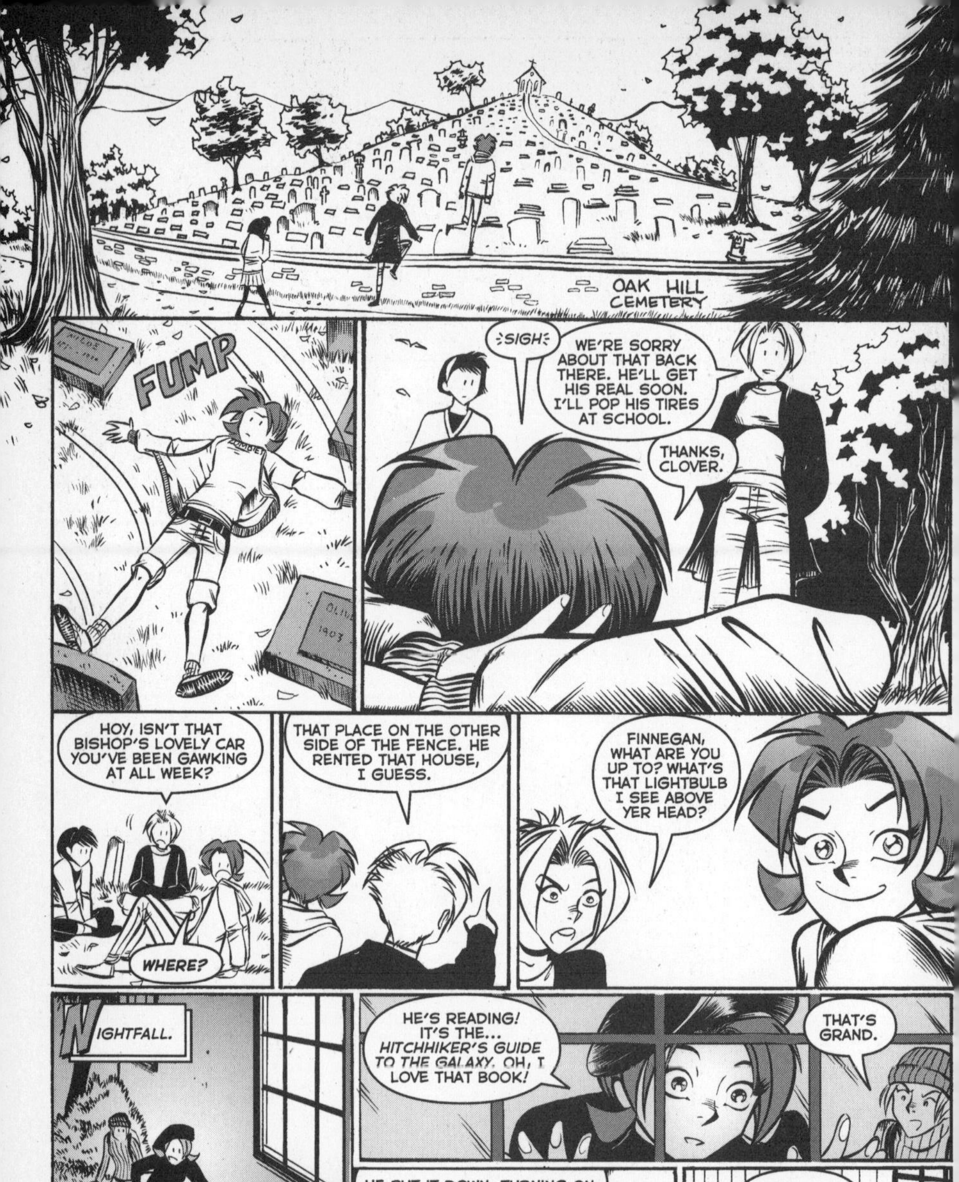
OAK HILL CEMETERY
FUMP
SIGH
WE'RE SORRY ABOUT THAT BACK THERE. HE'LL GET HIS REAL SOON. I'LL POP HIS TIRES AT SCHOOL.
THANKS, CLOVER.
HOY, ISN'T THAT BISHOP'S LOVELY CAR YOU'VE BEEN GAWKING AT ALL WEEK?
WHERE?
THAT PLACE ON THE OTHER SIDE OF THE FENCE. HE RENTED THAT HOUSE, I GUESS.
FINNEGAN, WHAT ARE YOU UP TO? WHAT'S THAT LIGHTBULB I SEE ABOVE YER HEAD?
NIGHTFALL.
I CAN'T BELIEVE IT! WE'RE JUST AS BAD AS ALAN AND VICTOR! I'LL TELL YOU, I DON'T WANT TO BE SEEIN' HIS THIRTY-YEAR-OLD, BARE ARSE, YOU BETTER JUST KEEP THE NAKED TALES TO YOURSELF.
HE'S READING! IT'S THE... *HITCHHIKER'S GUIDE TO THE GALAXY*. OH, I LOVE THAT BOOK!
THAT'S GRAND.
HE PUT IT DOWN. TURNING ON THE TELEVISION...OH NO, NOT "FULL HOUSE"!
WHEW, OKAY. HBO. OH, *MY GOD!* HE LEFT IT ON *HAROLD AND MAUDE!* OH, HE'S A *DREAM!*
GREAT. I'M FAMISHED, LET'S GO GET A BITE TO EAT NOW, ALL RIGHT?
AWWW, OKAY. I GUESS I'M HUNGRY, TOO. BYE, MR. B!

THIS ISN'T HEALTHY, BLEU. YOU NEED TO GET THIS GUY OUT OF YOUR HEAD. HE'S, LIKE, FIFTEEN YEARS OLDER THAN YOU, AND THE GUY IS YOUR TEACHER. YOU NEED TO FIND SOMEONE CLOSER TO OUR AGE!

YOU'RE RIGHT. I SHOULDN'T CARE ABOUT SOMEONE WHO'S NOT ONLY OLDER THAN ME, BUT ALSO NOT EVEN GOING TO BE HERE AFTER THIS FRIDAY.

‹SIGH›

DO YOU REALLY THINK IT'S BAD FOR HIM TO LIKE A FIFTEEN-YEAR-OLD?

YES! IT'S ILLEGAL!!!

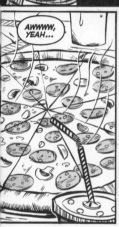

AWWWW, YEAH...

GOD BLESS THE ITALIANS FOR BRINGIN' PIZZA OVER AND LETTING AMERICA BASTARDIZE IT. THIS IS TH' BEST.

Foosh

THAT WAS MY LAST CHANCE TODAY. I GUESS THE ONLY LATE NIGHT CONTEST THEY HAD WAS LAST SATURDAY, SO MY ONLY HOPE IS TOMORROW. I'M SCREWED!

FWUMP

‹CHEW›
‹CHEW›

HI, GIRLS! IS THIS SEAT TAKEN? I'M BETTING IT ISN'T.

I DIDN'T THINK LIFE COULD GET ANY WORSE -- UNTIL YOU SHOWED UP!

WOP

DON'T BE AITIN ALL MY PIZZA!

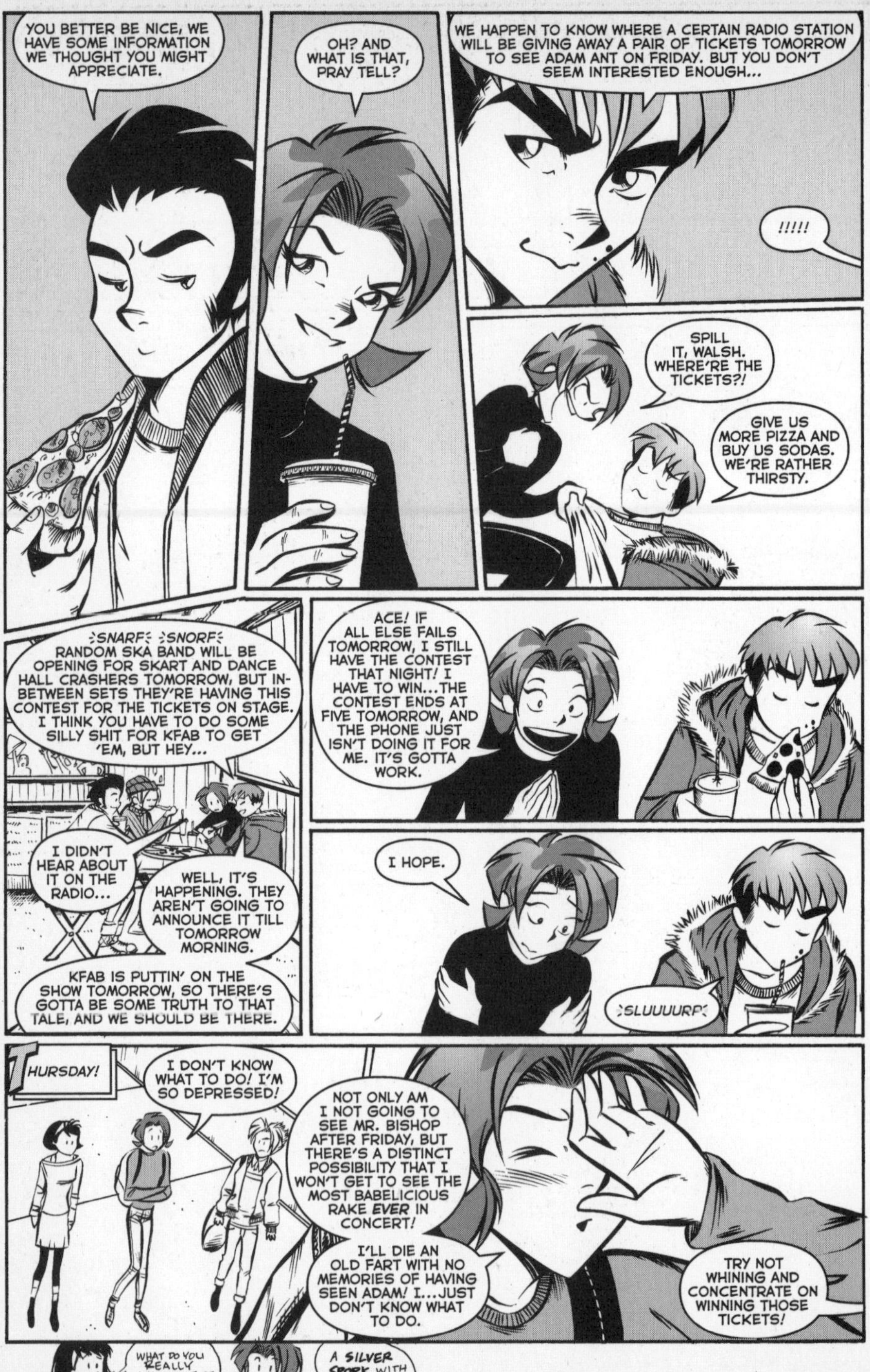
YOU BETTER BE NICE, WE HAVE SOME INFORMATION WE THOUGHT YOU MIGHT APPRECIATE.
OH? AND WHAT IS THAT, PRAY TELL?
WE HAPPEN TO KNOW WHERE A CERTAIN RADIO STATION WILL BE GIVING AWAY A PAIR OF TICKETS TOMORROW TO SEE ADAM ANT ON FRIDAY. BUT YOU DON'T SEEM INTERESTED ENOUGH...
!!!!!
SPILL IT, WALSH. WHERE'RE THE TICKETS?!
GIVE US MORE PIZZA AND BUY US SODAS. WE'RE RATHER THIRSTY.
SNARF SNORF
RANDOM SKA BAND WILL BE OPENING FOR SKART AND DANCE HALL CRASHERS TOMORROW, BUT IN-BETWEEN SETS THEY'RE HAVING THIS CONTEST FOR THE TICKETS ON STAGE. I THINK YOU HAVE TO DO SOME SILLY SHIT FOR KFAB TO GET 'EM, BUT HEY...
I DIDN'T HEAR ABOUT IT ON THE RADIO...
WELL, IT'S HAPPENING. THEY AREN'T GOING TO ANNOUNCE IT TILL TOMORROW MORNING.
KFAB IS PUTTIN' ON THE SHOW TOMORROW, SO THERE'S GOTTA BE SOME TRUTH TO THAT TALE, AND WE SHOULD BE THERE.
ACE! IF ALL ELSE FAILS TOMORROW, I STILL HAVE THE CONTEST THAT NIGHT! I HAVE TO WIN...THE CONTEST ENDS AT FIVE TOMORROW, AND THE PHONE JUST ISN'T DOING IT FOR ME. IT'S GOTTA WORK.
I HOPE.
SLUUUURP
THURSDAY!
I DON'T KNOW WHAT TO DO! I'M SO DEPRESSED!
NOT ONLY AM I NOT GOING TO SEE MR. BISHOP AFTER FRIDAY, BUT THERE'S A DISTINCT POSSIBILITY THAT I WON'T GET TO SEE THE MOST BABELICIOUS RAKE EVER IN CONCERT!
I'LL DIE AN OLD FART WITH NO MEMORIES OF HAVING SEEN ADAM! I...JUST DON'T KNOW WHAT TO DO.
TRY NOT WHINING AND CONCENTRATE ON WINNING THOSE TICKETS!
WHAT DO YOU REALLY WANT OUT OF LIFE, BLEU?
HMM.
A SILVER SPORK WITH THE NUMBER '19' ON THE BACK!
YEAH!
THAT'D BE COOL.

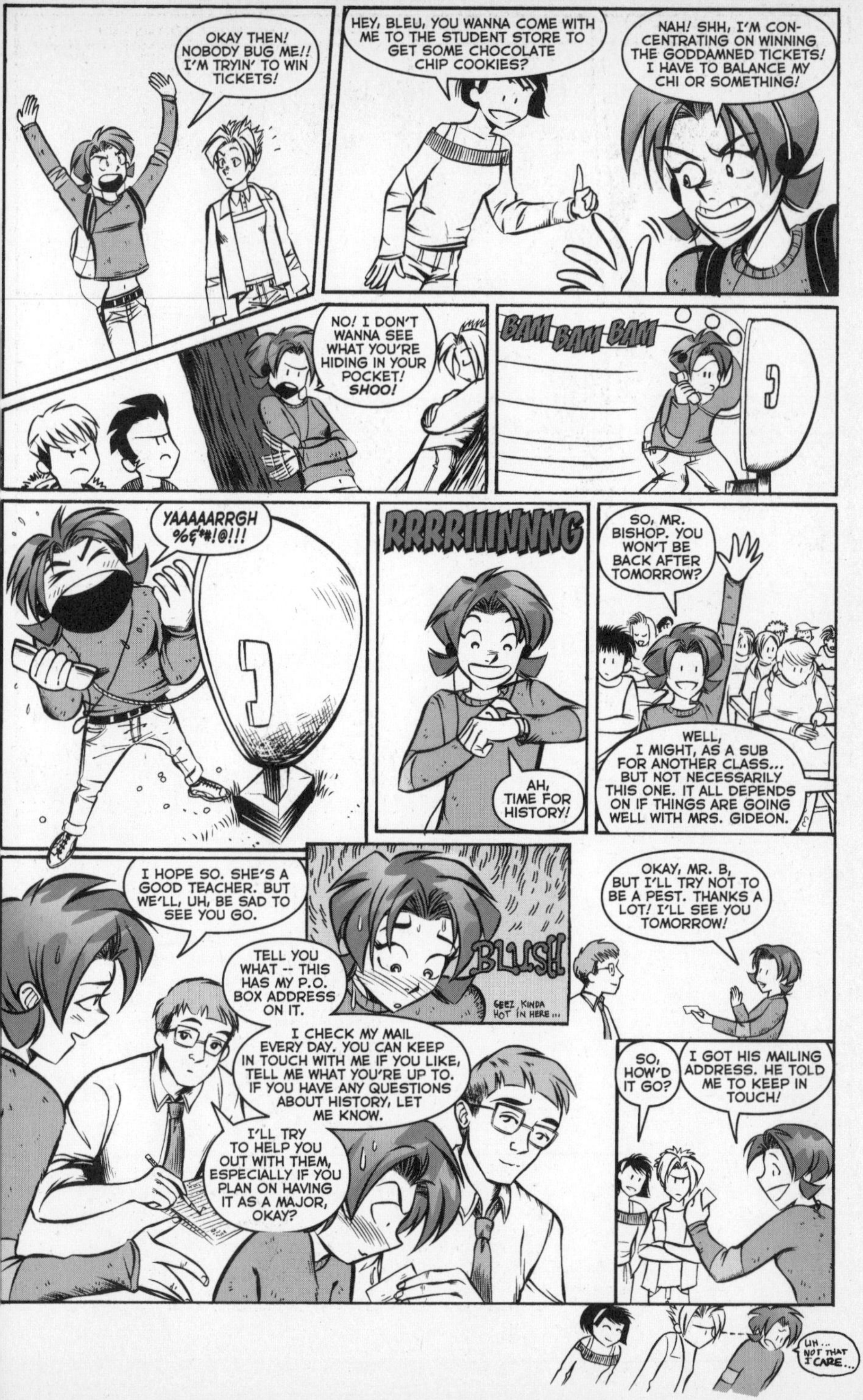
OKAY THEN! NOBODY BUG ME!! I'M TRYIN' TO WIN TICKETS!
HEY, BLEU, YOU WANNA COME WITH ME TO THE STUDENT STORE TO GET SOME CHOCOLATE CHIP COOKIES?
NAH! SHH, I'M CONCENTRATING ON WINNING THE GODDAMNED TICKETS! I HAVE TO BALANCE MY CHI OR SOMETHING!
NO! I DON'T WANNA SEE WHAT YOU'RE HIDING IN YOUR POCKET! SHOO!
BAM BAM BAM
YAAAAARRGH %$*#!@!!!
RRRRIIIINNNG
AH, TIME FOR HISTORY!
SO, MR. BISHOP. YOU WON'T BE BACK AFTER TOMORROW?
WELL, I MIGHT, AS A SUB FOR ANOTHER CLASS... BUT NOT NECESSARILY THIS ONE. IT ALL DEPENDS ON IF THINGS ARE GOING WELL WITH MRS. GIDEON.
I HOPE SO. SHE'S A GOOD TEACHER. BUT WE'LL, UH, BE SAD TO SEE YOU GO.
TELL YOU WHAT -- THIS HAS MY P.O. BOX ADDRESS ON IT.
I CHECK MY MAIL EVERY DAY. YOU CAN KEEP IN TOUCH WITH ME IF YOU LIKE, TELL ME WHAT YOU'RE UP TO. IF YOU HAVE ANY QUESTIONS ABOUT HISTORY, LET ME KNOW.
I'LL TRY TO HELP YOU OUT WITH THEM, ESPECIALLY IF YOU PLAN ON HAVING IT AS A MAJOR, OKAY?
BLUSH!
GEEZ, KINDA HOT IN HERE...
OKAY, MR. B, BUT I'LL TRY NOT TO BE A PEST. THANKS A LOT! I'LL SEE YOU TOMORROW!
SO, HOW'D IT GO?
I GOT HIS MAILING ADDRESS. HE TOLD ME TO KEEP IN TOUCH!
UH... NOT THAT I CARE...

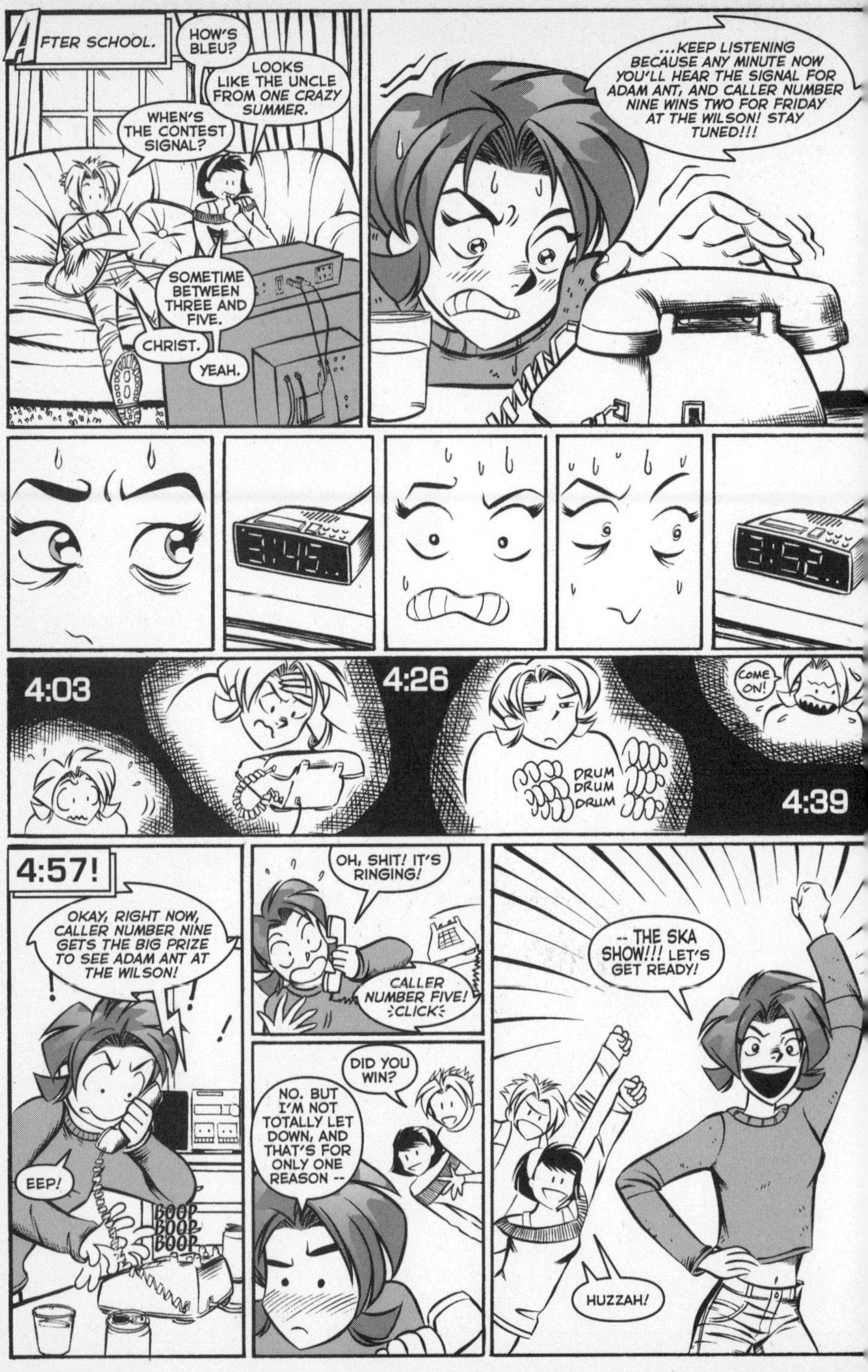
AFTER SCHOOL.
HOW'S BLEU?
LOOKS LIKE THE UNCLE FROM ONE CRAZY SUMMER.
WHEN'S THE CONTEST SIGNAL?
SOMETIME BETWEEN THREE AND FIVE.
CHRIST.
YEAH.
...KEEP LISTENING BECAUSE ANY MINUTE NOW YOU'LL HEAR THE SIGNAL FOR ADAM ANT, AND CALLER NUMBER NINE WINS TWO FOR FRIDAY AT THE WILSON! STAY TUNED!!!
3:45
3:52
4:03
4:26
DRUM DRUM DRUM
COME ON!
4:39
4:57!
OKAY, RIGHT NOW, CALLER NUMBER NINE GETS THE BIG PRIZE TO SEE ADAM ANT AT THE WILSON!
EEP!
BOOP BOOP BOOP
OH, SHIT! IT'S RINGING!
CALLER NUMBER FIVE! CLICK
DID YOU WIN?
NO. BUT I'M NOT TOTALLY LET DOWN, AND THAT'S FOR ONLY ONE REASON --
-- THE SKA SHOW!!! LET'S GET READY!
HUZZAH!

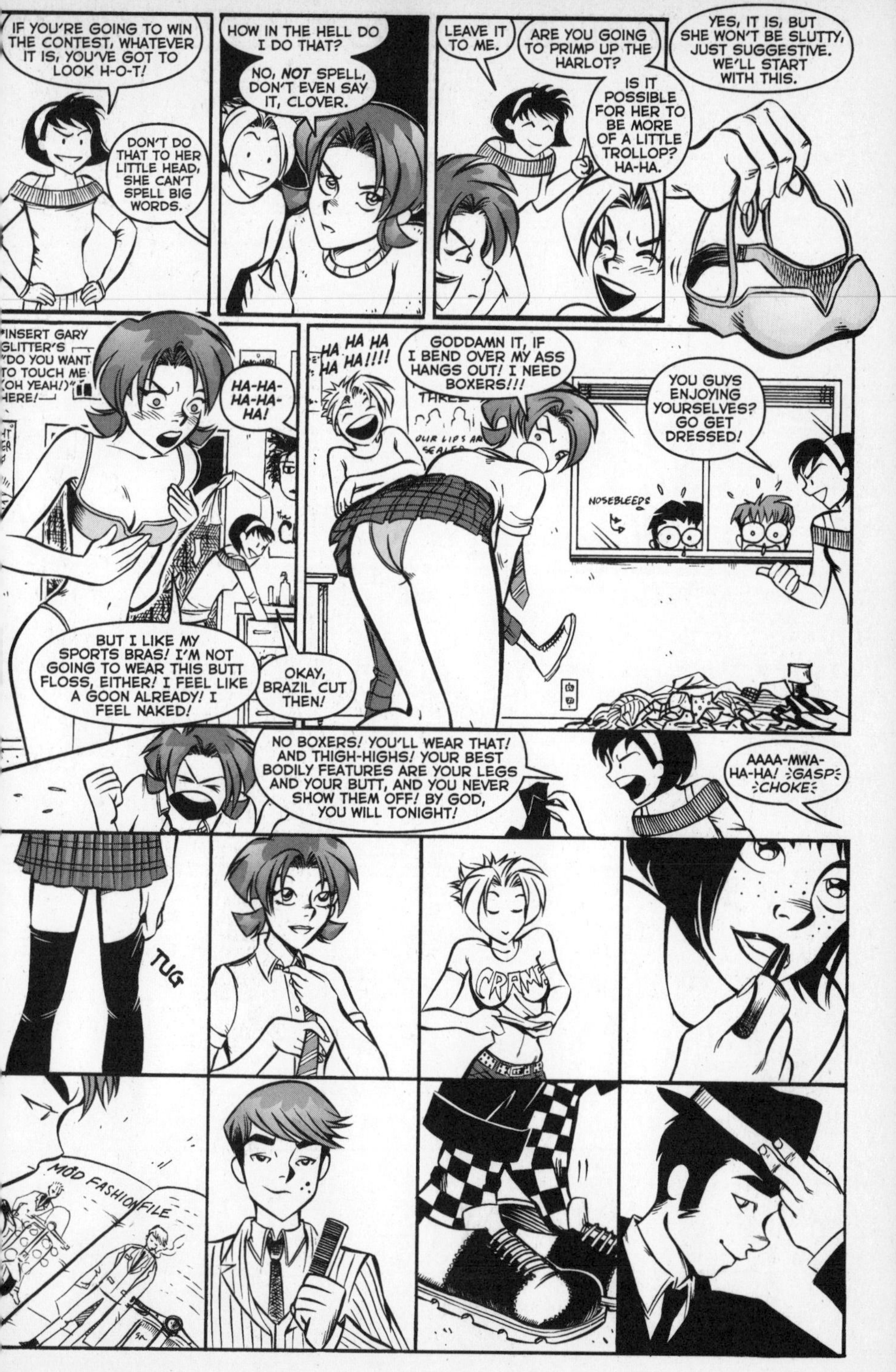
IF YOU'RE GOING TO WIN THE CONTEST, WHATEVER IT IS, YOU'VE GOT TO LOOK H-O-T!
DON'T DO THAT TO HER LITTLE HEAD, SHE CAN'T SPELL BIG WORDS.
HOW IN THE HELL DO I DO THAT?
NO, NOT SPELL, DON'T EVEN SAY IT, CLOVER.
LEAVE IT TO ME.
ARE YOU GOING TO PRIMP UP THE HARLOT?
IS IT POSSIBLE FOR HER TO BE MORE OF A LITTLE TROLLOP? HA-HA.
YES, IT IS, BUT SHE WON'T BE SLUTTY, JUST SUGGESTIVE. WE'LL START WITH THIS.
*INSERT GARY GLITTER'S "DO YOU WANT TO TOUCH ME (OH YEAH!)" HERE!
HA-HA-HA-HA-HA!
BUT I LIKE MY SPORTS BRAS! I'M NOT GOING TO WEAR THIS BUTT FLOSS, EITHER! I FEEL LIKE A GOON ALREADY! I FEEL NAKED!
OKAY, BRAZIL CUT THEN!
HA HA HA HA HA!!!!
GODDAMN IT, IF I BEND OVER MY ASS HANGS OUT! I NEED BOXERS!!!
YOU GUYS ENJOYING YOURSELVES? GO GET DRESSED!
NOSEBLEEDS
NO BOXERS! YOU'LL WEAR THAT! AND THIGH-HIGHS! YOUR BEST BODILY FEATURES ARE YOUR LEGS AND YOUR BUTT, AND YOU NEVER SHOW THEM OFF! BY GOD, YOU WILL TONIGHT!
AAAA-MWA-HA-HA! GASP CHOKE
TUG
MOD FASHION FILE

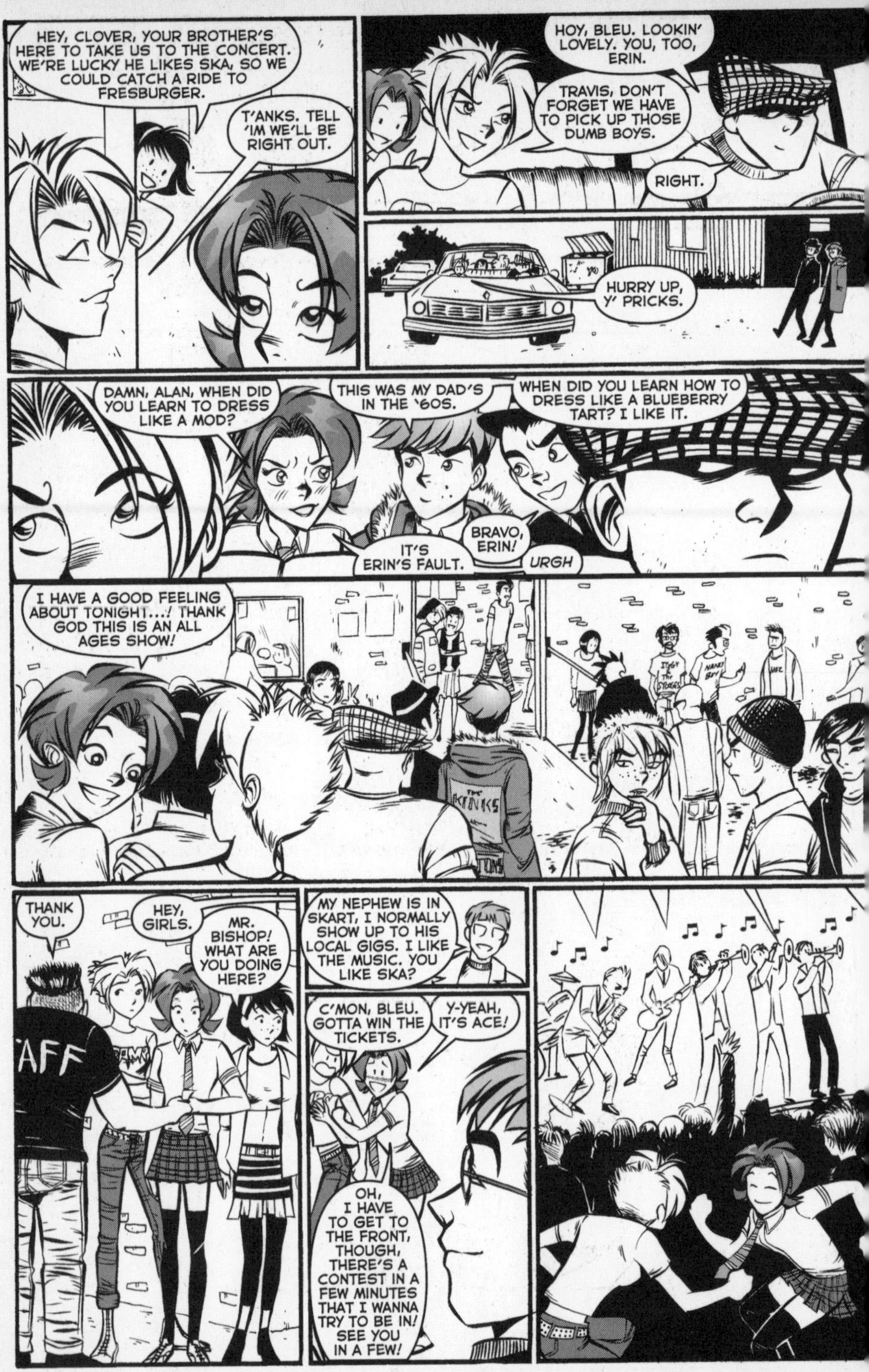
HEY, CLOVER, YOUR BROTHER'S HERE TO TAKE US TO THE CONCERT. WE'RE LUCKY HE LIKES SKA, SO WE COULD CATCH A RIDE TO FRESBURGER.
T'ANKS. TELL 'IM WE'LL BE RIGHT OUT.
HOY, BLEU. LOOKIN' LOVELY. YOU, TOO, ERIN.
TRAVIS, DON'T FORGET WE HAVE TO PICK UP THOSE DUMB BOYS.
RIGHT.
HURRY UP, Y' PRICKS.
DAMN, ALAN, WHEN DID YOU LEARN TO DRESS LIKE A MOD?
THIS WAS MY DAD'S IN THE '60S.
WHEN DID YOU LEARN HOW TO DRESS LIKE A BLUEBERRY TART? I LIKE IT.
IT'S ERIN'S FAULT.
BRAVO, ERIN!
URGH
I HAVE A GOOD FEELING ABOUT TONIGHT...! THANK GOD THIS IS AN ALL AGES SHOW!
THANK YOU.
HEY, GIRLS.
MR. BISHOP! WHAT ARE YOU DOING HERE?
MY NEPHEW IS IN SKART, I NORMALLY SHOW UP TO HIS LOCAL GIGS. I LIKE THE MUSIC. YOU LIKE SKA?
Y-YEAH, IT'S ACE!
C'MON, BLEU. GOTTA WIN THE TICKETS.
OH, I HAVE TO GET TO THE FRONT, THOUGH, THERE'S A CONTEST IN A FEW MINUTES THAT I WANNA TRY TO BE IN! SEE YOU IN A FEW!

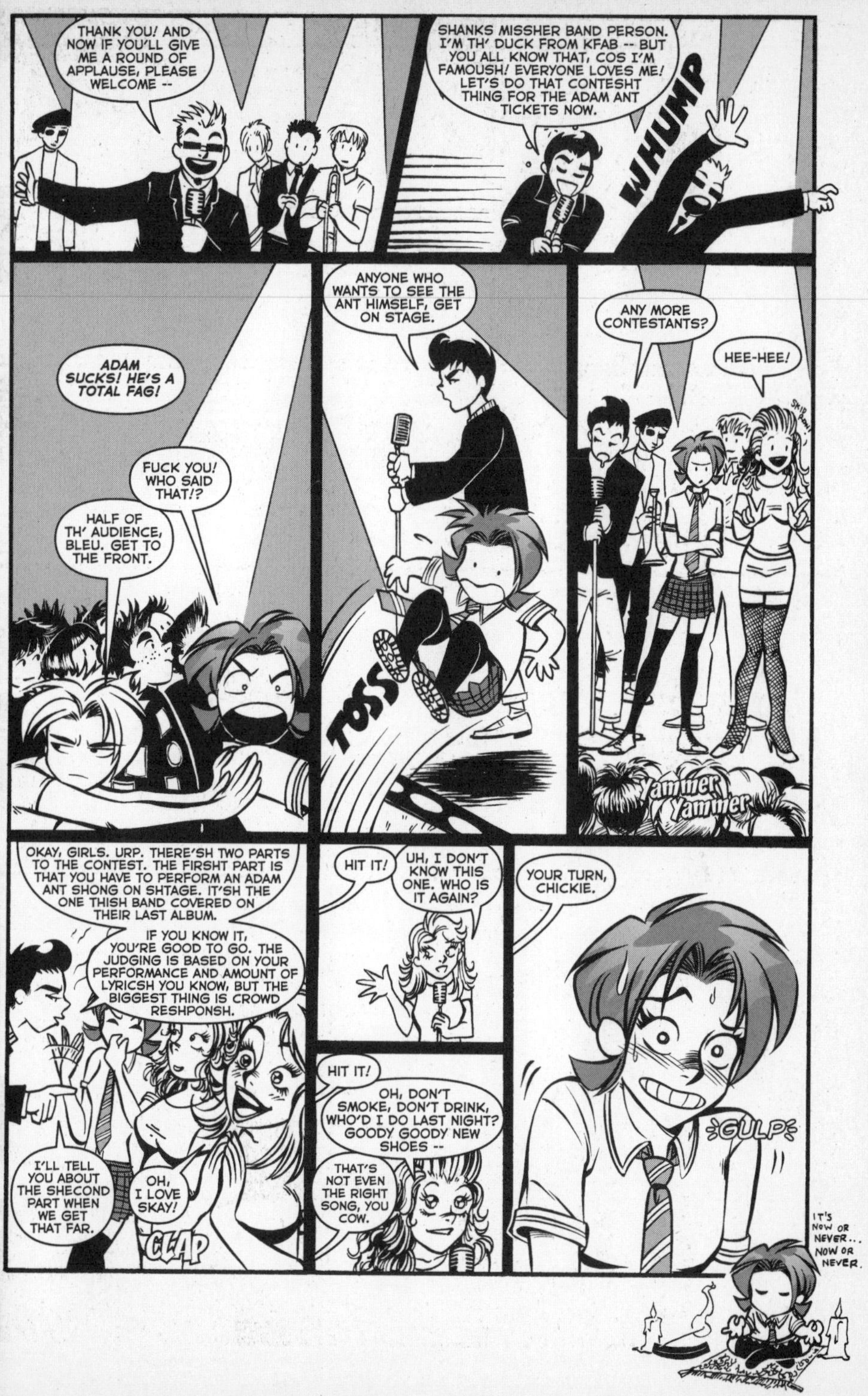
THANK YOU! AND NOW IF YOU'LL GIVE ME A ROUND OF APPLAUSE, PLEASE WELCOME --
SHANKS MISSHER BAND PERSON. I'M TH' DUCK FROM KFAB -- BUT YOU ALL KNOW THAT, COS I'M FAMOUSH! EVERYONE LOVES ME! LET'S DO THAT CONTESHT THING FOR THE ADAM ANT TICKETS NOW.
WHUMP
OH!
ADAM SUCKS! HE'S A TOTAL FAG!
FUCK YOU! WHO SAID THAT!?
HALF OF TH' AUDIENCE, BLEU. GET TO THE FRONT.
ANYONE WHO WANTS TO SEE THE ANT HIMSELF, GET ON STAGE.
TOSS
ANY MORE CONTESTANTS?
HEE-HEE!
SKIP BOW!
Yammer Yammer
OKAY, GIRLS. URP. THERE'SH TWO PARTS TO THE CONTEST. THE FIRSHT PART IS THAT YOU HAVE TO PERFORM AN ADAM ANT SHONG ON SHTAGE. IT'SH THE ONE THISH BAND COVERED ON THEIR LAST ALBUM.
IF YOU KNOW IT, YOU'RE GOOD TO GO. THE JUDGING IS BASED ON YOUR PERFORMANCE AND AMOUNT OF LYRICSH YOU KNOW, BUT THE BIGGEST THING IS CROWD RESHPONSH.
I'LL TELL YOU ABOUT THE SHECOND PART WHEN WE GET THAT FAR.
OH, I LOVE SKAY!
CLAP
HIT IT!
UH, I DON'T KNOW THIS ONE. WHO IS IT AGAIN?
HIT IT!
OH, DON'T SMOKE, DON'T DRINK, WHO'D I DO LAST NIGHT? GOODY GOODY NEW SHOES --
THAT'S NOT EVEN THE RIGHT SONG, YOU COW.
YOUR TURN, CHICKIE.
GULP
IT'S NOW OR NEVER... NOW OR NEVER.

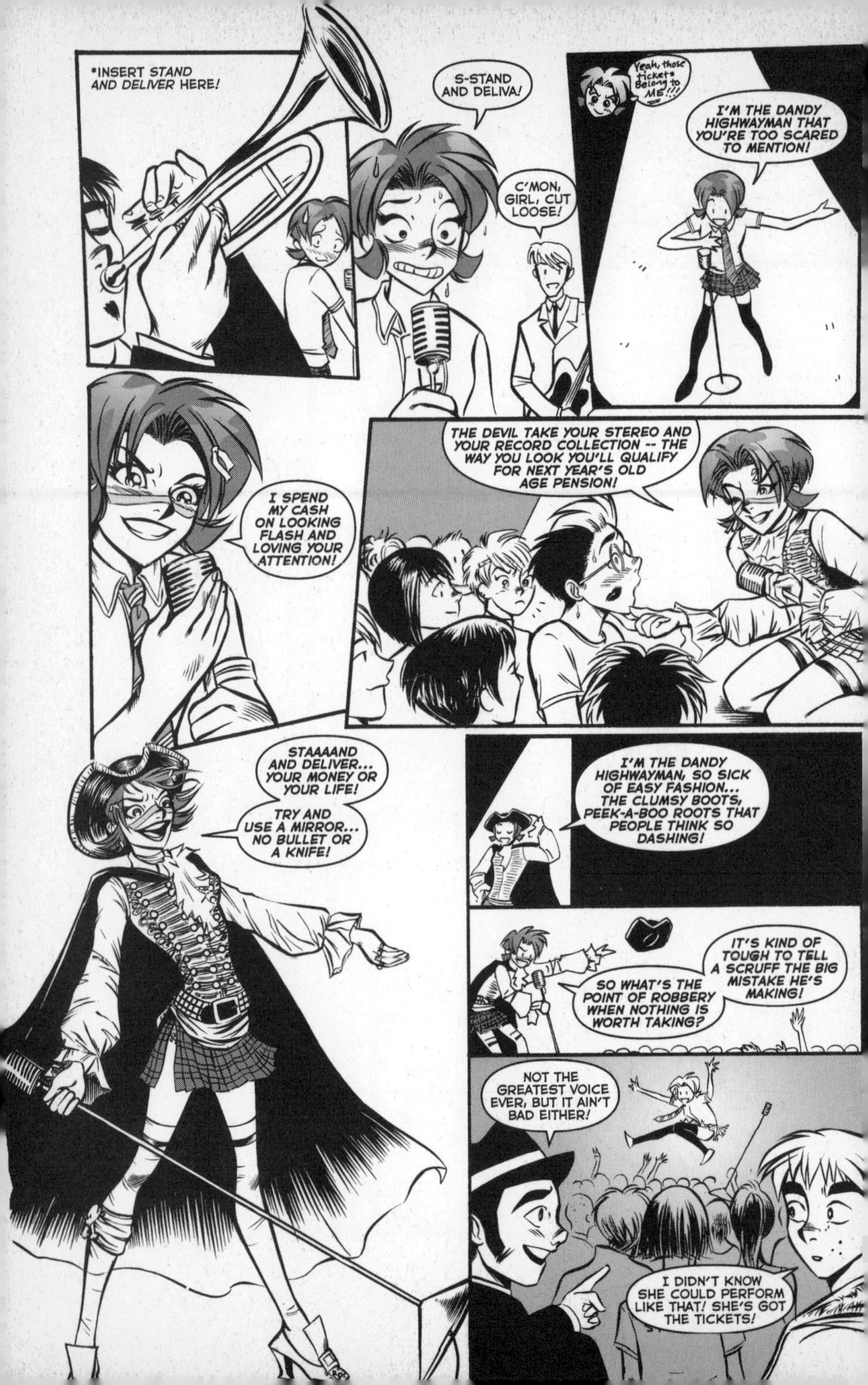
*INSERT STAND AND DELIVER HERE!
S-STAND AND DELIVA!
C'MON, GIRL, CUT LOOSE!
Yeah, those tickets Belong to ME!!!
I'M THE DANDY HIGHWAYMAN THAT YOU'RE TOO SCARED TO MENTION!
I SPEND MY CASH ON LOOKING FLASH AND LOVING YOUR ATTENTION!
THE DEVIL TAKE YOUR STEREO AND YOUR RECORD COLLECTION -- THE WAY YOU LOOK YOU'LL QUALIFY FOR NEXT YEAR'S OLD AGE PENSION!
STAAAAND AND DELIVER... YOUR MONEY OR YOUR LIFE!
TRY AND USE A MIRROR... NO BULLET OR A KNIFE!
I'M THE DANDY HIGHWAYMAN, SO SICK OF EASY FASHION... THE CLUMSY BOOTS, PEEK-A-BOO ROOTS THAT PEOPLE THINK SO DASHING!
IT'S KIND OF TOUGH TO TELL A SCRUFF THE BIG MISTAKE HE'S MAKING!
SO WHAT'S THE POINT OF ROBBERY WHEN NOTHING IS WORTH TAKING?
NOT THE GREATEST VOICE EVER, BUT IT AIN'T BAD EITHER!
I DIDN'T KNOW SHE COULD PERFORM LIKE THAT! SHE'S GOT THE TICKETS!

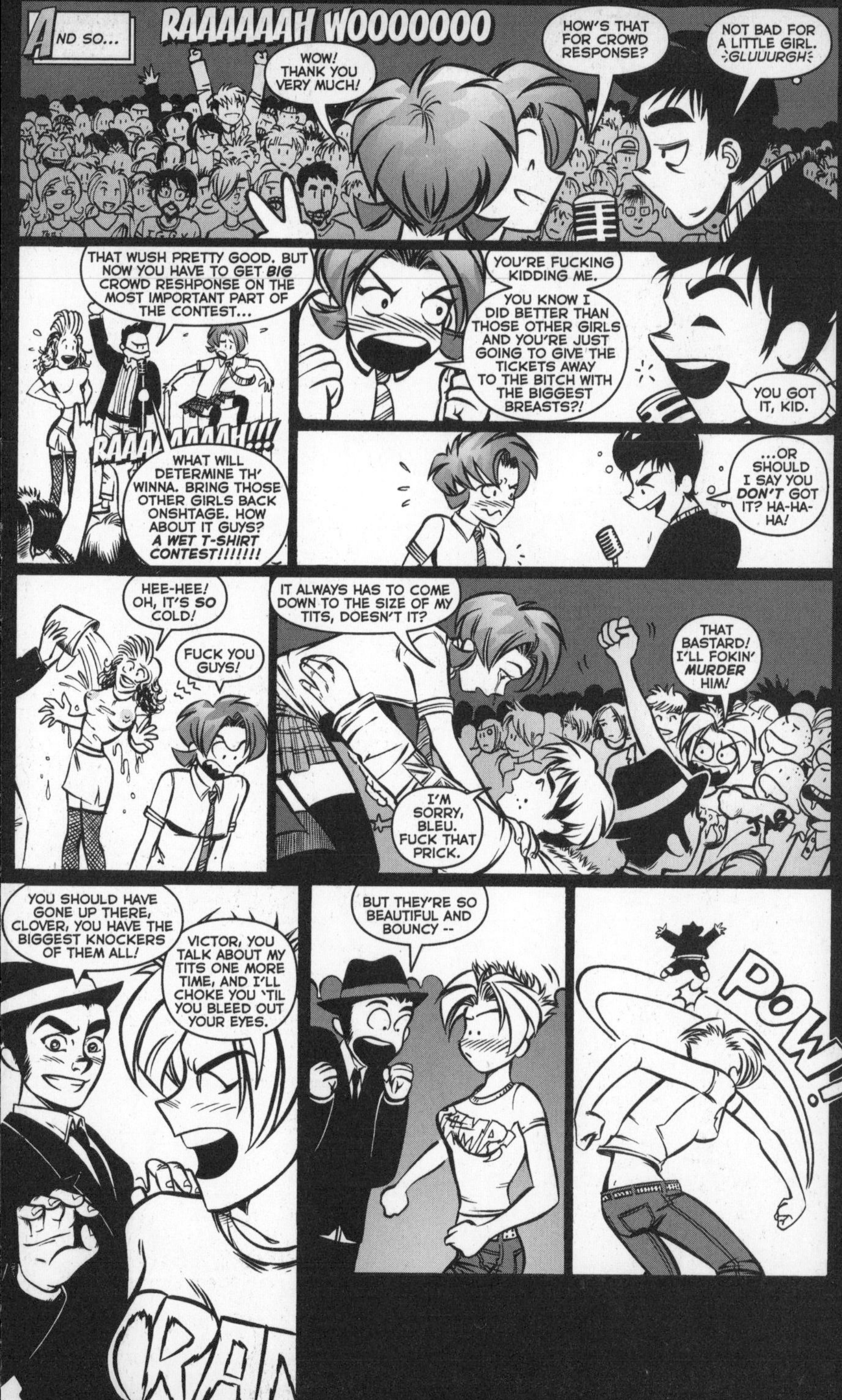
AND SO...
RAAAAAAH WOOOOOOO
WOW! THANK YOU VERY MUCH!
HOW'S THAT FOR CROWD RESPONSE?
NOT BAD FOR A LITTLE GIRL. GLUUURGH
THAT WUSH PRETTY GOOD. BUT NOW YOU HAVE TO GET BIG CROWD RESHPONSE ON THE MOST IMPORTANT PART OF THE CONTEST...
RAAAAAAAAH!!!
WHAT WILL DETERMINE TH' WINNA. BRING THOSE OTHER GIRLS BACK ONSHTAGE. HOW ABOUT IT GUYS? A WET T-SHIRT CONTEST!!!!!!!
YOU'RE FUCKING KIDDING ME.
YOU KNOW I DID BETTER THAN THOSE OTHER GIRLS AND YOU'RE JUST GOING TO GIVE THE TICKETS AWAY TO THE BITCH WITH THE BIGGEST BREASTS?!
YOU GOT IT, KID.
...OR SHOULD I SAY YOU DON'T GOT IT? HA-HA-HA!
HEE-HEE! OH, IT'S SO COLD!
FUCK YOU GUYS!
IT ALWAYS HAS TO COME DOWN TO THE SIZE OF MY TITS, DOESN'T IT?
THAT BASTARD! I'LL FOKIN' MURDER HIM!
I'M SORRY, BLEU. FUCK THAT PRICK.
YOU SHOULD HAVE GONE UP THERE, CLOVER, YOU HAVE THE BIGGEST KNOCKERS OF THEM ALL!
VICTOR, YOU TALK ABOUT MY TITS ONE MORE TIME, AND I'LL CHOKE YOU 'TIL YOU BLEED OUT YOUR EYES.
CRAIN
BUT THEY'RE SO BEAUTIFUL AND BOUNCY --
POW!

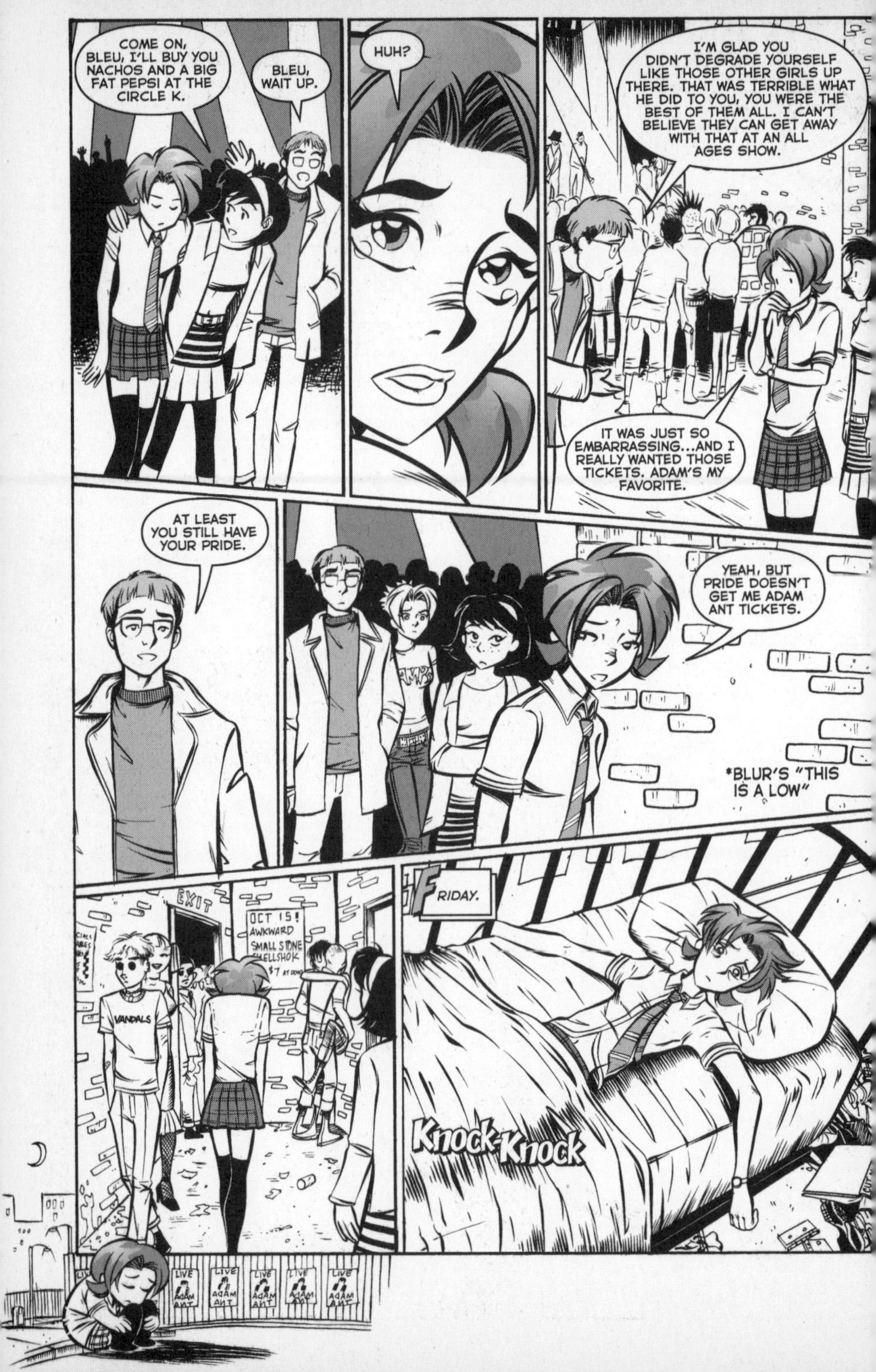
COME ON, BLEU, I'LL BUY YOU NACHOS AND A BIG FAT PEPSI AT THE CIRCLE K.
BLEU, WAIT UP.
HUH?
I'M GLAD YOU DIDN'T DEGRADE YOURSELF LIKE THOSE OTHER GIRLS UP THERE. THAT WAS TERRIBLE WHAT HE DID TO YOU, YOU WERE THE BEST OF THEM ALL. I CAN'T BELIEVE THEY CAN GET AWAY WITH THAT AT AN ALL AGES SHOW.
IT WAS JUST SO EMBARRASSING...AND I REALLY WANTED THOSE TICKETS. ADAM'S MY FAVORITE.
AT LEAST YOU STILL HAVE YOUR PRIDE.
YEAH, BUT PRIDE DOESN'T GET ME ADAM ANT TICKETS.
*BLUR'S "THIS IS A LOW"
EXIT
OCT 15!
AWKWARD
SMALL STONE
VANDALS
LIVE ADAM ANT
FRIDAY.
Knock-Knock

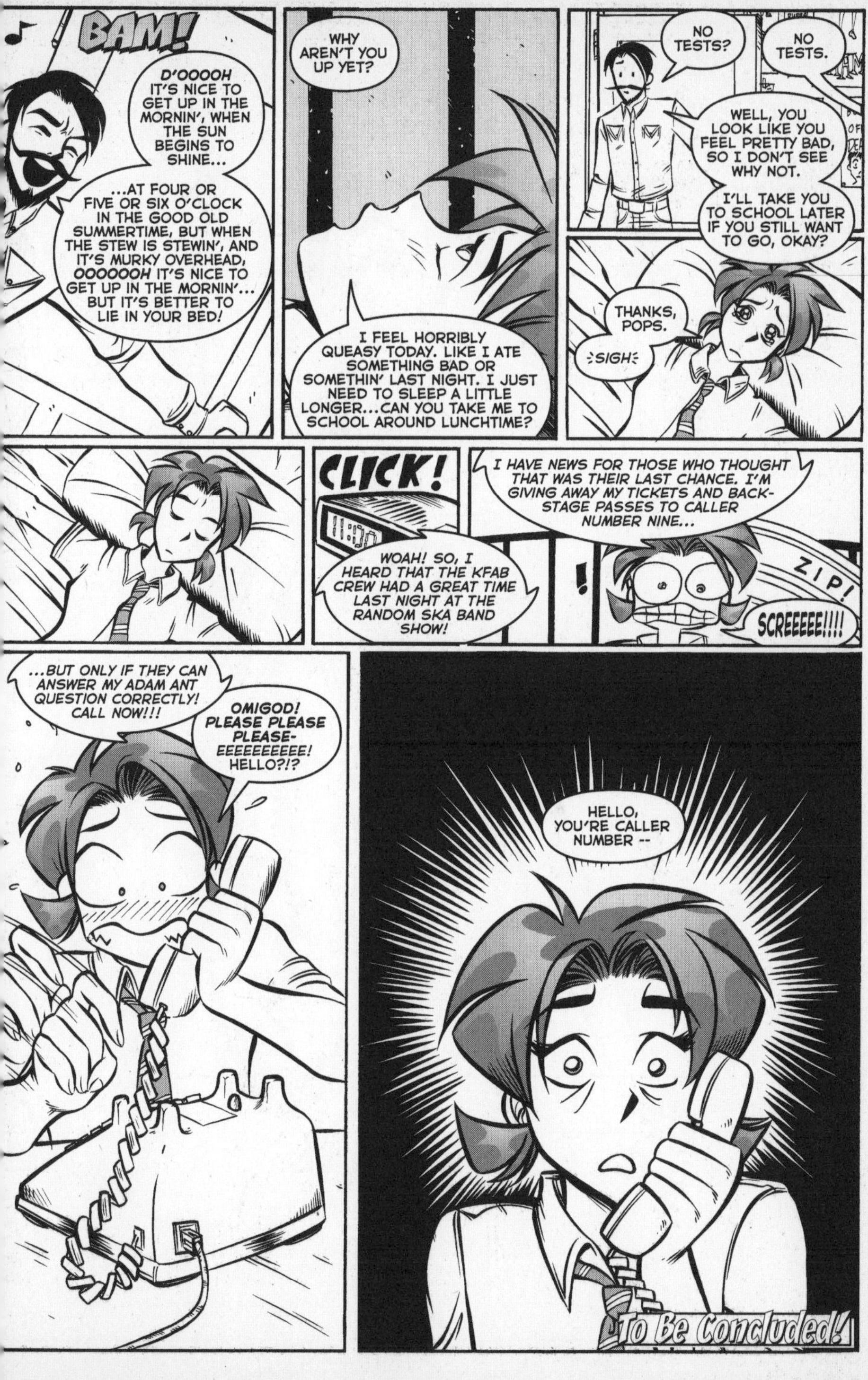
BAM!
D'OOOOH IT'S NICE TO GET UP IN THE MORNIN', WHEN THE SUN BEGINS TO SHINE...
...AT FOUR OR FIVE OR SIX O'CLOCK IN THE GOOD OLD SUMMERTIME, BUT WHEN THE STEW IS STEWIN', AND IT'S MURKY OVERHEAD, OOOOOOH IT'S NICE TO GET UP IN THE MORNIN'... BUT IT'S BETTER TO LIE IN YOUR BED!
WHY AREN'T YOU UP YET?
I FEEL HORRIBLY QUEASY TODAY. LIKE I ATE SOMETHING BAD OR SOMETHIN' LAST NIGHT. I JUST NEED TO SLEEP A LITTLE LONGER...CAN YOU TAKE ME TO SCHOOL AROUND LUNCHTIME?
NO TESTS?
NO TESTS.
WELL, YOU LOOK LIKE YOU FEEL PRETTY BAD, SO I DON'T SEE WHY NOT.
I'LL TAKE YOU TO SCHOOL LATER IF YOU STILL WANT TO GO, OKAY?
THANKS, POPS.
SIGH
CLICK!
WOAH! SO, I HEARD THAT THE KFAB CREW HAD A GREAT TIME LAST NIGHT AT THE RANDOM SKA BAND SHOW!
I HAVE NEWS FOR THOSE WHO THOUGHT THAT WAS THEIR LAST CHANCE. I'M GIVING AWAY MY TICKETS AND BACK-STAGE PASSES TO CALLER NUMBER NINE...
!
ZIP!
SCREEEEE!!!!
...BUT ONLY IF THEY CAN ANSWER MY ADAM ANT QUESTION CORRECTLY! CALL NOW!!!
OMIGOD! PLEASE PLEASE PLEASE-EEEEEEEEEE! HELLO?!?
HELLO, YOU'RE CALLER NUMBER --
To Be Concluded!

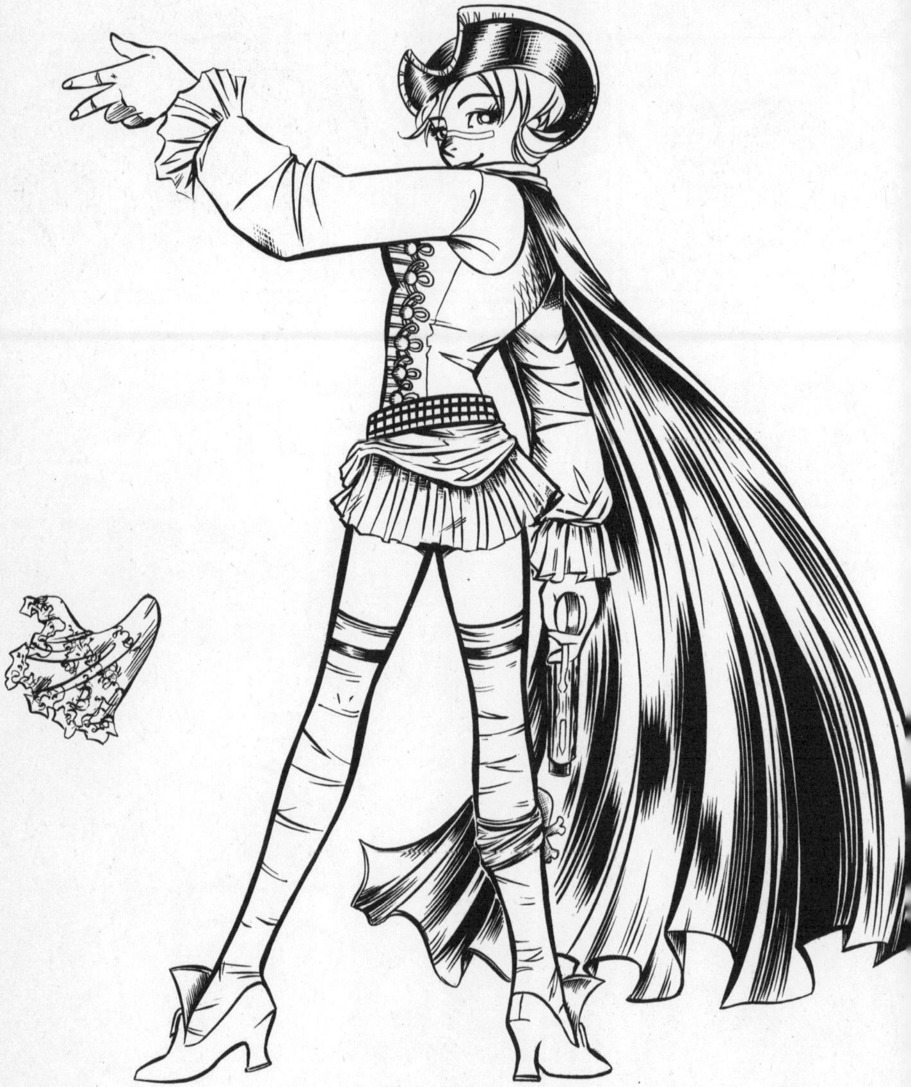

chapter three:

# "TRY THIS FOR SIGHS"

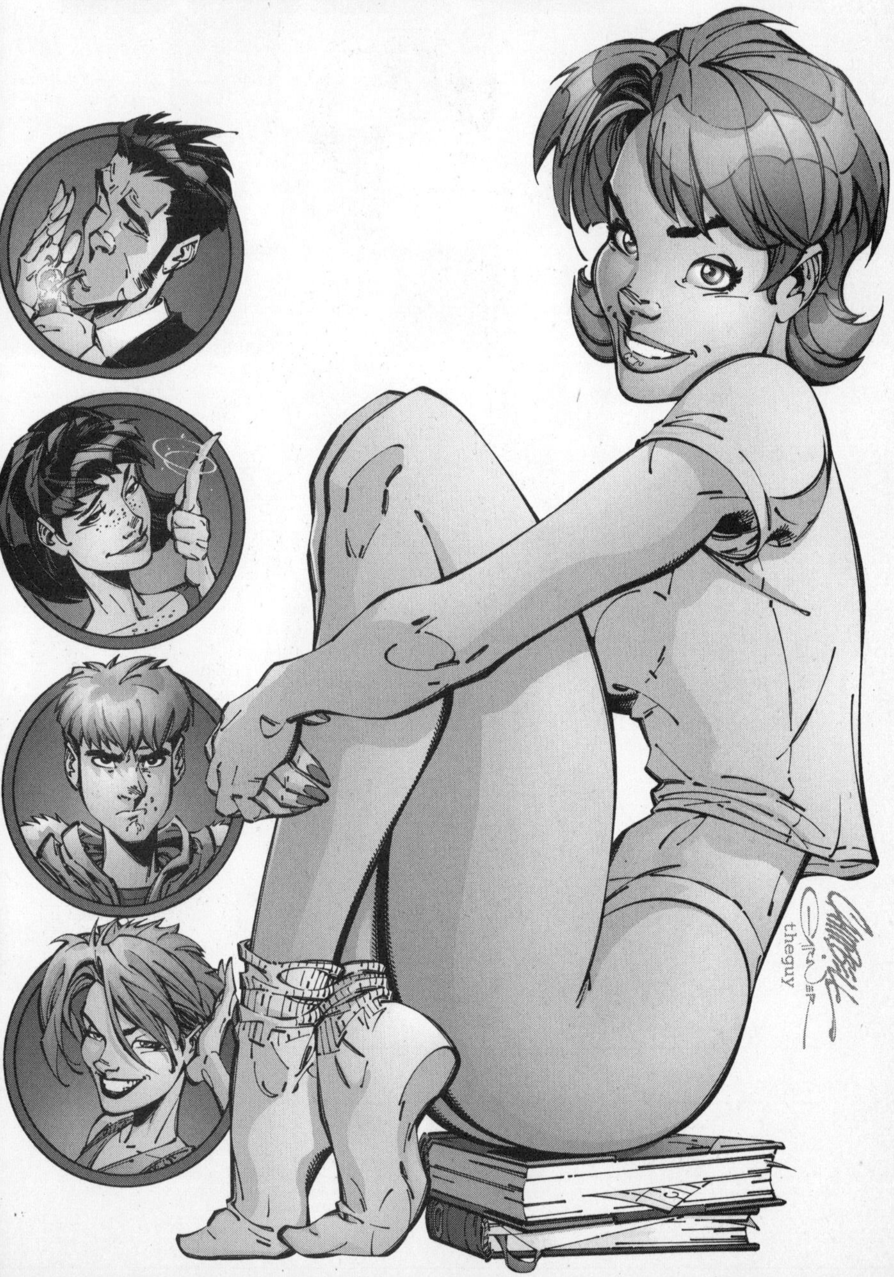
theguy

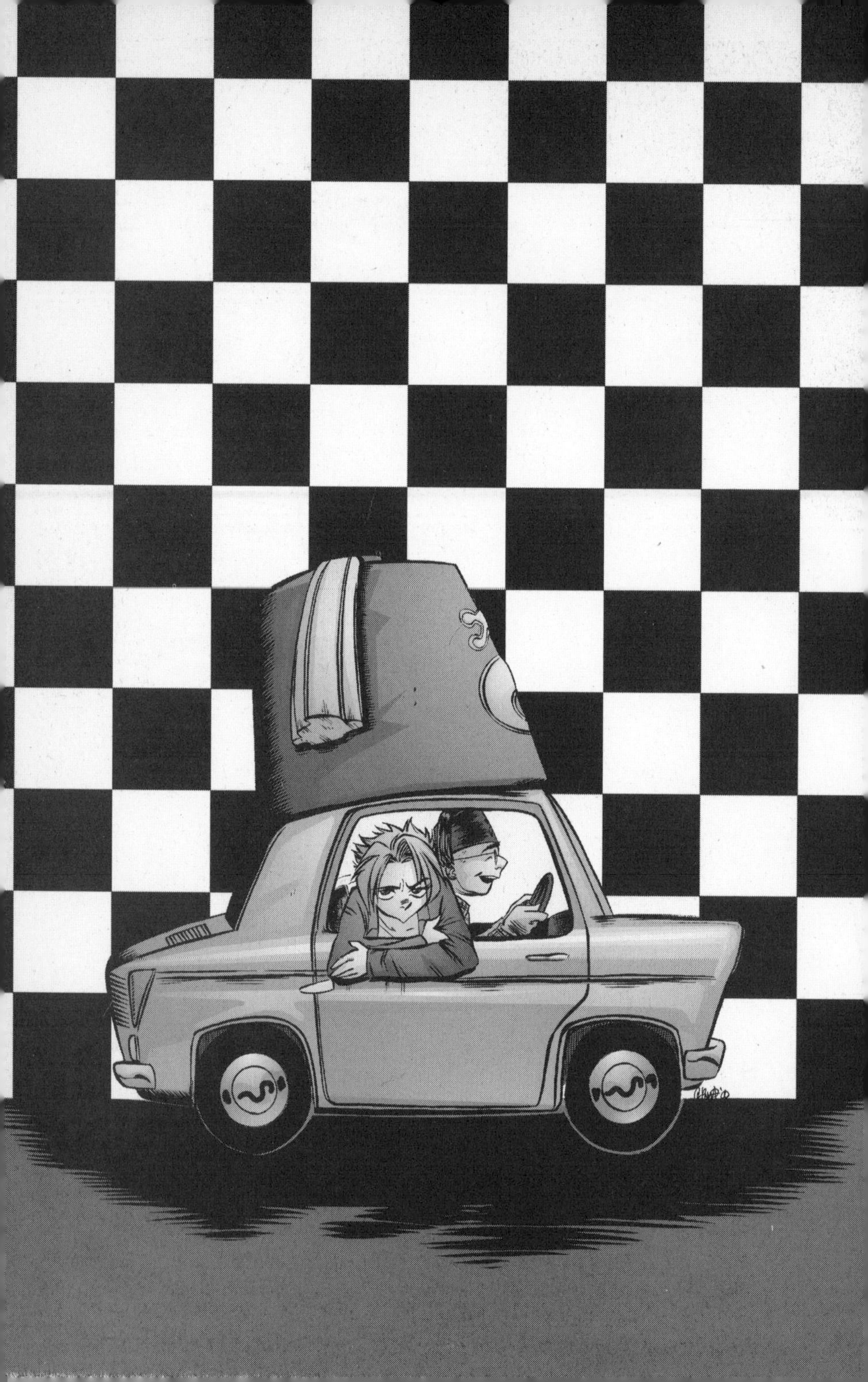

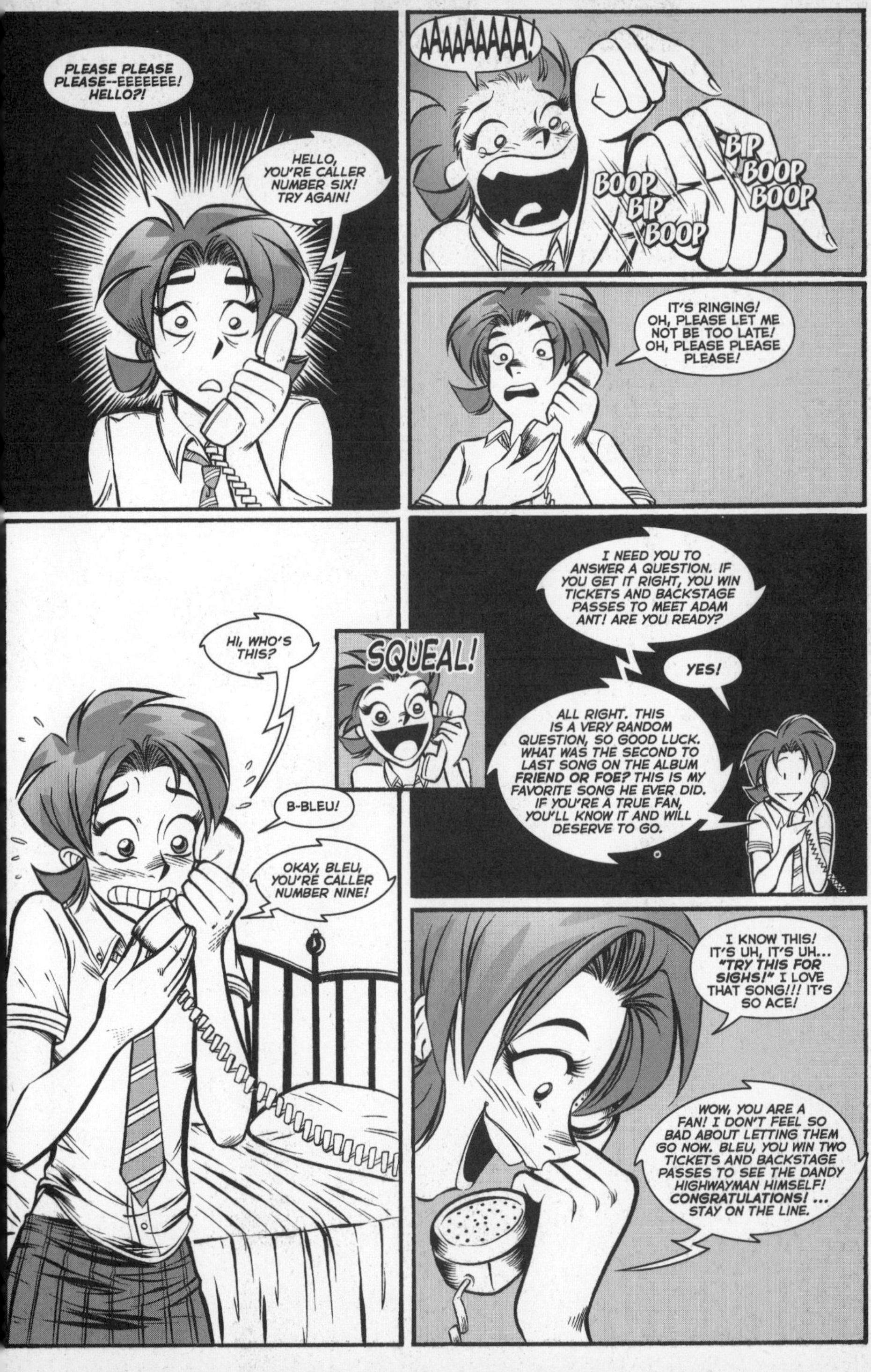
PLEASE PLEASE PLEASE--EEEEEEE! HELLO?!
HELLO, YOU'RE CALLER NUMBER SIX! TRY AGAIN!
AAAAAAAAA!
BOOP BIP BOOP
BIP BOOP BOOP
IT'S RINGING! OH, PLEASE LET ME NOT BE TOO LATE! OH, PLEASE PLEASE PLEASE!
HI, WHO'S THIS?
B-BLEU!
OKAY, BLEU, YOU'RE CALLER NUMBER NINE!
SQUEAL!
I NEED YOU TO ANSWER A QUESTION. IF YOU GET IT RIGHT, YOU WIN TICKETS AND BACKSTAGE PASSES TO MEET ADAM ANT! ARE YOU READY?
YES!
ALL RIGHT. THIS IS A VERY RANDOM QUESTION, SO GOOD LUCK. WHAT WAS THE SECOND TO LAST SONG ON THE ALBUM FRIEND OR FOE? THIS IS MY FAVORITE SONG HE EVER DID. IF YOU'RE A TRUE FAN, YOU'LL KNOW IT AND WILL DESERVE TO GO.
I KNOW THIS! IT'S UH, IT'S UH... "TRY THIS FOR SIGHS!" I LOVE THAT SONG!!! IT'S SO ACE!
WOW, YOU ARE A FAN! I DON'T FEEL SO BAD ABOUT LETTING THEM GO NOW. BLEU, YOU WIN TWO TICKETS AND BACKSTAGE PASSES TO SEE THE DANDY HIGHWAYMAN HIMSELF! CONGRATULATIONS! ... STAY ON THE LINE.

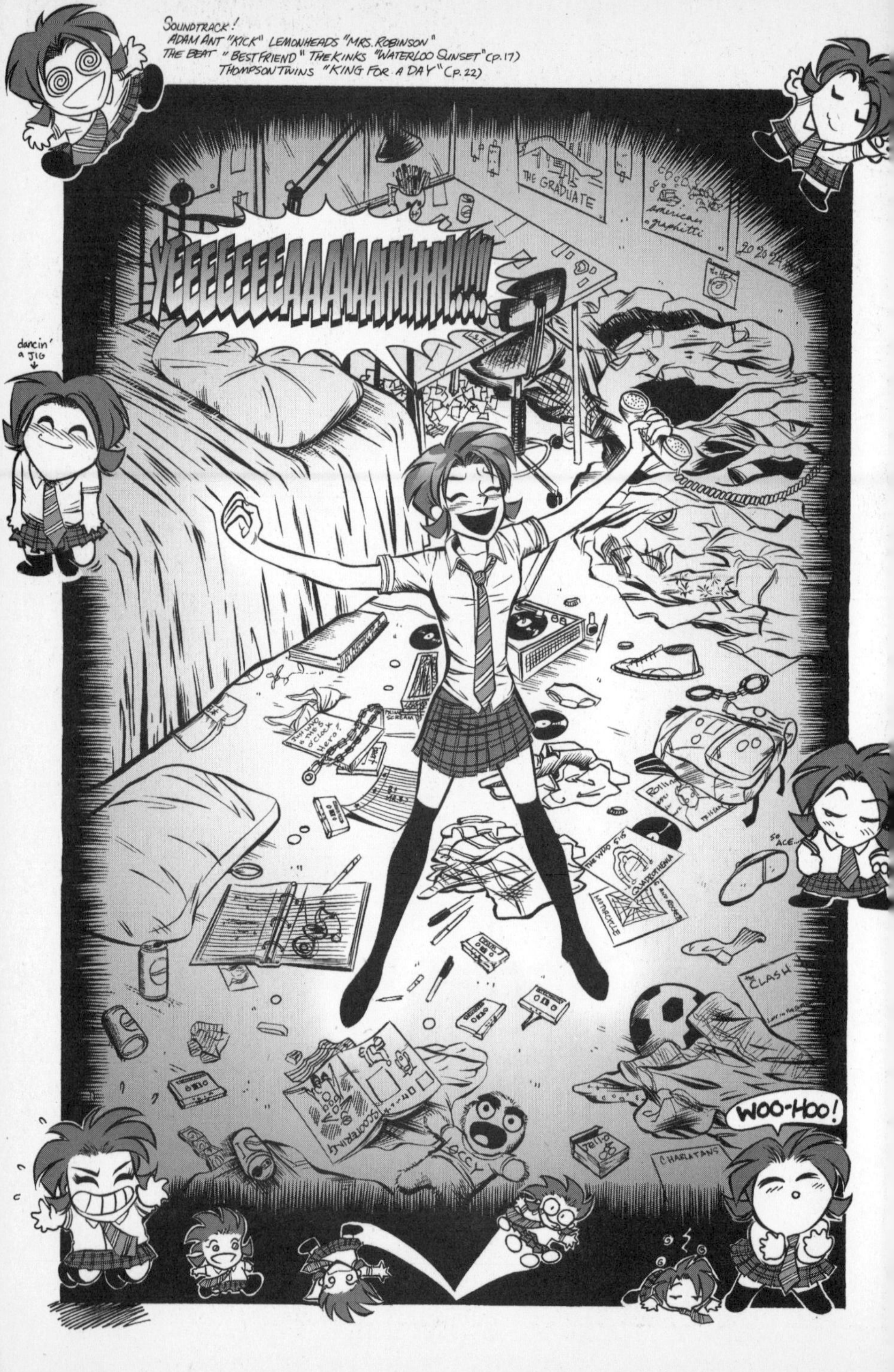
SOUNDTRACK!
ADAM ANT "KICK" LEMONHEADS "MRS. ROBINSON"
THE BEAT "BEST FRIEND" THE KINKS "WATERLOO SUNSET" (p.17)
THOMPSON TWINS "KING FOR A DAY" (p.22)
YEEEEEEEAAAAAAHHHHH!!!!!.....
THE GRADUATE
american graphitti
dancin' a JIG
SO ACE...
THE CLASH
WOO-HOO!

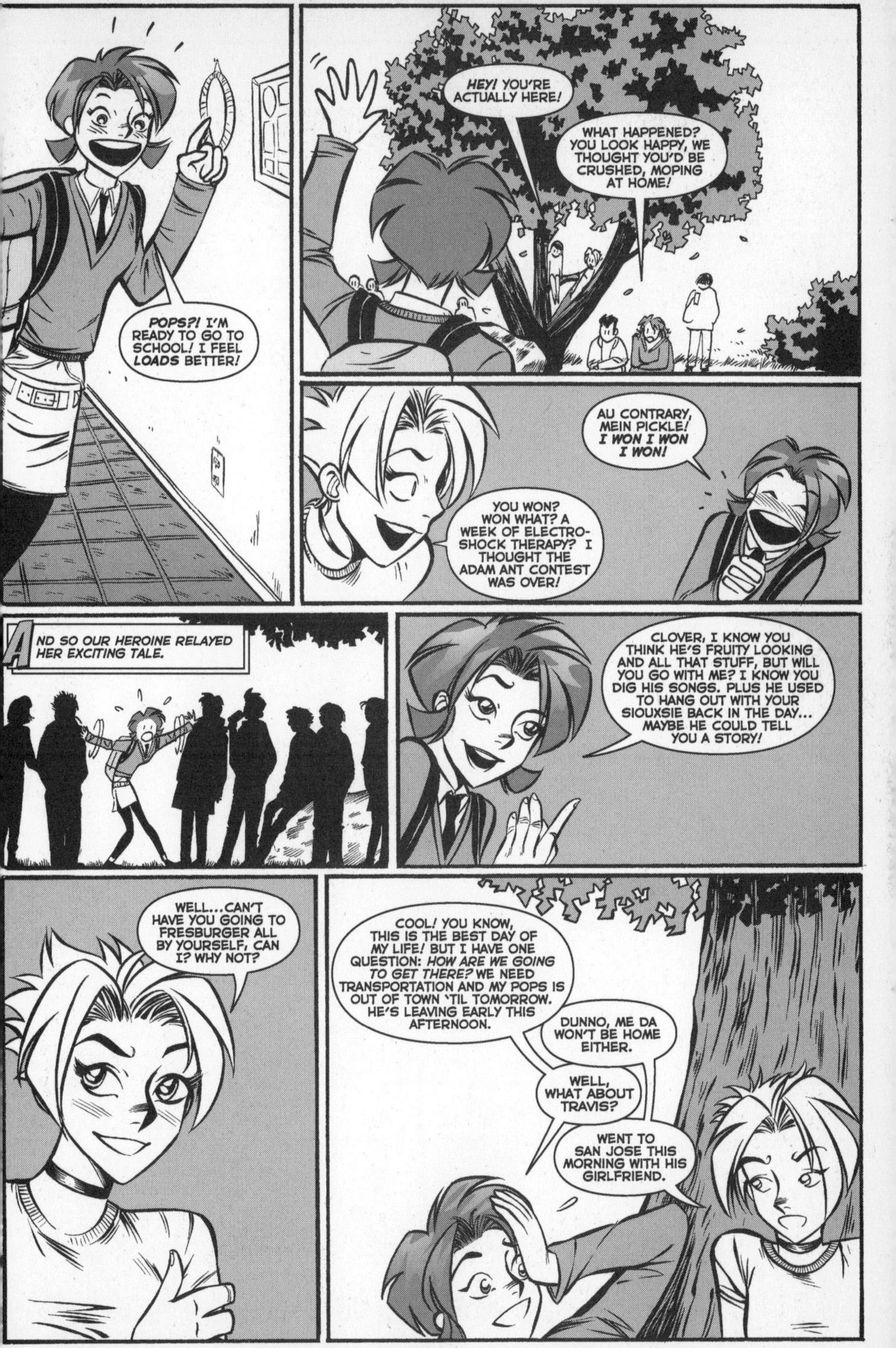
POPS?! I'M READY TO GO TO SCHOOL! I FEEL LOADS BETTER!
HEY! YOU'RE ACTUALLY HERE!
WHAT HAPPENED? YOU LOOK HAPPY, WE THOUGHT YOU'D BE CRUSHED, MOPING AT HOME!
AU CONTRARY, MEIN PICKLE! I WON I WON I WON!
YOU WON? WON WHAT? A WEEK OF ELECTRO-SHOCK THERAPY? I THOUGHT THE ADAM ANT CONTEST WAS OVER!
AND SO OUR HEROINE RELAYED HER EXCITING TALE.
CLOVER, I KNOW YOU THINK HE'S FRUITY LOOKING AND ALL THAT STUFF, BUT WILL YOU GO WITH ME? I KNOW YOU DIG HIS SONGS. PLUS HE USED TO HANG OUT WITH YOUR SIOUXSIE BACK IN THE DAY... MAYBE HE COULD TELL YOU A STORY!
WELL...CAN'T HAVE YOU GOING TO FRESBURGER ALL BY YOURSELF, CAN I? WHY NOT?
COOL! YOU KNOW, THIS IS THE BEST DAY OF MY LIFE! BUT I HAVE ONE QUESTION: HOW ARE WE GOING TO GET THERE? WE NEED TRANSPORTATION AND MY POPS IS OUT OF TOWN 'TIL TOMORROW. HE'S LEAVING EARLY THIS AFTERNOON.
DUNNO, ME DA WON'T BE HOME EITHER.
WELL, WHAT ABOUT TRAVIS?
WENT TO SAN JOSE THIS MORNING WITH HIS GIRLFRIEND.

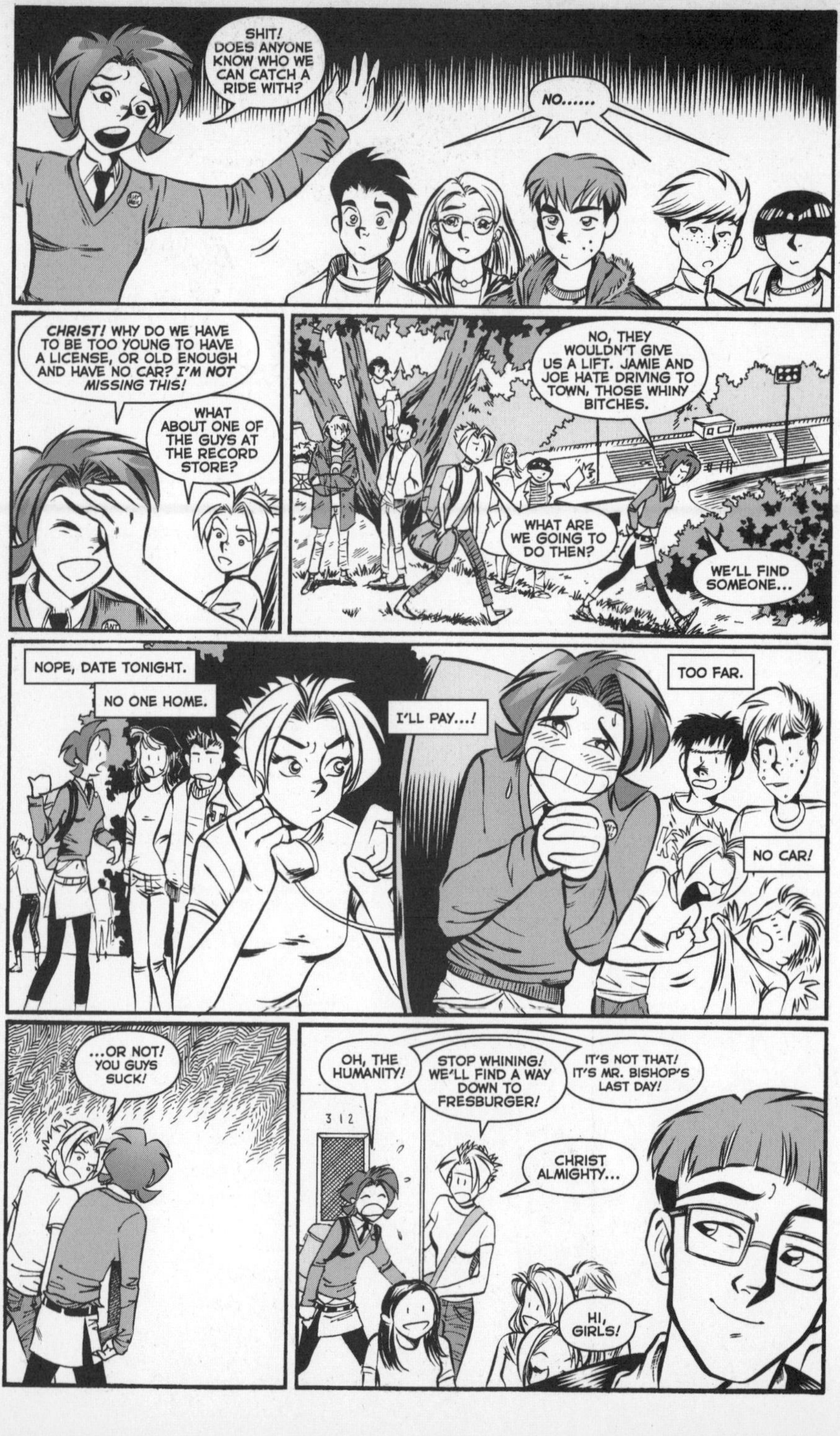
SHIT! DOES ANYONE KNOW WHO WE CAN CATCH A RIDE WITH?
NO......
CHRIST! WHY DO WE HAVE TO BE TOO YOUNG TO HAVE A LICENSE, OR OLD ENOUGH AND HAVE NO CAR? I'M NOT MISSING THIS!
WHAT ABOUT ONE OF THE GUYS AT THE RECORD STORE?
NO, THEY WOULDN'T GIVE US A LIFT. JAMIE AND JOE HATE DRIVING TO TOWN, THOSE WHINY BITCHES.
WHAT ARE WE GOING TO DO THEN?
WE'LL FIND SOMEONE...
NOPE, DATE TONIGHT.
NO ONE HOME.
I'LL PAY...!
TOO FAR.
NO CAR!
...OR NOT! YOU GUYS SUCK!
OH, THE HUMANITY!
STOP WHINING! WE'LL FIND A WAY DOWN TO FRESBURGER!
IT'S NOT THAT! IT'S MR. BISHOP'S LAST DAY!
312
CHRIST ALMIGHTY...
HI, GIRLS!

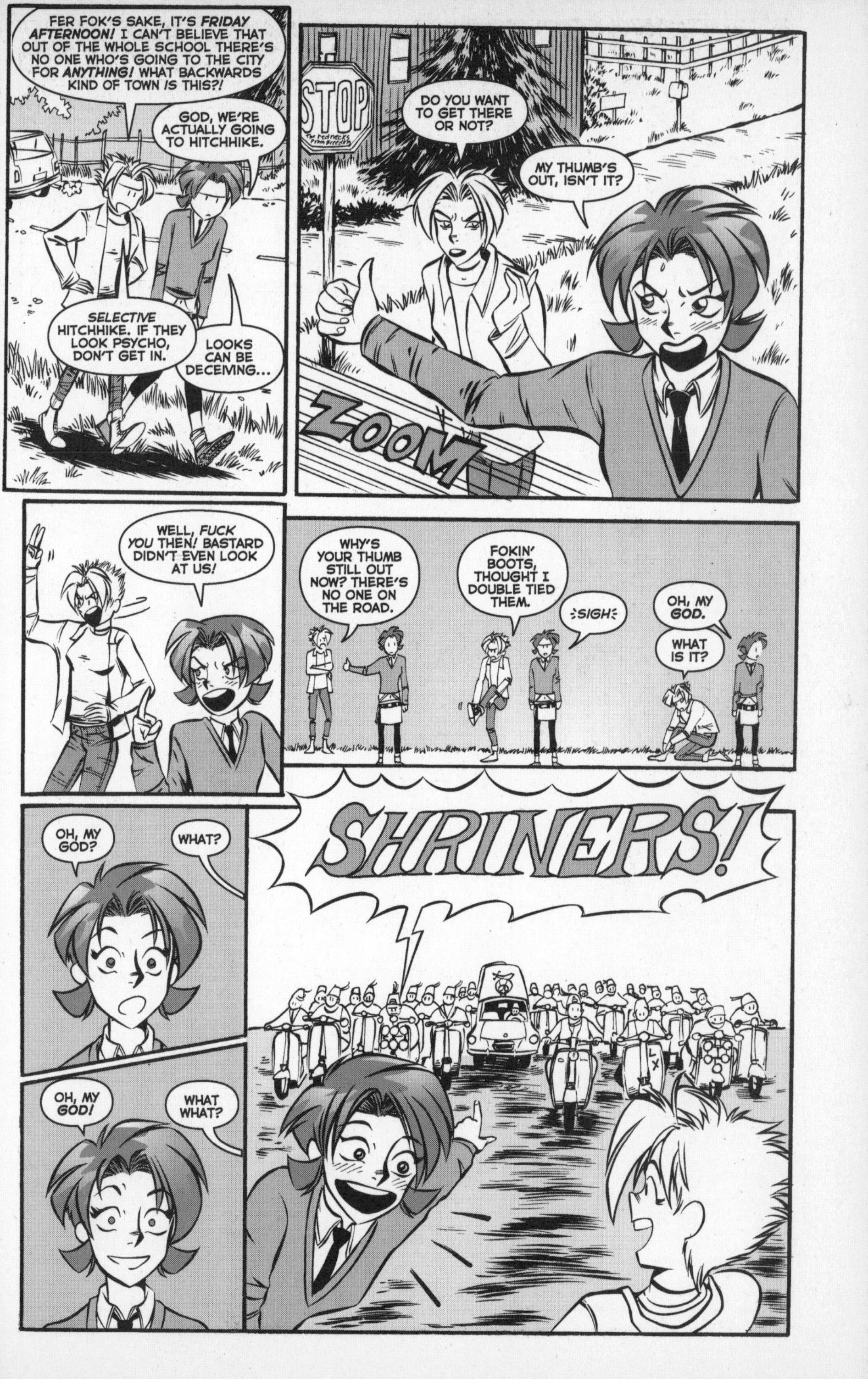
FER FOK'S SAKE, IT'S *FRIDAY AFTERNOON!* I CAN'T BELIEVE THAT OUT OF THE WHOLE SCHOOL THERE'S NO ONE WHO'S GOING TO THE CITY FOR *ANYTHING!* WHAT BACKWARDS KIND OF TOWN *IS* THIS?!
GOD, WE'RE ACTUALLY GOING TO HITCHHIKE.
*SELECTIVE* HITCHHIKE. IF THEY LOOK PSYCHO, DON'T GET IN.
LOOKS CAN BE DECEIVING...
STOP
DO YOU WANT TO GET THERE OR NOT?
MY THUMB'S OUT, ISN'T IT?
ZOOM
WELL, *FUCK YOU* THEN! BASTARD DIDN'T EVEN LOOK AT US!
WHY'S YOUR THUMB STILL OUT NOW? THERE'S NO ONE ON THE ROAD.
FOKIN' BOOTS, THOUGHT I DOUBLE TIED THEM.
*SIGH*
OH, MY *GOD.*
WHAT IS IT?
OH, MY GOD?
WHAT?
OH, MY *GOD!*
WHAT WHAT?
SHRINERS!

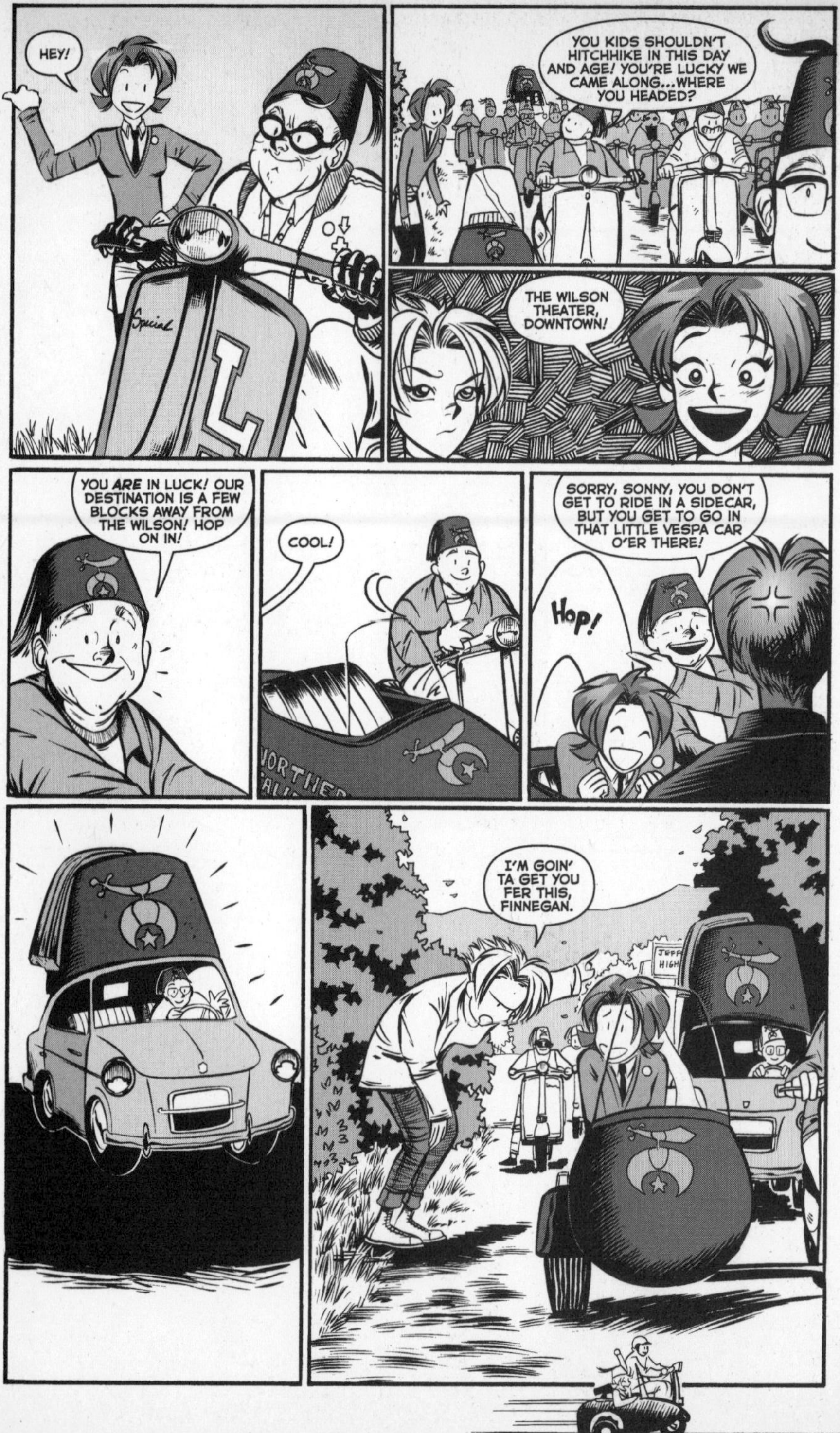
HEY!
YOU KIDS SHOULDN'T HITCHHIKE IN THIS DAY AND AGE! YOU'RE LUCKY WE CAME ALONG...WHERE YOU HEADED?
THE WILSON THEATER, DOWNTOWN!
YOU ARE IN LUCK! OUR DESTINATION IS A FEW BLOCKS AWAY FROM THE WILSON! HOP ON IN!
COOL!
SORRY, SONNY, YOU DON'T GET TO RIDE IN A SIDECAR, BUT YOU GET TO GO IN THAT LITTLE VESPA CAR O'ER THERE!
HOP!
I'M GOIN' TA GET YOU FER THIS, FINNEGAN.

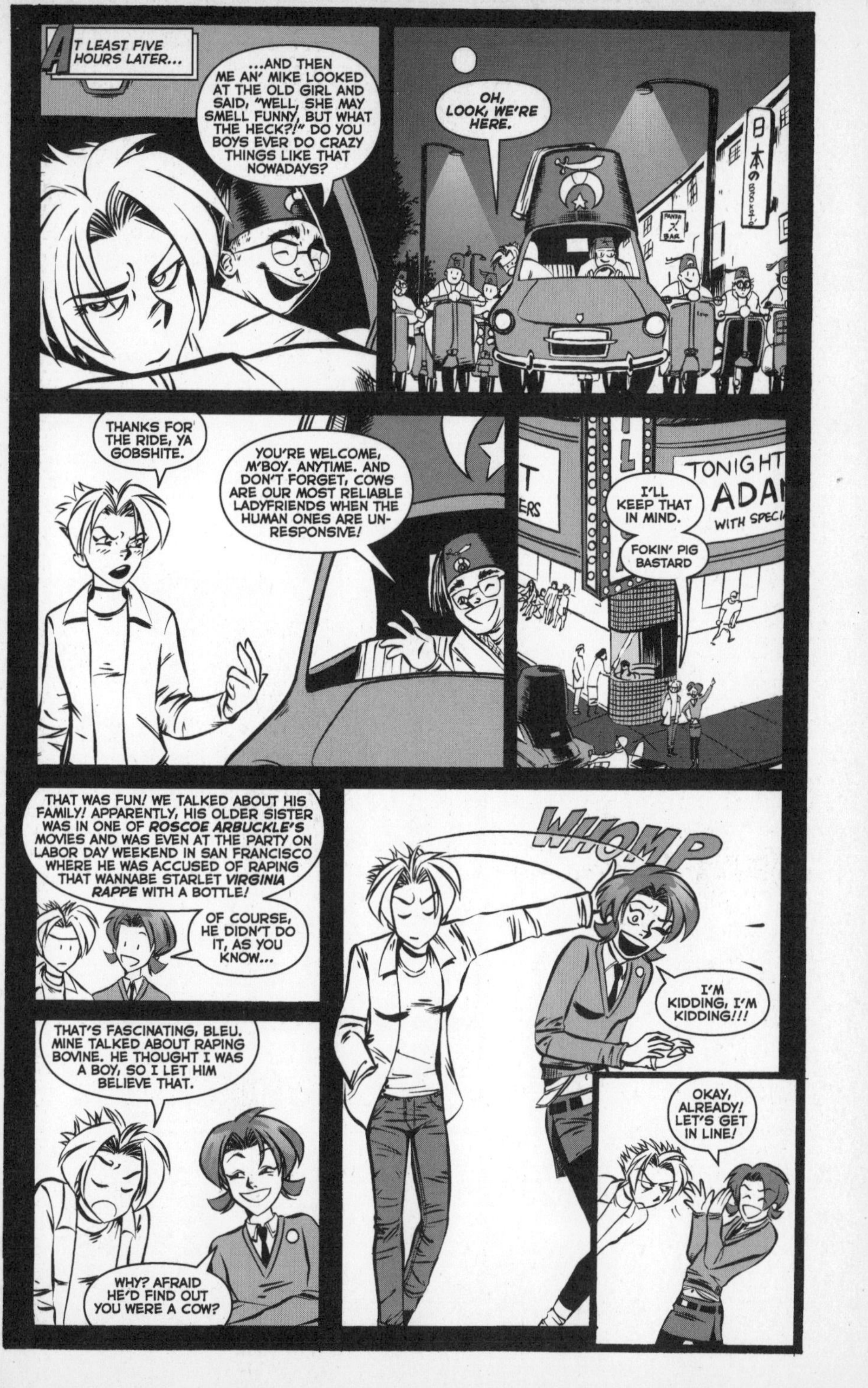
AT LEAST FIVE HOURS LATER...
...AND THEN ME AN' MIKE LOOKED AT THE OLD GIRL AND SAID, "WELL, SHE MAY SMELL FUNNY, BUT WHAT THE HECK?!" DO YOU BOYS EVER DO CRAZY THINGS LIKE THAT NOWADAYS?
OH, LOOK, WE'RE HERE.
THANKS FOR THE RIDE, YA GOBSHITE.
YOU'RE WELCOME, M'BOY. ANYTIME. AND DON'T FORGET, COWS ARE OUR MOST RELIABLE LADYFRIENDS WHEN THE HUMAN ONES ARE UN-RESPONSIVE!
TONIGHT
I'LL KEEP THAT IN MIND.
FOKIN' PIG BASTARD
THAT WAS FUN! WE TALKED ABOUT HIS FAMILY! APPARENTLY, HIS OLDER SISTER WAS IN ONE OF ***ROSCOE ARBUCKLE'S*** MOVIES AND WAS EVEN AT THE PARTY ON LABOR DAY WEEKEND IN SAN FRANCISCO WHERE HE WAS ACCUSED OF RAPING THAT WANNABE STARLET ***VIRGINIA RAPPE*** WITH A BOTTLE!
OF COURSE, HE DIDN'T DO IT, AS YOU KNOW...
THAT'S FASCINATING, BLEU. MINE TALKED ABOUT RAPING BOVINE. HE THOUGHT I WAS A BOY, SO I LET HIM BELIEVE THAT.
WHY? AFRAID HE'D FIND OUT YOU WERE A COW?
WHOMP
I'M KIDDING, I'M KIDDING!!!
OKAY, ALREADY! LET'S GET IN LINE!

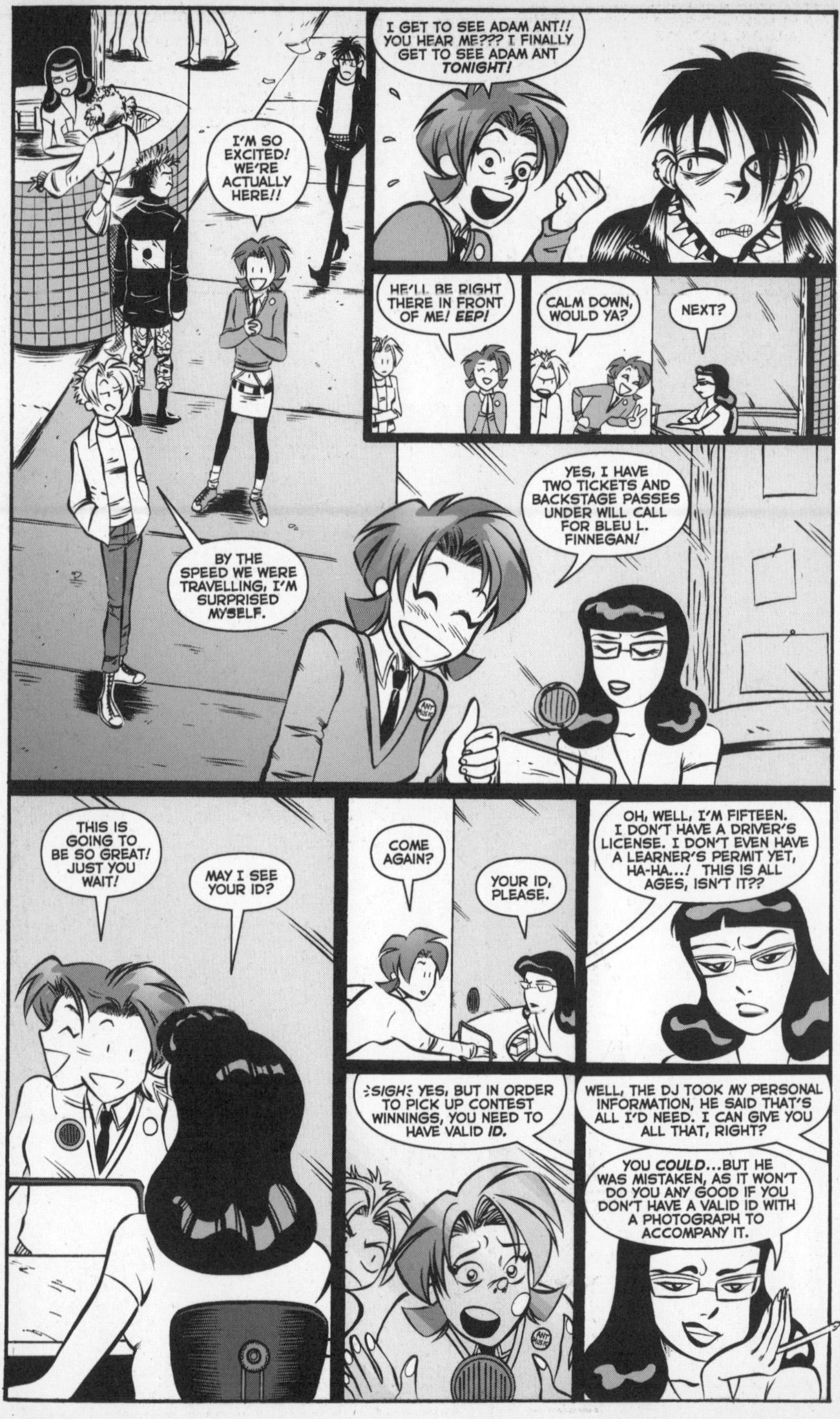
I'M SO EXCITED! WE'RE ACTUALLY HERE!!
BY THE SPEED WE WERE TRAVELLING, I'M SURPRISED MYSELF.
I GET TO SEE ADAM ANT!! YOU HEAR ME??? I FINALLY GET TO SEE ADAM ANT TONIGHT!
HE'LL BE RIGHT THERE IN FRONT OF ME! EEP!
CALM DOWN, WOULD YA?
NEXT?
YES, I HAVE TWO TICKETS AND BACKSTAGE PASSES UNDER WILL CALL FOR BLEU L. FINNEGAN!
ANT MUSIC
THIS IS GOING TO BE SO GREAT! JUST YOU WAIT!
MAY I SEE YOUR ID?
COME AGAIN?
YOUR ID, PLEASE.
OH, WELL, I'M FIFTEEN. I DON'T HAVE A DRIVER'S LICENSE. I DON'T EVEN HAVE A LEARNER'S PERMIT YET, HA-HA...! THIS IS ALL AGES, ISN'T IT??
SIGH YES, BUT IN ORDER TO PICK UP CONTEST WINNINGS, YOU NEED TO HAVE VALID ID.
WELL, THE DJ TOOK MY PERSONAL INFORMATION, HE SAID THAT'S ALL I'D NEED. I CAN GIVE YOU ALL THAT, RIGHT?
YOU COULD...BUT HE WAS MISTAKEN, AS IT WON'T DO YOU ANY GOOD IF YOU DON'T HAVE A VALID ID WITH A PHOTOGRAPH TO ACCOMPANY IT.
ANT MUSIC

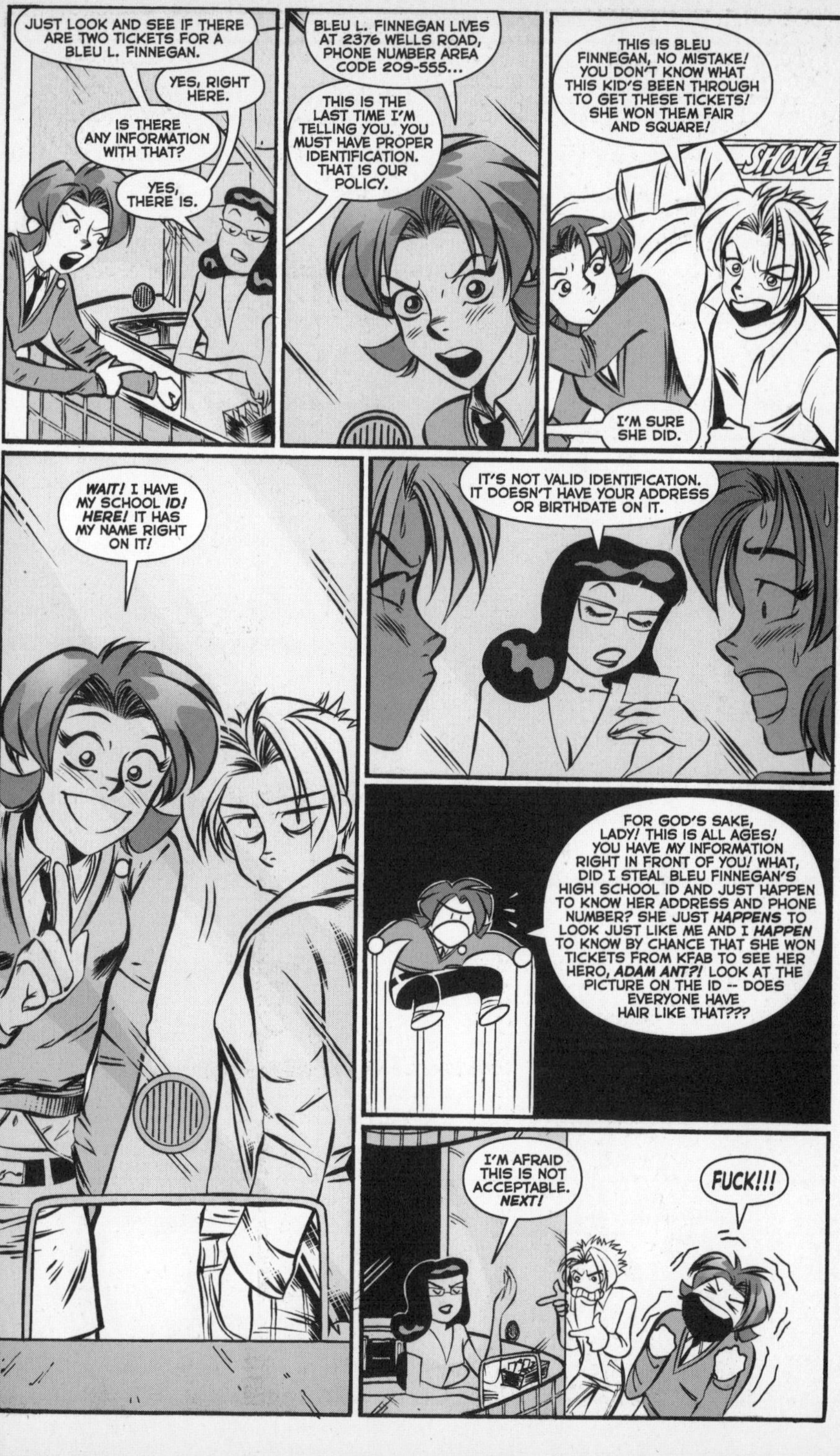

JUST LOOK AND SEE IF THERE ARE TWO TICKETS FOR A BLEU L. FINNEGAN.
YES, RIGHT HERE.
IS THERE ANY INFORMATION WITH THAT?
YES, THERE IS.
BLEU L. FINNEGAN LIVES AT 2376 WELLS ROAD, PHONE NUMBER AREA CODE 209-555...
THIS IS THE LAST TIME I'M TELLING YOU. YOU MUST HAVE PROPER IDENTIFICATION. THAT IS OUR POLICY.
THIS IS BLEU FINNEGAN, NO MISTAKE! YOU DON'T KNOW WHAT THIS KID'S BEEN THROUGH TO GET THESE TICKETS! SHE WON THEM FAIR AND SQUARE!
SHOVE
I'M SURE SHE DID.
WAIT! I HAVE MY SCHOOL ID! HERE! IT HAS MY NAME RIGHT ON IT!
IT'S NOT VALID IDENTIFICATION. IT DOESN'T HAVE YOUR ADDRESS OR BIRTHDATE ON IT.
FOR GOD'S SAKE, LADY! THIS IS ALL AGES! YOU HAVE MY INFORMATION RIGHT IN FRONT OF YOU! WHAT, DID I STEAL BLEU FINNEGAN'S HIGH SCHOOL ID AND JUST HAPPEN TO KNOW HER ADDRESS AND PHONE NUMBER? SHE JUST HAPPENS TO LOOK JUST LIKE ME AND I HAPPEN TO KNOW BY CHANCE THAT SHE WON TICKETS FROM KFAB TO SEE HER HERO, ADAM ANT?! LOOK AT THE PICTURE ON THE ID -- DOES EVERYONE HAVE HAIR LIKE THAT???
I'M AFRAID THIS IS NOT ACCEPTABLE. NEXT!
FUCK!!!

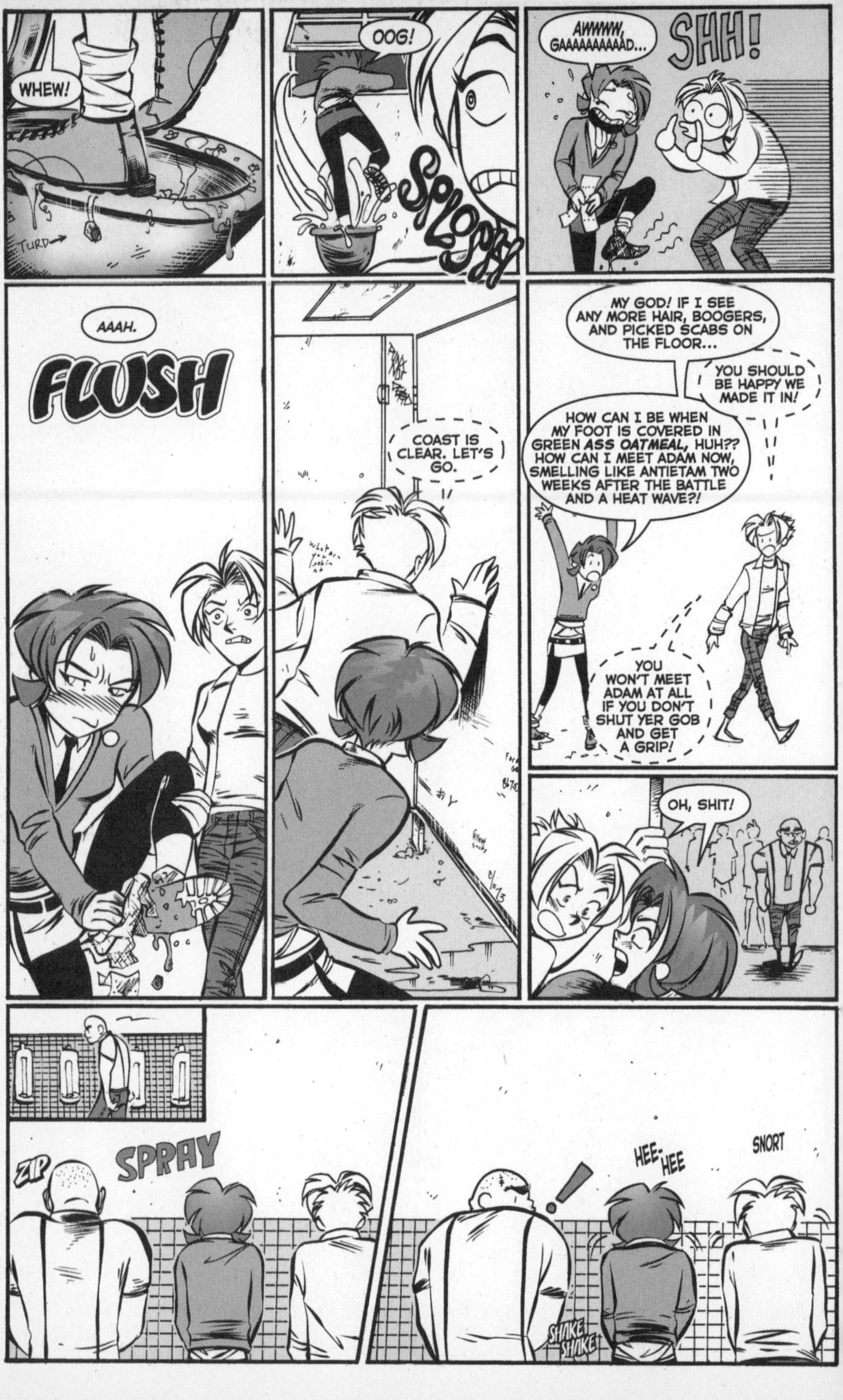
WHEW!
TURD
OOG!
SPLOOSH
AWWWW, GAAAAAAAAAAD...
SHH!
AAAH.
FLUSH
COAST IS CLEAR. LET'S GO.
MY GOD! IF I SEE ANY MORE HAIR, BOOGERS, AND PICKED SCABS ON THE FLOOR...
YOU SHOULD BE HAPPY WE MADE IT IN!
HOW CAN I BE WHEN MY FOOT IS COVERED IN GREEN ASS OATMEAL, HUH?? HOW CAN I MEET ADAM NOW, SMELLING LIKE ANTIETAM TWO WEEKS AFTER THE BATTLE AND A HEAT WAVE?!
YOU WON'T MEET ADAM AT ALL IF YOU DON'T SHUT YER GOB AND GET A GRIP!
OH, SHIT!
ZIP
SPRAY
HEE-HEE
SNORT
SHAKE SHAKE

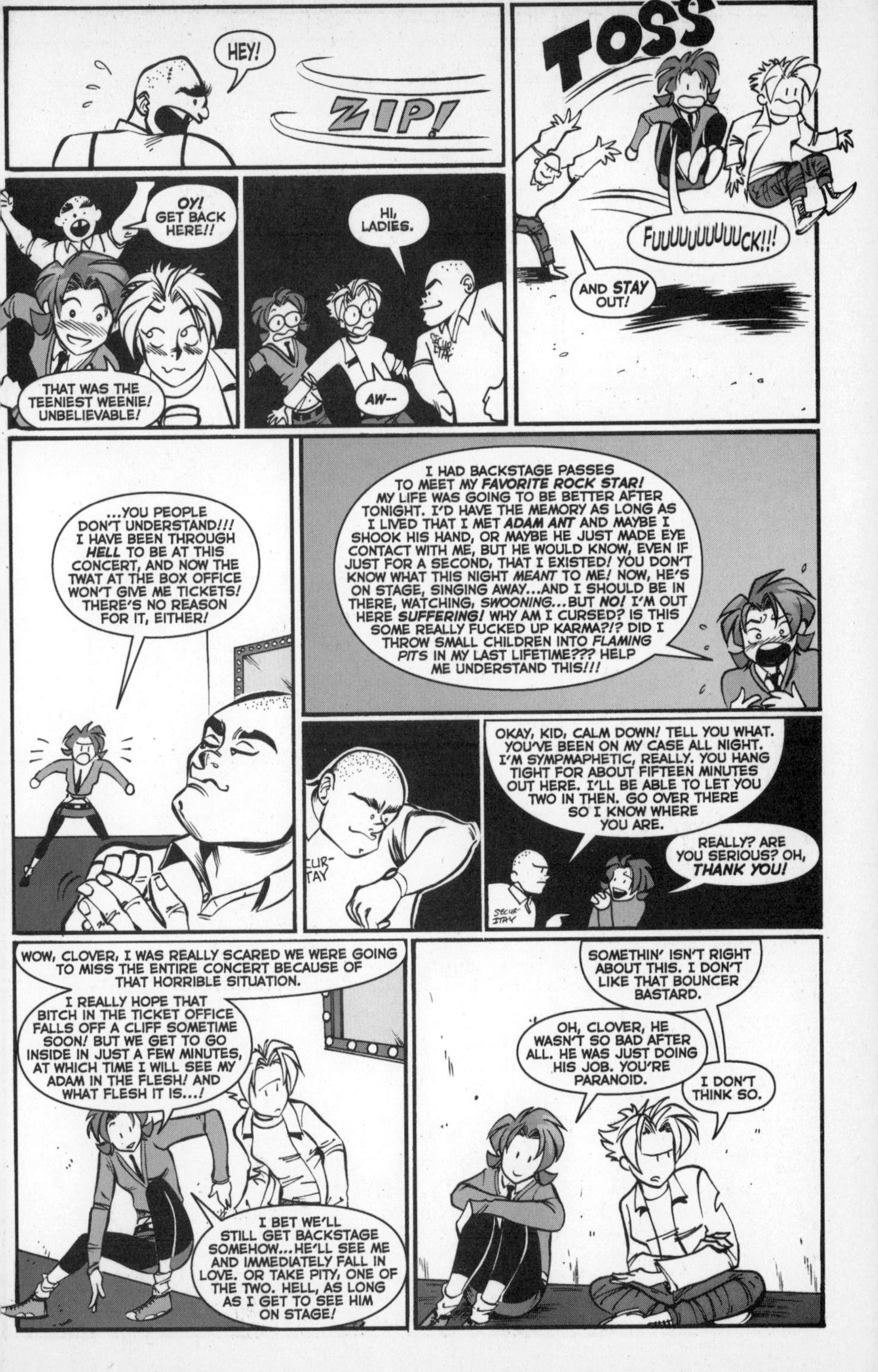
HEY!
ZIP!
TOSS
OY! GET BACK HERE!!
THAT WAS THE TEENIEST WEENIE! UNBELIEVABLE!
HI, LADIES.
AW--
SECUR-ITAY
FUUUUUUUUUCK!!!
AND STAY OUT!
...YOU PEOPLE DON'T UNDERSTAND!!! I HAVE BEEN THROUGH HELL TO BE AT THIS CONCERT, AND NOW THE TWAT AT THE BOX OFFICE WON'T GIVE ME TICKETS! THERE'S NO REASON FOR IT, EITHER!
I HAD BACKSTAGE PASSES TO MEET MY FAVORITE ROCK STAR! MY LIFE WAS GOING TO BE BETTER AFTER TONIGHT. I'D HAVE THE MEMORY AS LONG AS I LIVED THAT I MET ADAM ANT AND MAYBE I SHOOK HIS HAND, OR MAYBE HE JUST MADE EYE CONTACT WITH ME, BUT HE WOULD KNOW, EVEN IF JUST FOR A SECOND, THAT I EXISTED! YOU DON'T KNOW WHAT THIS NIGHT MEANT TO ME! NOW, HE'S ON STAGE, SINGING AWAY...AND I SHOULD BE IN THERE, WATCHING, SWOONING...BUT NO! I'M OUT HERE SUFFERING! WHY AM I CURSED? IS THIS SOME REALLY FUCKED UP KARMA?!? DID I THROW SMALL CHILDREN INTO FLAMING PITS IN MY LAST LIFETIME??? HELP ME UNDERSTAND THIS!!!
OKAY, KID, CALM DOWN! TELL YOU WHAT. YOU'VE BEEN ON MY CASE ALL NIGHT. I'M SYMPMAPHETIC, REALLY. YOU HANG TIGHT FOR ABOUT FIFTEEN MINUTES OUT HERE. I'LL BE ABLE TO LET YOU TWO IN THEN. GO OVER THERE SO I KNOW WHERE YOU ARE.
REALLY? ARE YOU SERIOUS? OH, THANK YOU!
SECUR-ITAY
WOW, CLOVER, I WAS REALLY SCARED WE WERE GOING TO MISS THE ENTIRE CONCERT BECAUSE OF THAT HORRIBLE SITUATION.
I REALLY HOPE THAT BITCH IN THE TICKET OFFICE FALLS OFF A CLIFF SOMETIME SOON! BUT WE GET TO GO INSIDE IN JUST A FEW MINUTES, AT WHICH TIME I WILL SEE MY ADAM IN THE FLESH! AND WHAT FLESH IT IS...!
I BET WE'LL STILL GET BACKSTAGE SOMEHOW...HE'LL SEE ME AND IMMEDIATELY FALL IN LOVE. OR TAKE PITY, ONE OF THE TWO. HELL, AS LONG AS I GET TO SEE HIM ON STAGE!
SOMETHIN' ISN'T RIGHT ABOUT THIS. I DON'T LIKE THAT BOUNCER BASTARD.
OH, CLOVER, HE WASN'T SO BAD AFTER ALL. HE WAS JUST DOING HIS JOB. YOU'RE PARANOID.
I DON'T THINK SO.

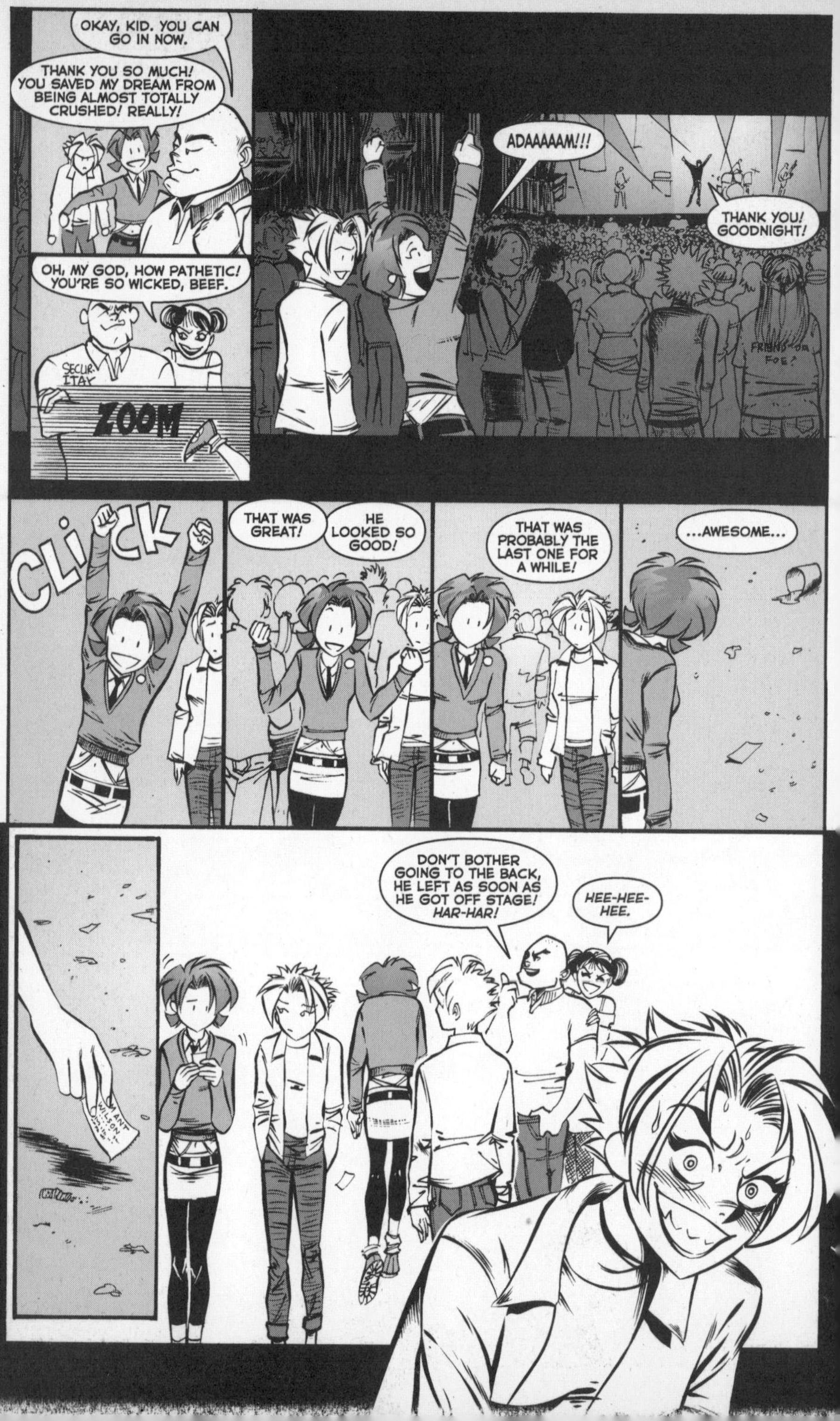
OKAY, KID. YOU CAN GO IN NOW.
THANK YOU SO MUCH! YOU SAVED MY DREAM FROM BEING ALMOST TOTALLY CRUSHED! REALLY!
OH, MY GOD, HOW PATHETIC! YOU'RE SO WICKED, BEEF.
SECUR-ITAY
ZOOM
ADAAAAAM!!!
THANK YOU! GOODNIGHT!
FRIEND OR FOE?
CLICK
THAT WAS GREAT!
HE LOOKED SO GOOD!
THAT WAS PROBABLY THE LAST ONE FOR A WHILE!
...AWESOME...
DON'T BOTHER GOING TO THE BACK, HE LEFT AS SOON AS HE GOT OFF STAGE! HAR-HAR!
HEE-HEE-HEE.

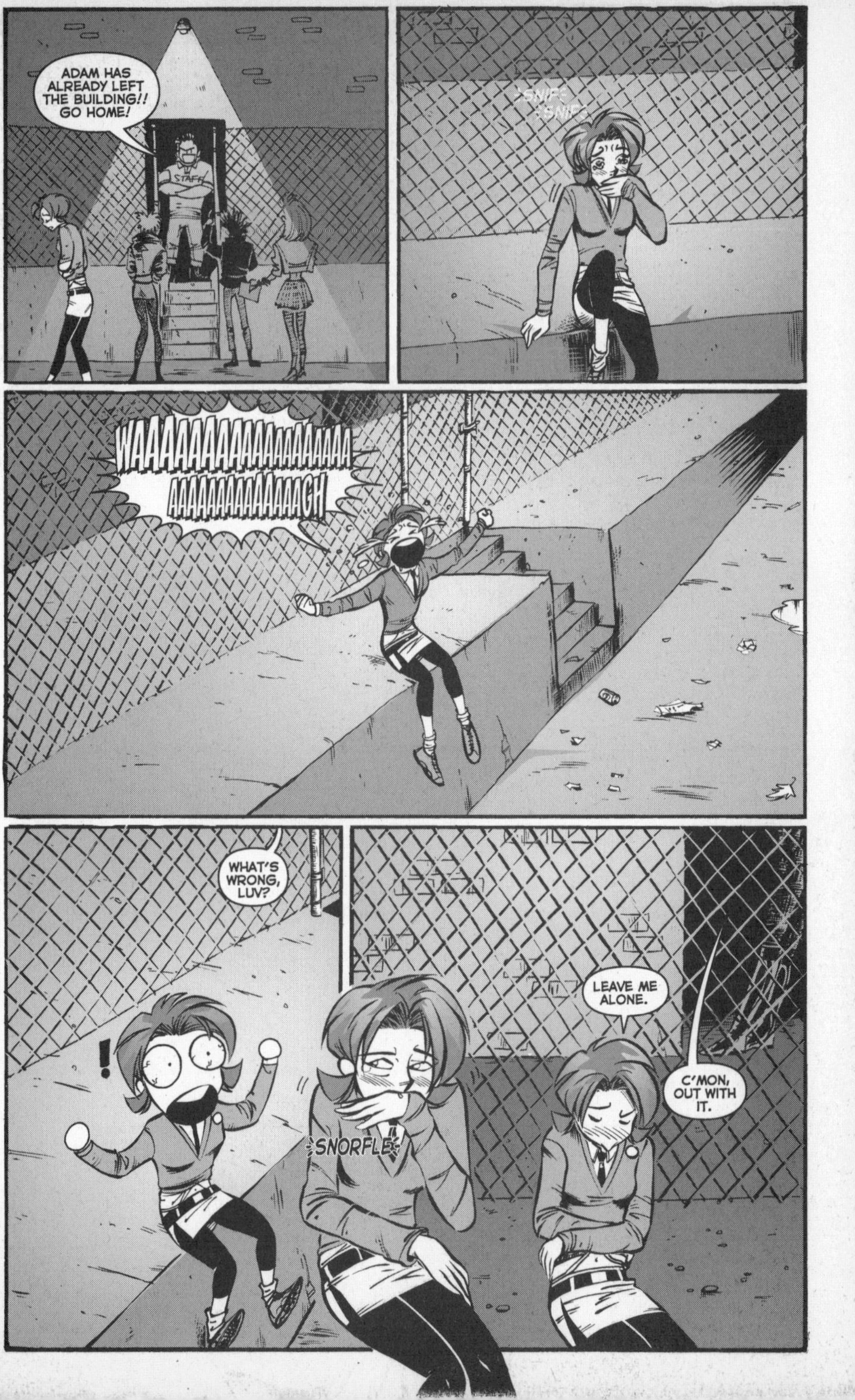
ADAM HAS ALREADY LEFT THE BUILDING!! GO HOME!
STAFF
SNIF
SNIF
WAAAAAAAAAAAAAAAAAAA AAAAAAAAAAAAAGH
WHAT'S WRONG, LUV?
!
SNORFLE
LEAVE ME ALONE.
C'MON, OUT WITH IT.

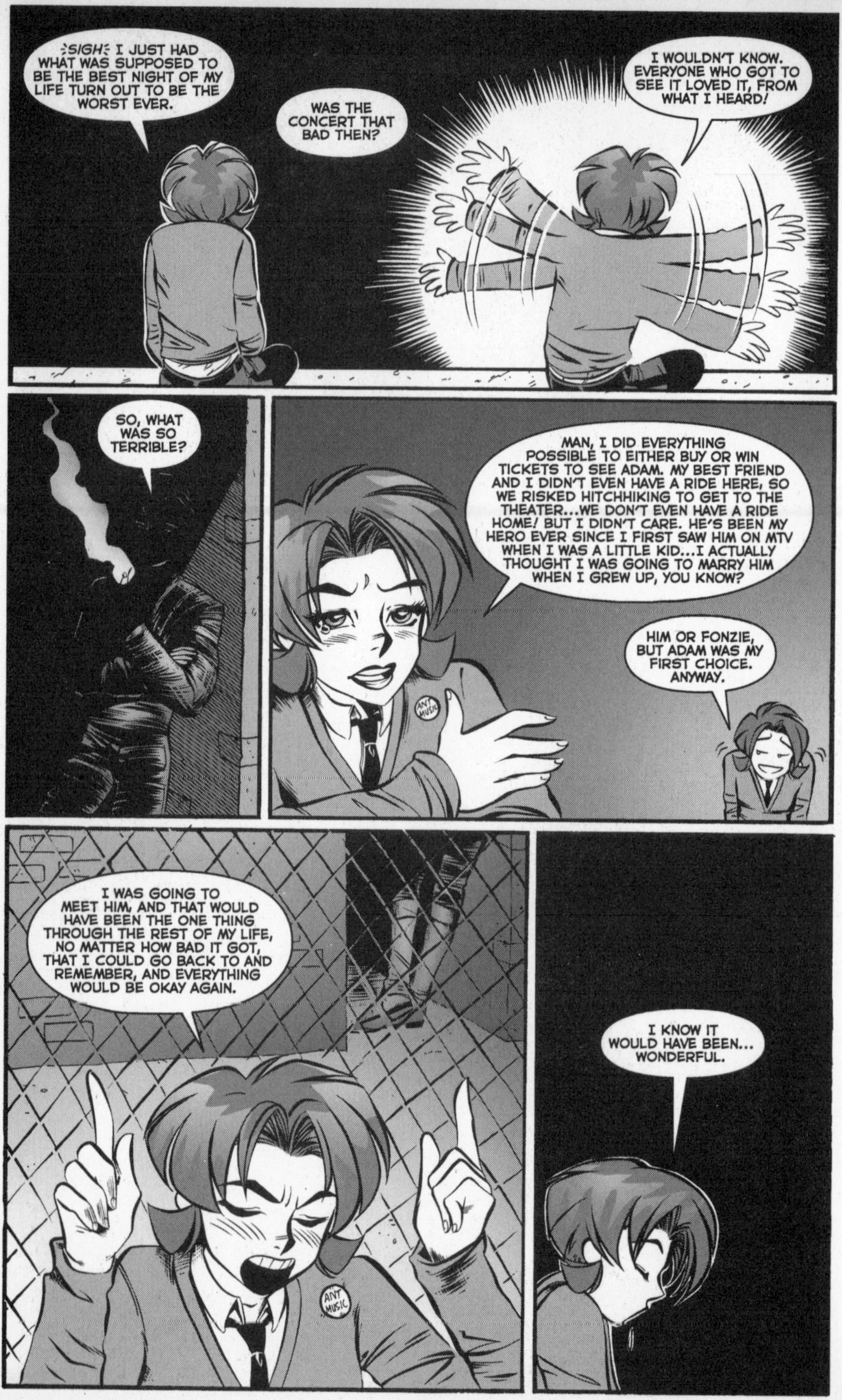

:SIGH: I JUST HAD WHAT WAS SUPPOSED TO BE THE BEST NIGHT OF MY LIFE TURN OUT TO BE THE WORST EVER.
WAS THE CONCERT THAT BAD THEN?
I WOULDN'T KNOW. EVERYONE WHO GOT TO SEE IT LOVED IT, FROM WHAT I HEARD!
SO, WHAT WAS SO TERRIBLE?
MAN, I DID EVERYTHING POSSIBLE TO EITHER BUY OR WIN TICKETS TO SEE ADAM. MY BEST FRIEND AND I DIDN'T EVEN HAVE A RIDE HERE, SO WE RISKED HITCHHIKING TO GET TO THE THEATER...WE DON'T EVEN HAVE A RIDE HOME! BUT I DIDN'T CARE. HE'S BEEN MY HERO EVER SINCE I FIRST SAW HIM ON MTV WHEN I WAS A LITTLE KID...I ACTUALLY THOUGHT I WAS GOING TO MARRY HIM WHEN I GREW UP, YOU KNOW?
HIM OR FONZIE, BUT ADAM WAS MY FIRST CHOICE. ANYWAY.
ANT MUSIC
I WAS GOING TO MEET HIM, AND THAT WOULD HAVE BEEN THE ONE THING THROUGH THE REST OF MY LIFE, NO MATTER HOW BAD IT GOT, THAT I COULD GO BACK TO AND REMEMBER, AND EVERYTHING WOULD BE OKAY AGAIN.
ANT MUSIC
I KNOW IT WOULD HAVE BEEN... WONDERFUL.

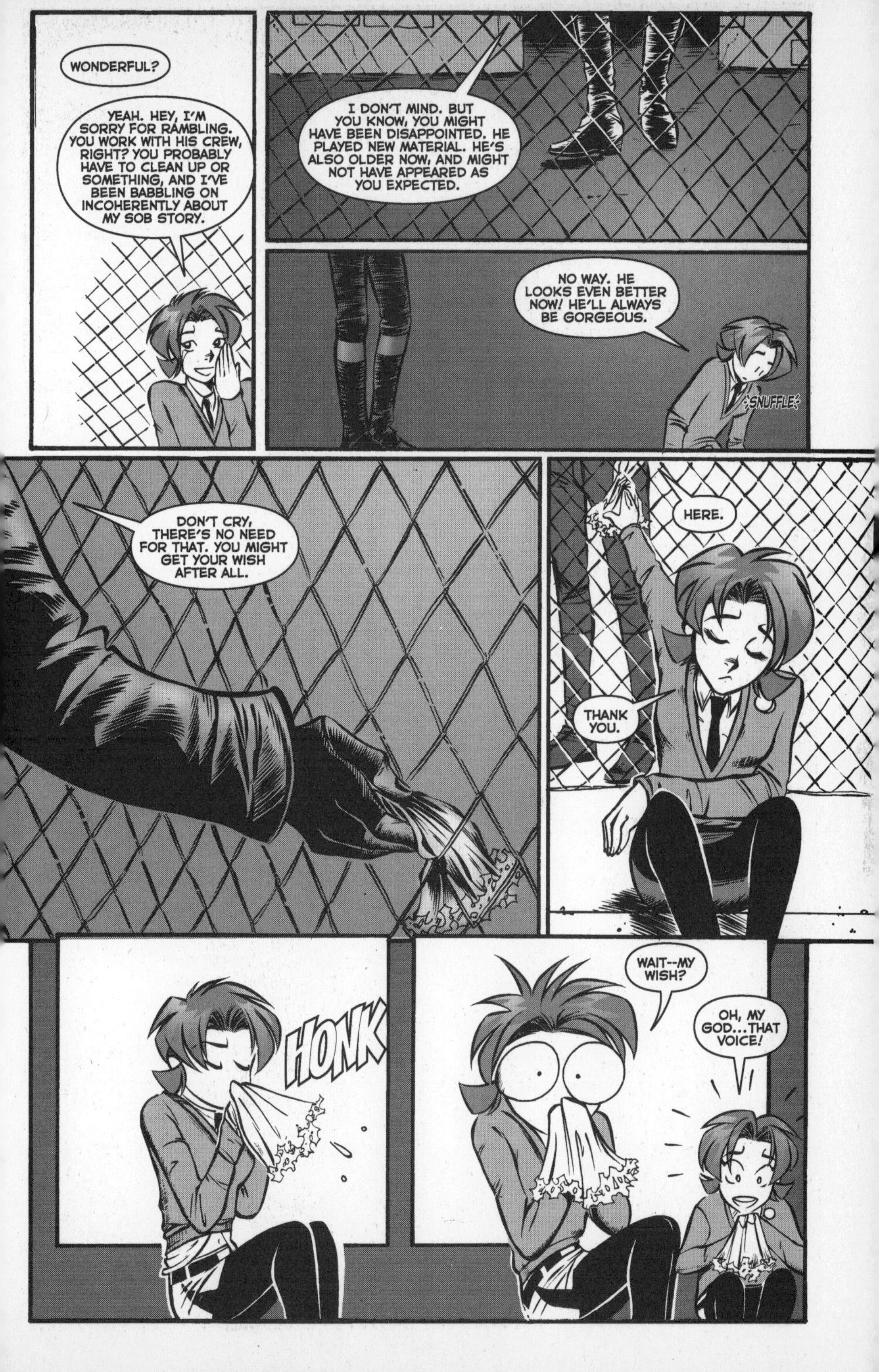
WONDERFUL?
YEAH. HEY, I'M SORRY FOR RAMBLING. YOU WORK WITH HIS CREW, RIGHT? YOU PROBABLY HAVE TO CLEAN UP OR SOMETHING, AND I'VE BEEN BABBLING ON INCOHERENTLY ABOUT MY SOB STORY.
I DON'T MIND. BUT YOU KNOW, YOU MIGHT HAVE BEEN DISAPPOINTED. HE PLAYED NEW MATERIAL. HE'S ALSO OLDER NOW, AND MIGHT NOT HAVE APPEARED AS YOU EXPECTED.
NO WAY. HE LOOKS EVEN BETTER NOW! HE'LL ALWAYS BE GORGEOUS.
SNUFFLE
DON'T CRY, THERE'S NO NEED FOR THAT. YOU MIGHT GET YOUR WISH AFTER ALL.
HERE.
THANK YOU.
HONK
WAIT--MY WISH?
OH, MY GOD...THAT VOICE!

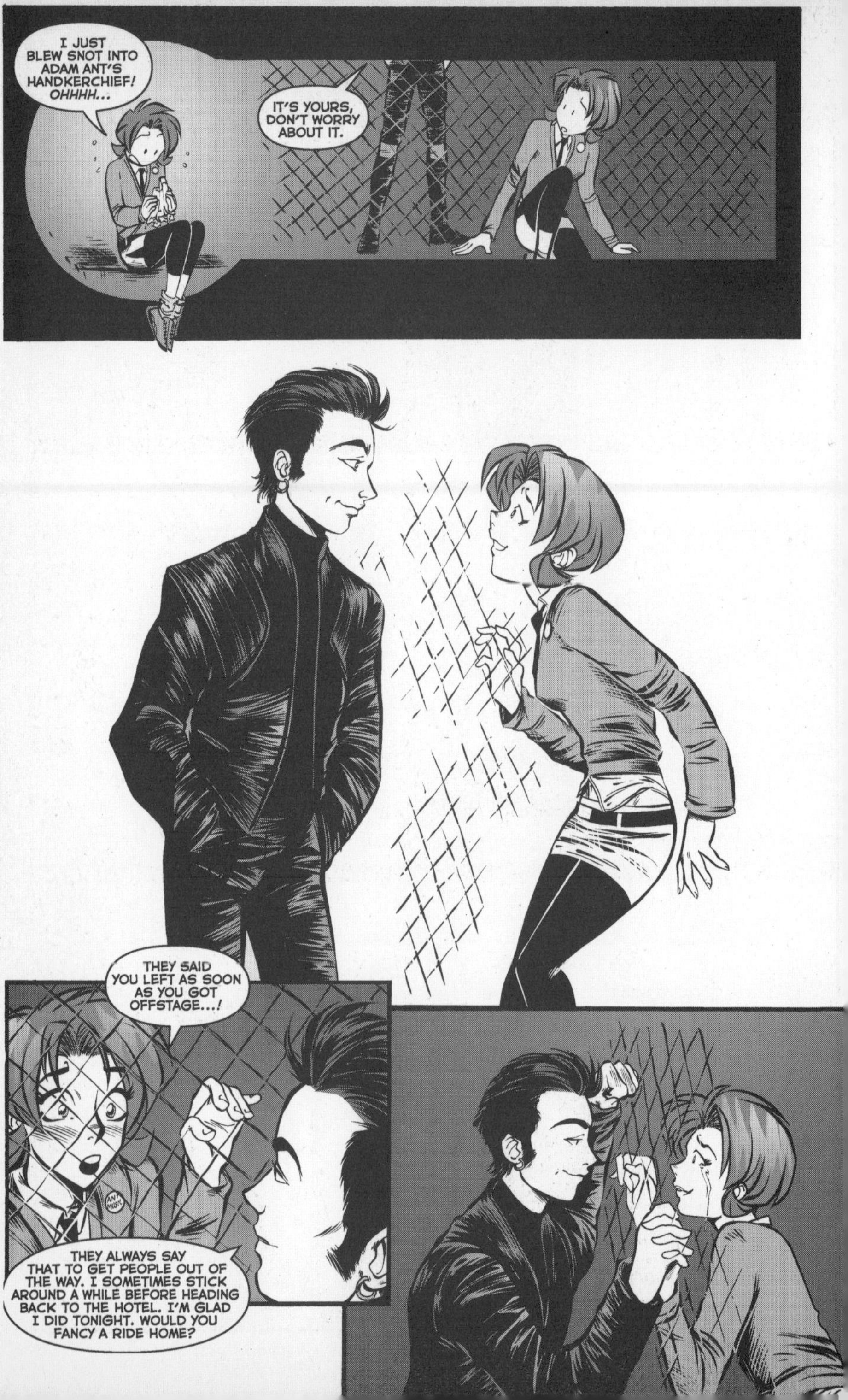
I JUST BLEW SNOT INTO ADAM ANT'S HANDKERCHIEF! OHHHH...
IT'S YOURS, DON'T WORRY ABOUT IT.
THEY SAID YOU LEFT AS SOON AS YOU GOT OFFSTAGE...!
THEY ALWAYS SAY THAT TO GET PEOPLE OUT OF THE WAY. I SOMETIMES STICK AROUND A WHILE BEFORE HEADING BACK TO THE HOTEL. I'M GLAD I DID TONIGHT. WOULD YOU FANCY A RIDE HOME?

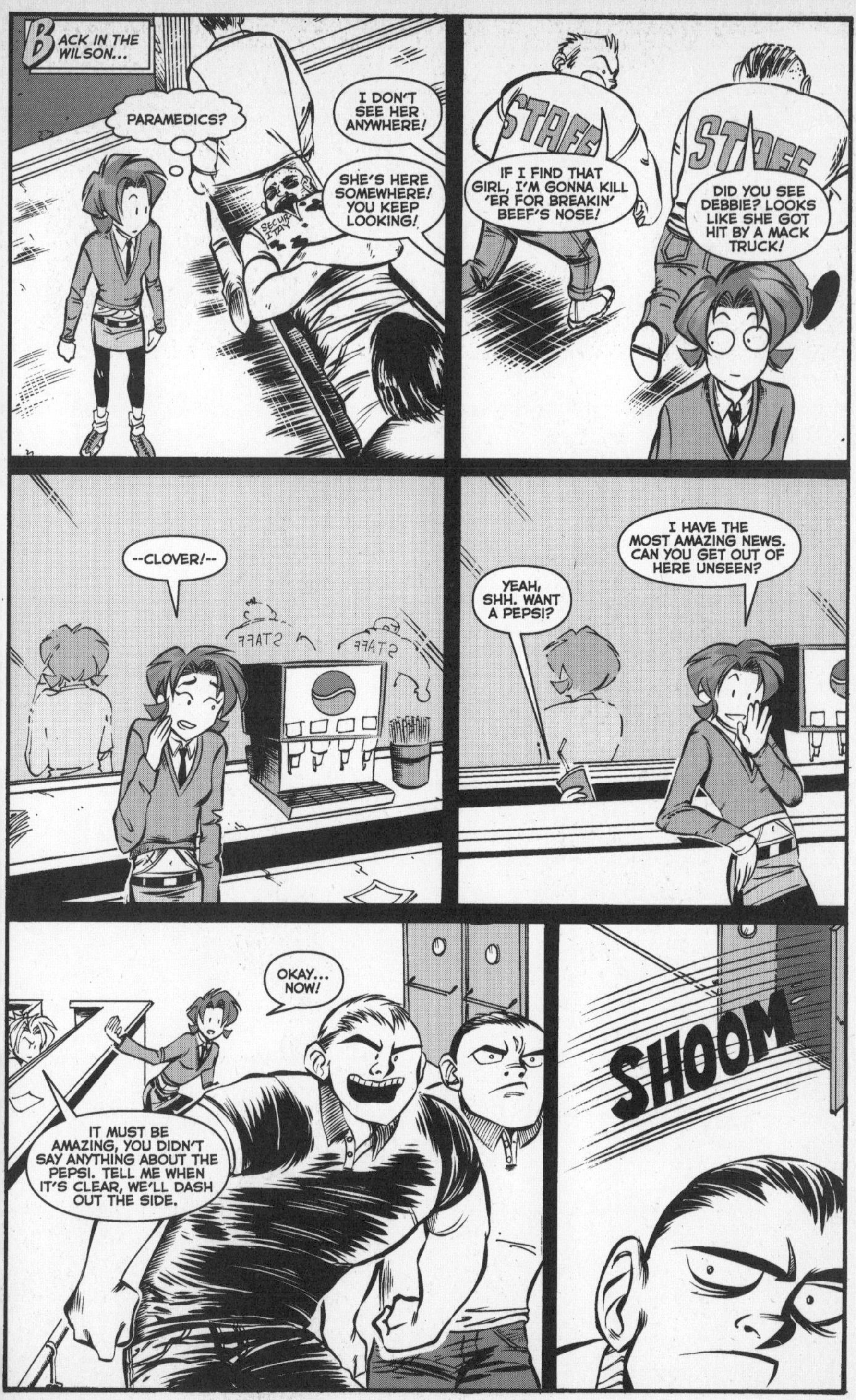
BACK IN THE WILSON...
PARAMEDICS?
I DON'T SEE HER ANYWHERE!
SHE'S HERE SOMEWHERE! YOU KEEP LOOKING!
SECURITAY
STAFF
STAFF
IF I FIND THAT GIRL, I'M GONNA KILL 'ER FOR BREAKIN' BEEF'S NOSE!
DID YOU SEE DEBBIE? LOOKS LIKE SHE GOT HIT BY A MACK TRUCK!
--CLOVER!--
STAFF
STAFF
I HAVE THE MOST AMAZING NEWS. CAN YOU GET OUT OF HERE UNSEEN?
YEAH, SHH. WANT A PEPSI?
IT MUST BE AMAZING, YOU DIDN'T SAY ANYTHING ABOUT THE PEPSI. TELL ME WHEN IT'S CLEAR, WE'LL DASH OUT THE SIDE.
OKAY... NOW!
SHOOM

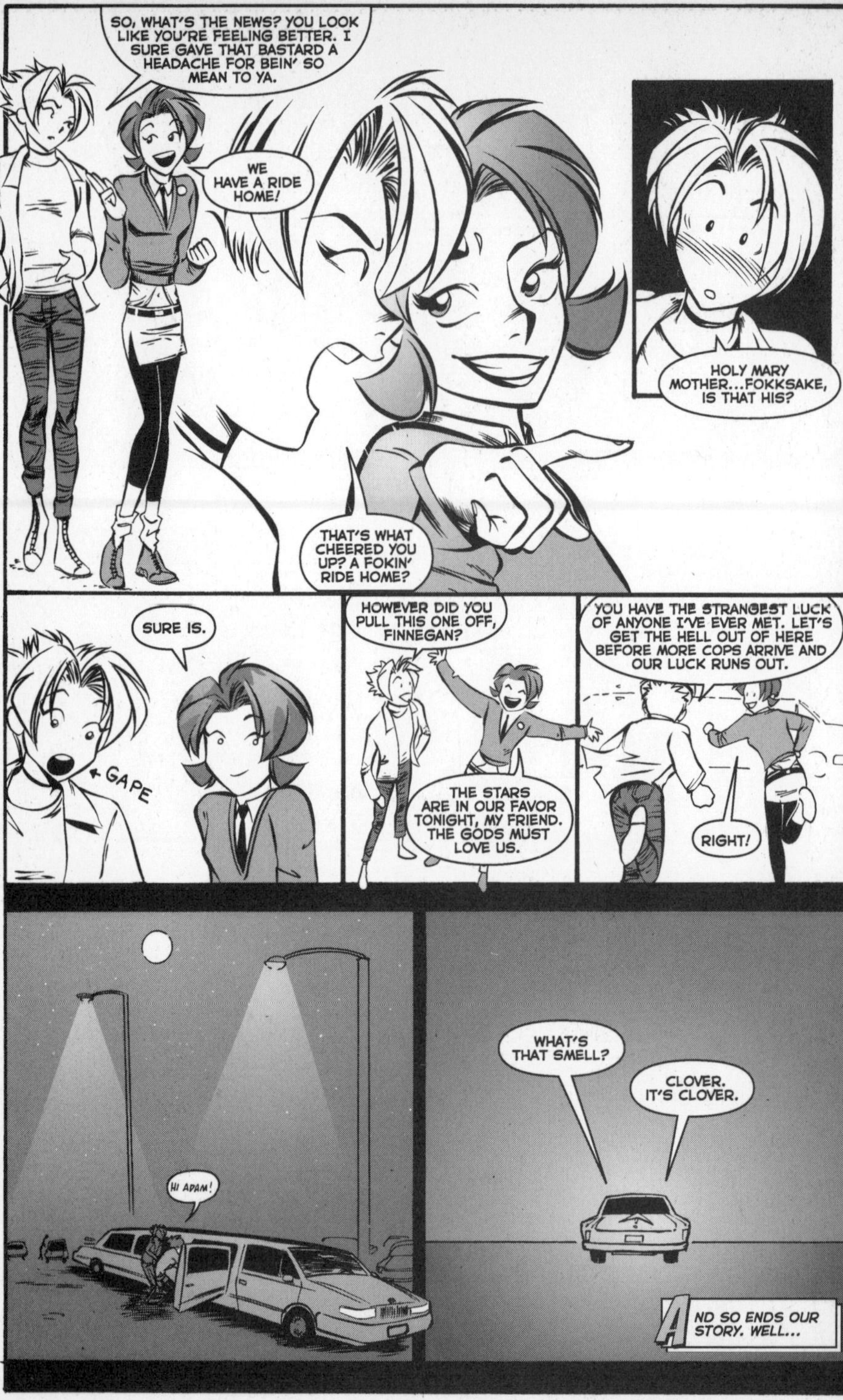
SO, WHAT'S THE NEWS? YOU LOOK LIKE YOU'RE FEELING BETTER. I SURE GAVE THAT BASTARD A HEADACHE FOR BEIN' SO MEAN TO YA.
WE HAVE A RIDE HOME!
THAT'S WHAT CHEERED YOU UP? A FOKIN' RIDE HOME?
HOLY MARY MOTHER...FOKKSAKE, IS THAT HIS?
SURE IS.
GAPE
HOWEVER DID YOU PULL THIS ONE OFF, FINNEGAN?
THE STARS ARE IN OUR FAVOR TONIGHT, MY FRIEND. THE GODS MUST LOVE US.
YOU HAVE THE STRANGEST LUCK OF ANYONE I'VE EVER MET. LET'S GET THE HELL OUT OF HERE BEFORE MORE COPS ARRIVE AND OUR LUCK RUNS OUT.
RIGHT!
HI ADAM!
WHAT'S THAT SMELL?
CLOVER. IT'S CLOVER.
AND SO ENDS OUR STORY. WELL...

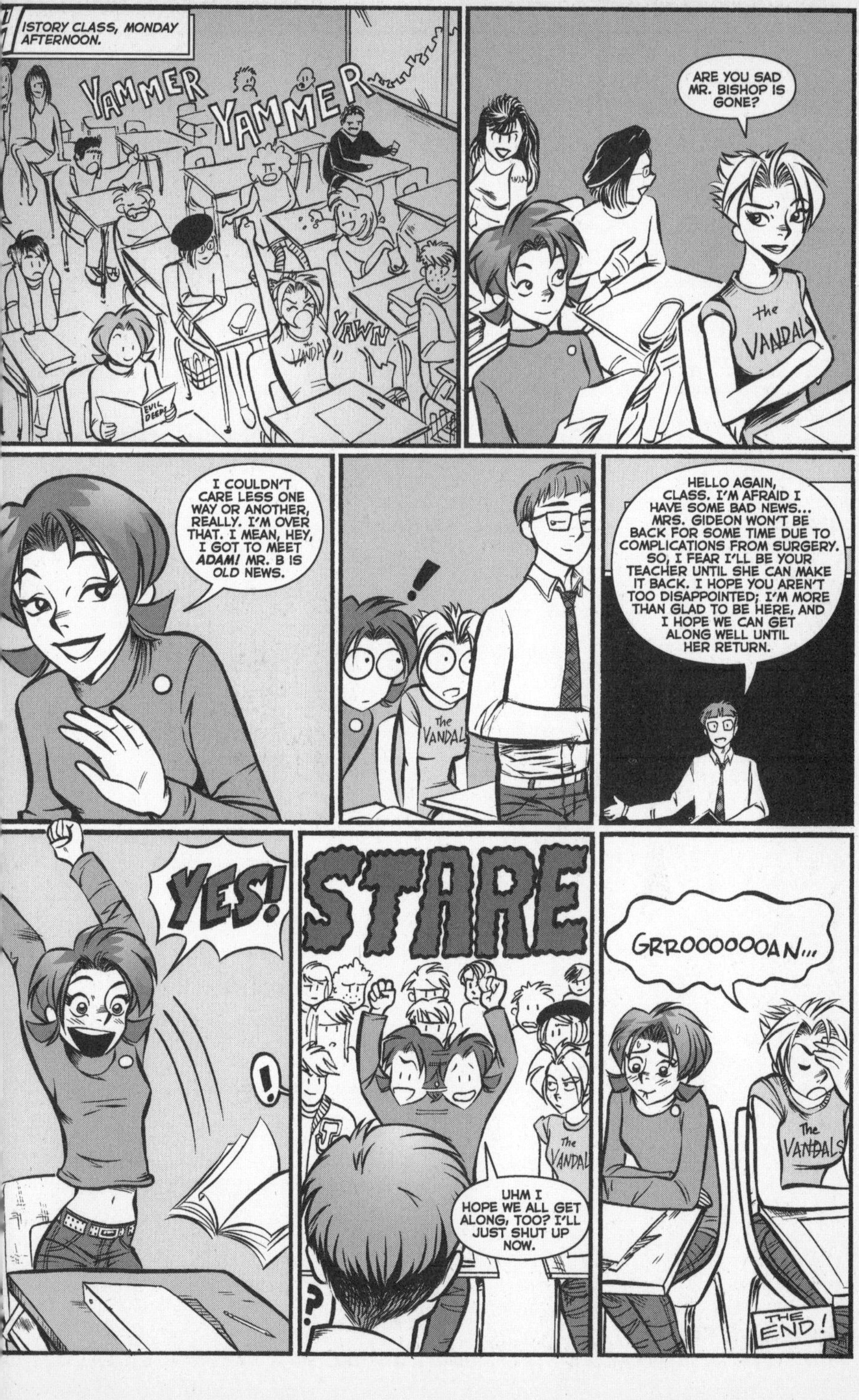
ISTORY CLASS, MONDAY AFTERNOON.
YAMMER YAMMER
YAWN
EVIL DEEP
ARE YOU SAD MR. BISHOP IS GONE?
I COULDN'T CARE LESS ONE WAY OR ANOTHER, REALLY. I'M OVER THAT. I MEAN, HEY, I GOT TO MEET ADAM! MR. B IS OLD NEWS.
!
HELLO AGAIN, CLASS. I'M AFRAID I HAVE SOME BAD NEWS... MRS. GIDEON WON'T BE BACK FOR SOME TIME DUE TO COMPLICATIONS FROM SURGERY. SO, I FEAR I'LL BE YOUR TEACHER UNTIL SHE CAN MAKE IT BACK. I HOPE YOU AREN'T TOO DISAPPOINTED; I'M MORE THAN GLAD TO BE HERE, AND I HOPE WE CAN GET ALONG WELL UNTIL HER RETURN.
YES!
!
STARE
UHM I HOPE WE ALL GET ALONG, TOO? I'LL JUST SHUT UP NOW.
?
GRROOOOOOAN...
THE END!

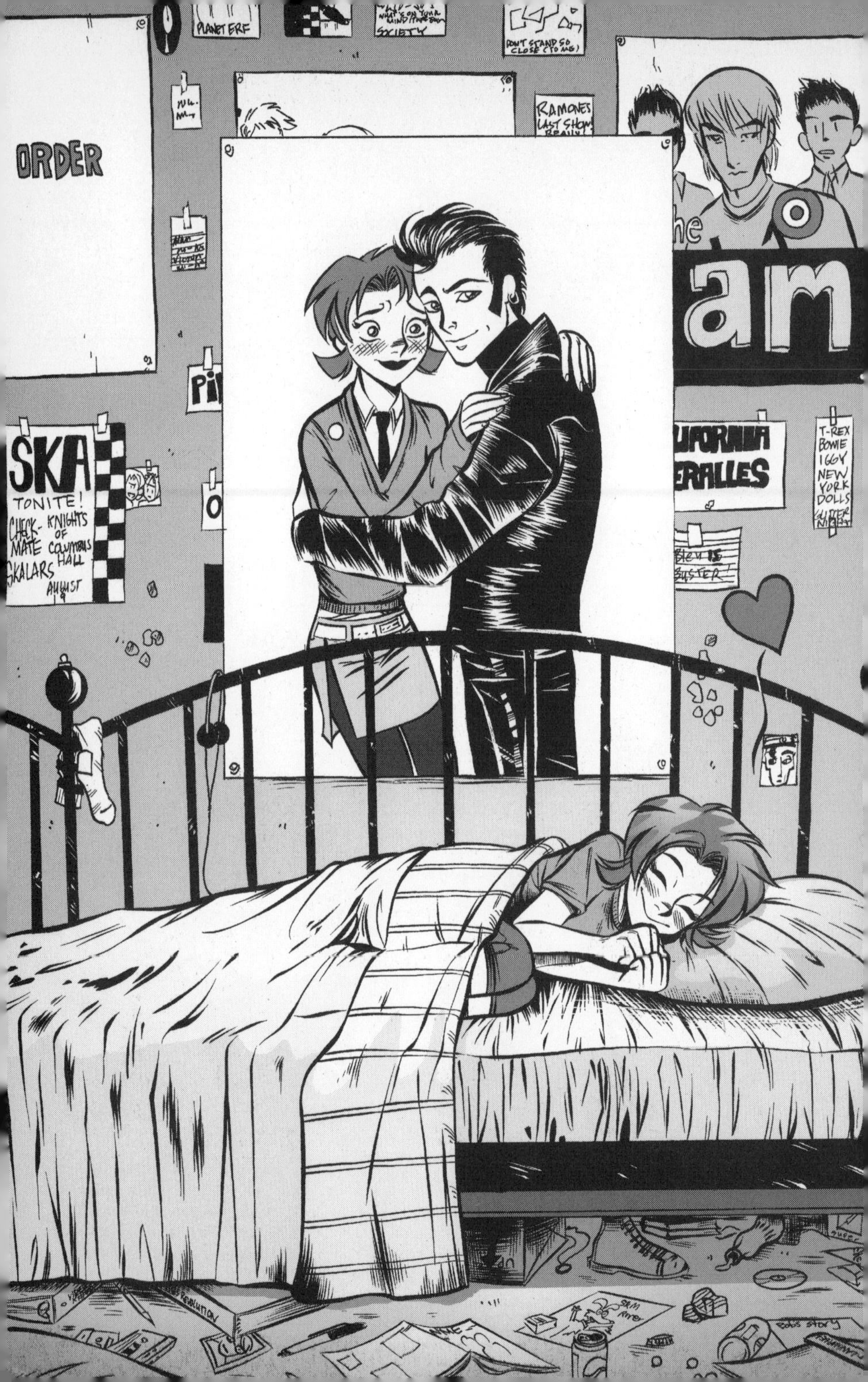

PLANET ERF
SOCIETY
DON'T STAND SO CLOSE (TO ME)
RAMONES LAST SHOW
ORDER
SKA TONITE! CHECK-MATE SKALARS KNIGHTS OF COLUMBUS HALL AUGUST 9
ERALLES
T-REX BOWIE IGGY NEW YORK DOLLS

# THE SHORT STORIES

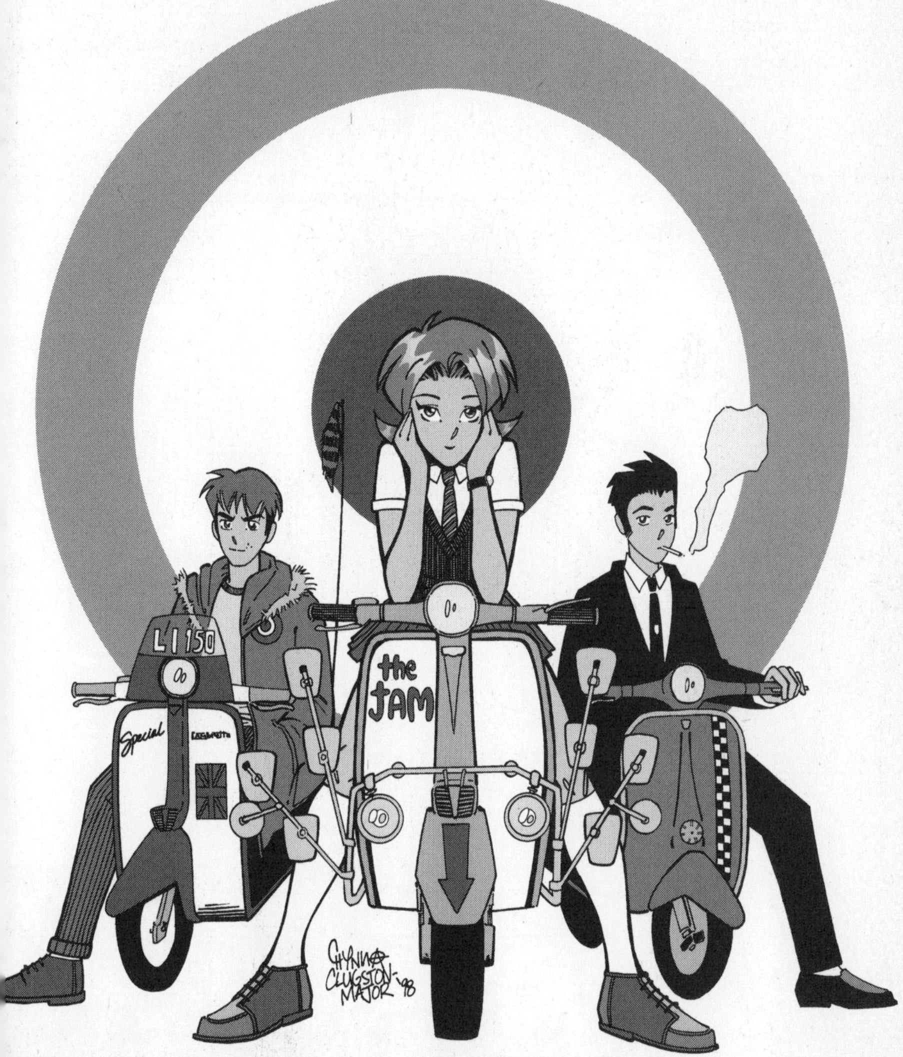
LI 150
Special
the JAM
CHYNNA CLUGSTON-MAJOR '98

*e following pages contain the many short stories that preceded the miniseries* The Kids Are Alright. *They are printed here in near chronological order to show the progression of the characters from their debut in* Dark *rse* Presents *to the last couple of stories Chynna did before starting the series. At the tail end of the stories, we are also reprinting the three original promotional ads for the series in their original form.*

*An unprinted pin-up*

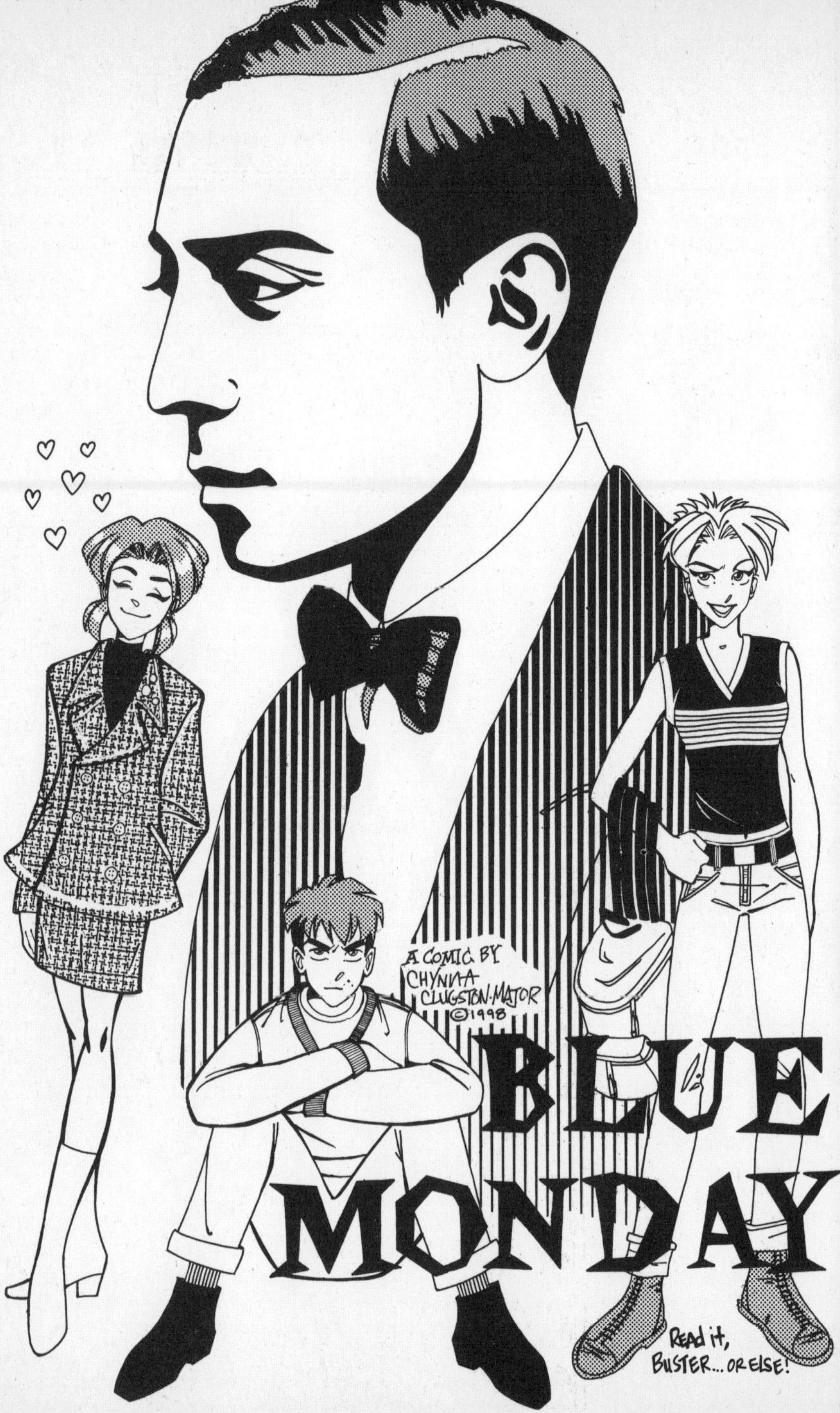
A COMIC BY CHYNNA CLUGSTON-MAJOR ©1998
BLUE MONDAY
Read it, BUSTER... OR ELSE!

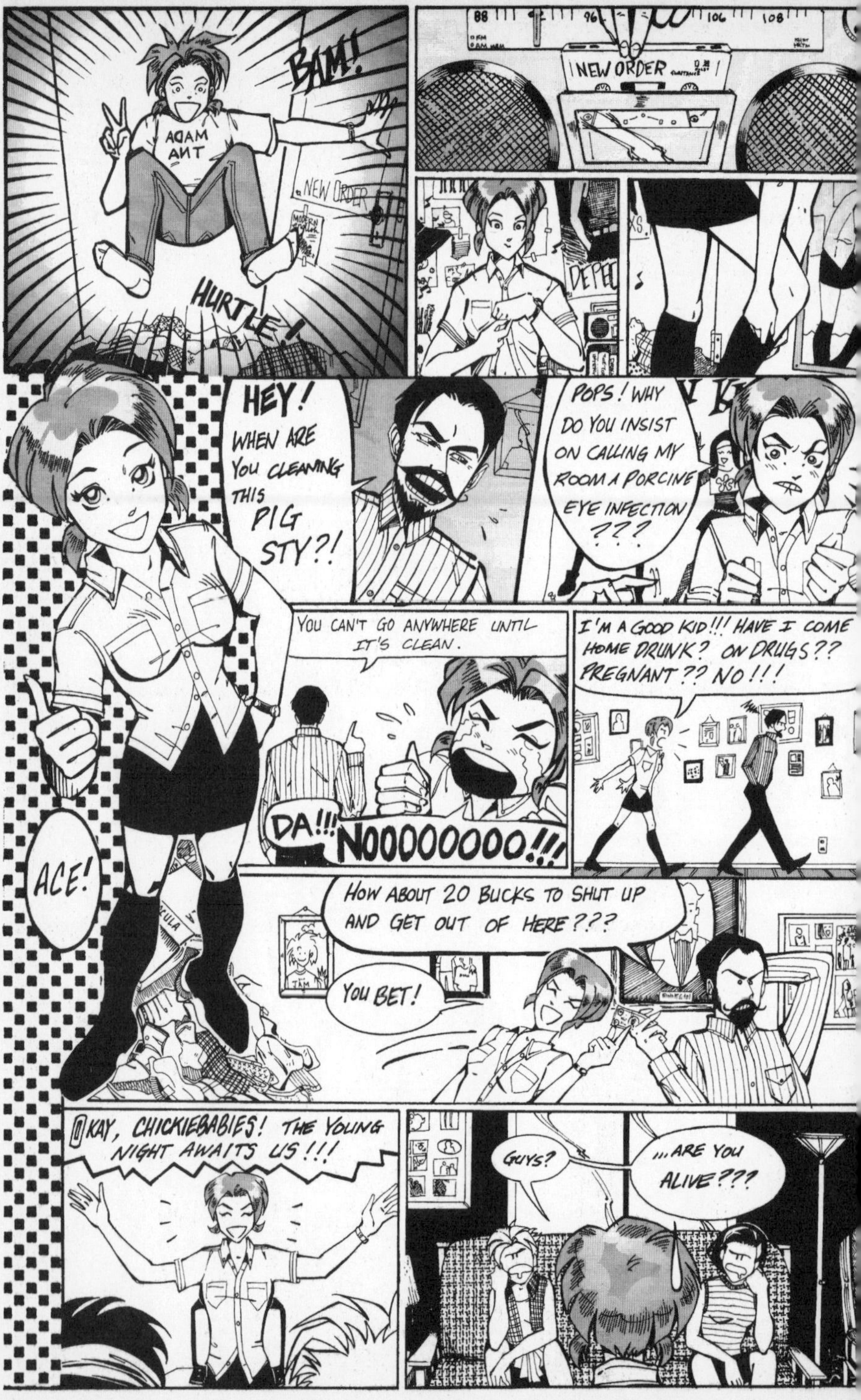
BAM!
ADAM ANT
NEW ORDER
HURTLE!
NEW ORDER
HEY! WHEN ARE YOU CLEANING THIS PIG STY?!
POPS! WHY DO YOU INSIST ON CALLING MY ROOM A PORCINE EYE INFECTION???
ACE!
YOU CAN'T GO ANYWHERE UNTIL IT'S CLEAN.
DA!!! NOOOOOOOO!!!
I'M A GOOD KID!!! HAVE I COME HOME DRUNK? ON DRUGS?? PREGNANT?? NO!!!
HOW ABOUT 20 BUCKS TO SHUT UP AND GET OUT OF HERE???
YOU BET!
OKAY, CHICKIEBABIES! THE YOUNG NIGHT AWAITS US!!!
GUYS?
...ARE YOU ALIVE???

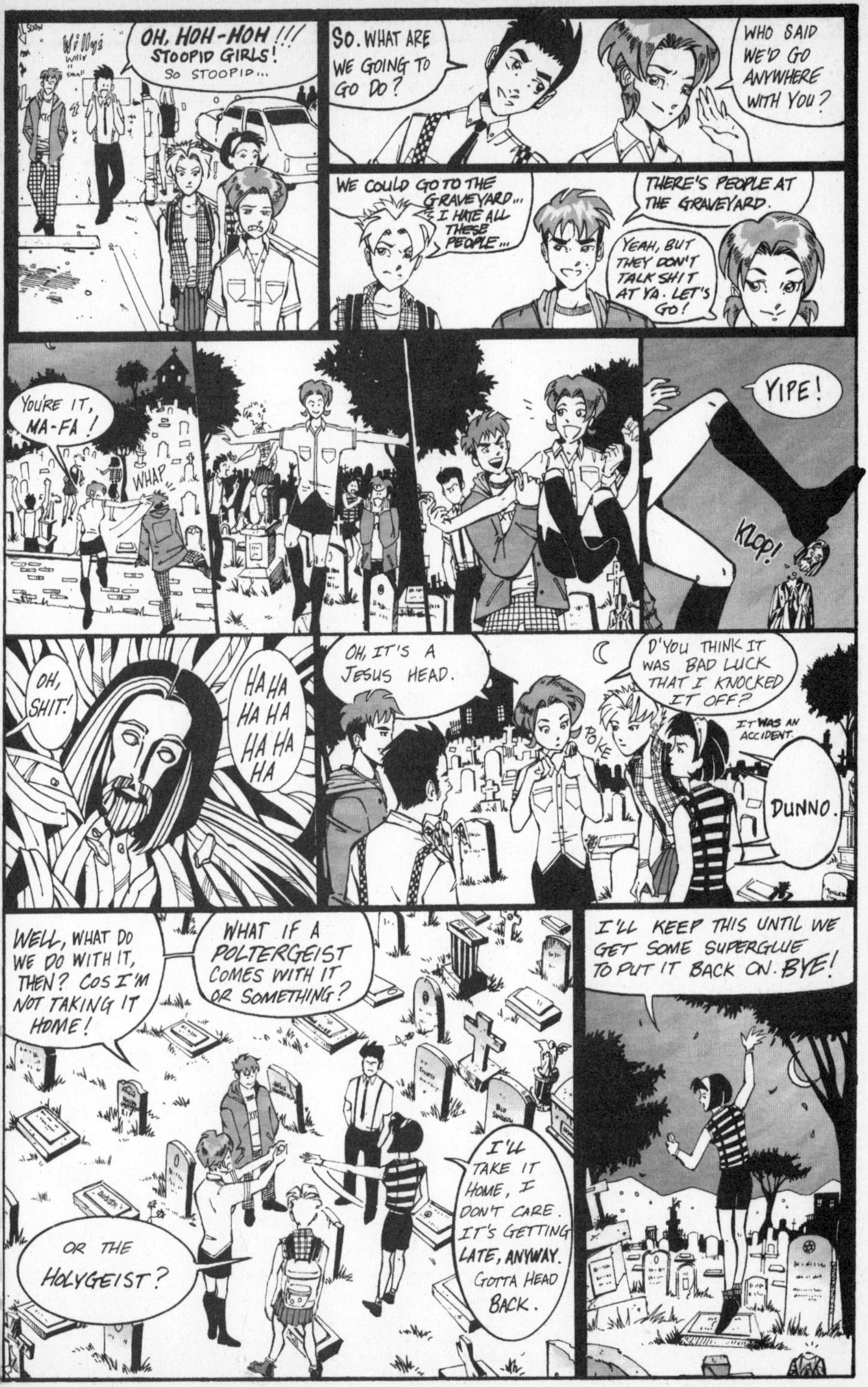
OH, HOH-HOH!!! STOOPID GIRLS! SO STOOPID...
SO. WHAT ARE WE GOING TO GO DO?
WHO SAID WE'D GO ANYWHERE WITH YOU?
WE COULD GO TO THE GRAVEYARD... I HATE ALL THESE PEOPLE...
THERE'S PEOPLE AT THE GRAVEYARD.
YEAH, BUT THEY DON'T TALK SHIT AT YA. LET'S GO!
YOU'RE IT, MA-FA!
WHAP
YIPE!
KLOP!
OH, SHIT!
HA HA HA HA HA HA HA
OH, IT'S A JESUS HEAD.
D'YOU THINK IT WAS BAD LUCK THAT I KNOCKED IT OFF?
POKE
IT WAS AN ACCIDENT.
DUNNO.
WELL, WHAT DO WE DO WITH IT, THEN? COS I'M NOT TAKING IT HOME!
WHAT IF A POLTERGEIST COMES WITH IT OR SOMETHING?
OR THE HOLYGEIST?
I'LL TAKE IT HOME, I DON'T CARE. IT'S GETTING LATE, ANYWAY. GOTTA HEAD BACK.
I'LL KEEP THIS UNTIL WE GET SOME SUPERGLUE TO PUT IT BACK ON. BYE!

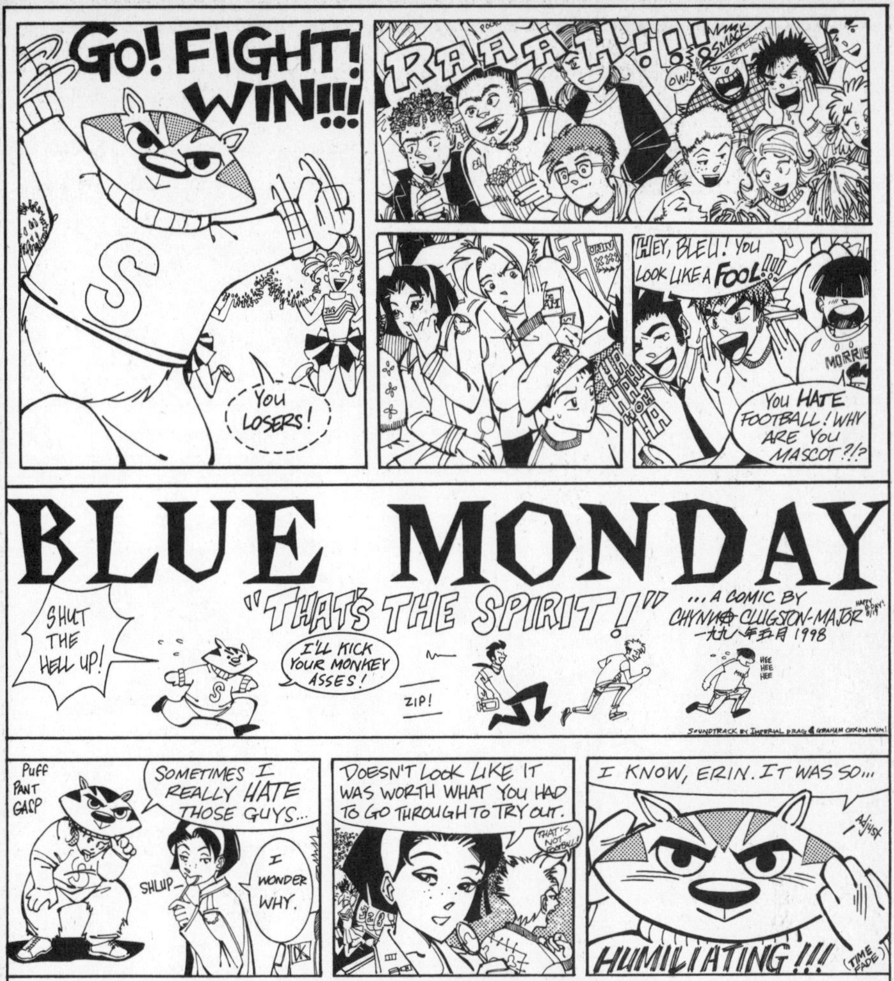
GO! FIGHT! WIN!!!
RAAAAH!!!
SMACK
OW!
You LOSERS!
HEY, BLEU! You LOOK LIKE A FOOL!!!
HA HA HA
You HATE FOOTBALL! WHY ARE You MASCOT?!?
BLUE MONDAY
"THAT'S THE SPIRIT!"
...A COMIC BY CHYNNA CLUGSTON-MAJOR 一九九八年五月 1998
SHUT THE HELL UP!
I'LL KICK YOUR MONKEY ASSES!
ZIP!
HEE HEE HEE
Puff PANT GASP
SOMETIMES I REALLY HATE THOSE GUYS...
SHLUP
I WONDER WHY.
DOESN'T LOOK LIKE IT WAS WORTH WHAT YOU HAD TO GO THROUGH TO TRY OUT.
I KNOW, ERIN. IT WAS SO...
Adjust
HUMILIATING!!!
(TIME FADE)
LAST WEEK...
HEY! THEY'RE HAVIN' MASCOT TRYOUTS THIS WEEK! I'LL GO ASK ABOUT IT!!!
!
BAM!
FICE
SIGN ME UP! I'M "MASCOT MATERIAL"!!!
...
THERE'S THREE OTHER GIRLS WHO WANT TO BE MASCOT...
SO, YOU'LL HAVE TO TRY OUT WEDNESDAY. HERE'S WHAT YOU HAVE TO LEARN.

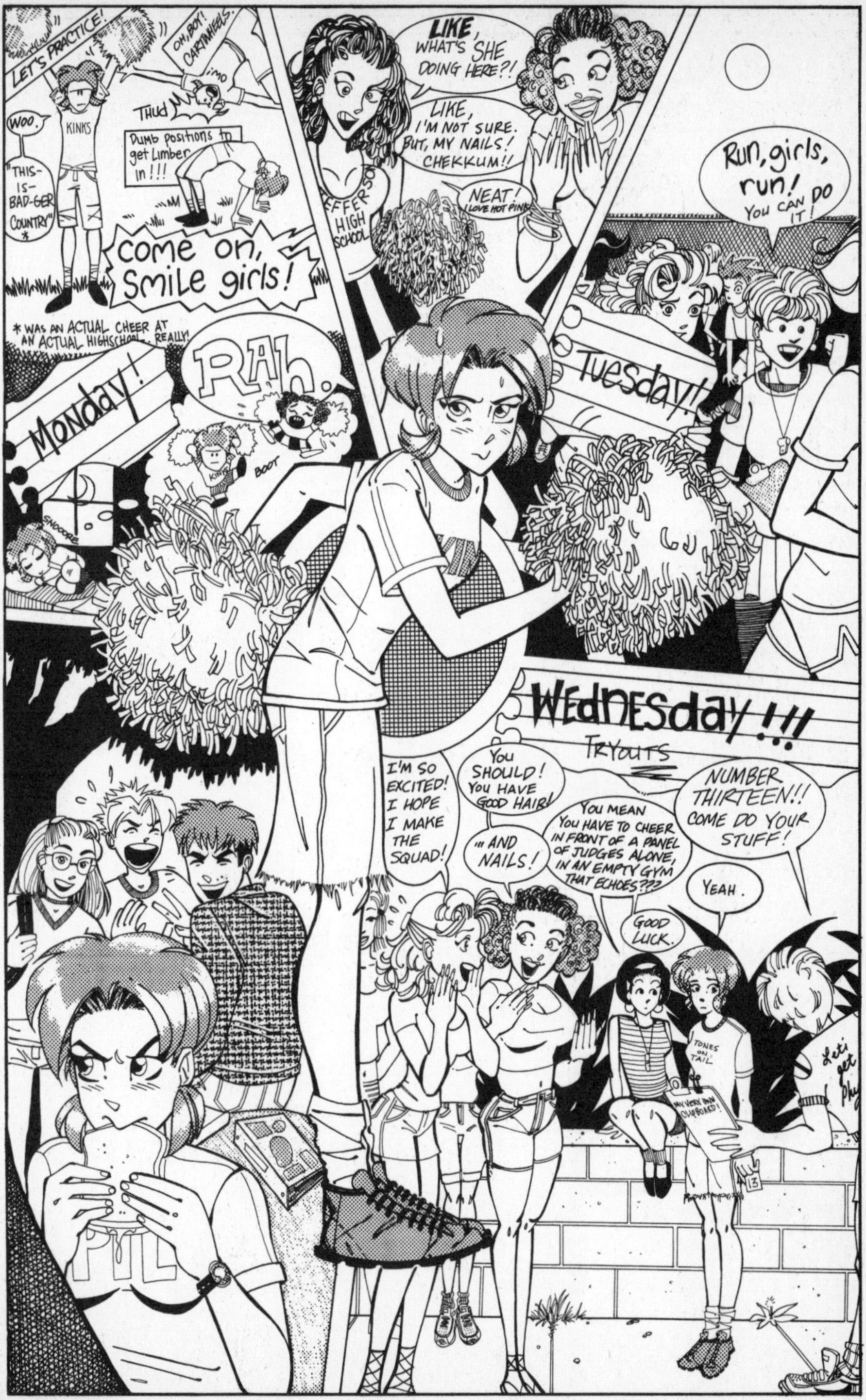
LET'S PRACTICE!
OH, BOY! CARTWHEELS.
THUD
WOO.
KINKS
"THIS-IS-BAD-GER COUNTRY" *
Dumb positions to get Limber in!!!
Come on, Smile girls!
* WAS AN ACTUAL CHEER AT AN ACTUAL HIGHSCHOOL... REALLY!
LIKE, WHAT'S SHE DOING HERE?!
LIKE, I'M NOT SURE. BUT, MY NAILS! CHEKKUM!!
NEAT! I LOVE HOT PINK!
JEFFERSON HIGH SCHOOL
Run, girls, run! You CAN DO IT!
Monday!
RAh.
SNOOORE
BOOT
Tuesday!!
WEDNESDAY!!!
TRYOUTS
I'M SO EXCITED! I HOPE I MAKE THE SQUAD!
You SHOULD! You HAVE GOOD HAIR!
... AND NAILS!
You MEAN You HAVE TO CHEER IN FRONT OF A PANEL OF JUDGES ALONE, IN AN EMPTY GYM THAT ECHOES???
NUMBER THIRTEEN!! COME DO YOUR STUFF!
YEAH.
GOOD LUCK.
TONES ON TAIL
MY VERY OWN CLIPBOARD!
13

# BLUE MONDAY
## "THE Curse OF THE Jesus Head"

A COMIC BY CHYNNA CLUGSTON-MAJOR SEP 1998

SOUNDTRACK BY ADAM ANT, (YUM) THE STONE ROSES, & "M".

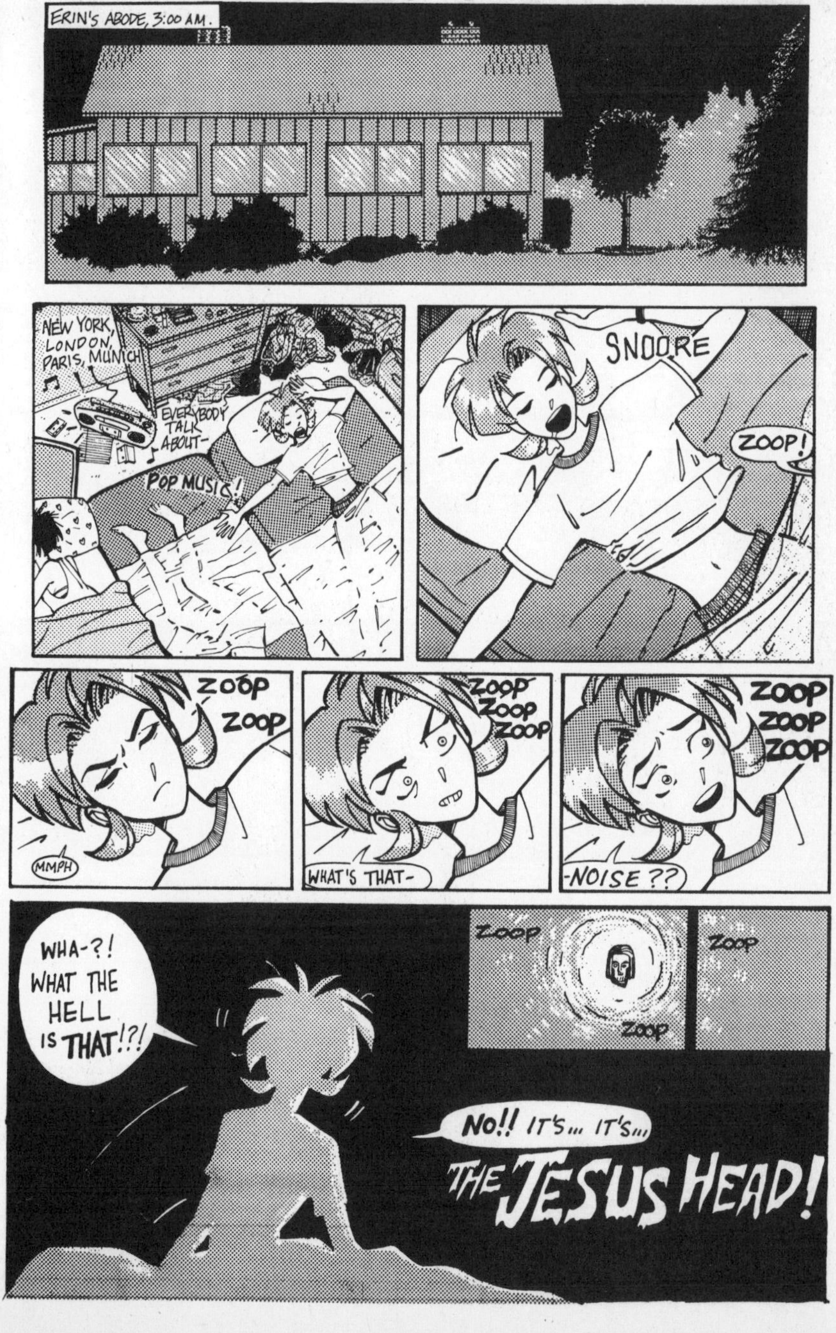

ERIN'S ABODE, 3:00 AM.
NEW YORK, LONDON, PARIS, MUNICH
EVERYBODY TALK ABOUT-
POP MUSIC!
SNOORE
ZOOP!
ZOOP ZOOP
MMPH
ZOOP ZOOP ZOOP
WHAT'S THAT-
ZOOP ZOOP ZOOP
-NOISE??
WHA-?! WHAT THE HELL IS THAT!?!
ZOOP
ZOOP
ZOOP
NO!! IT'S... IT'S...
THE JESUS HEAD!

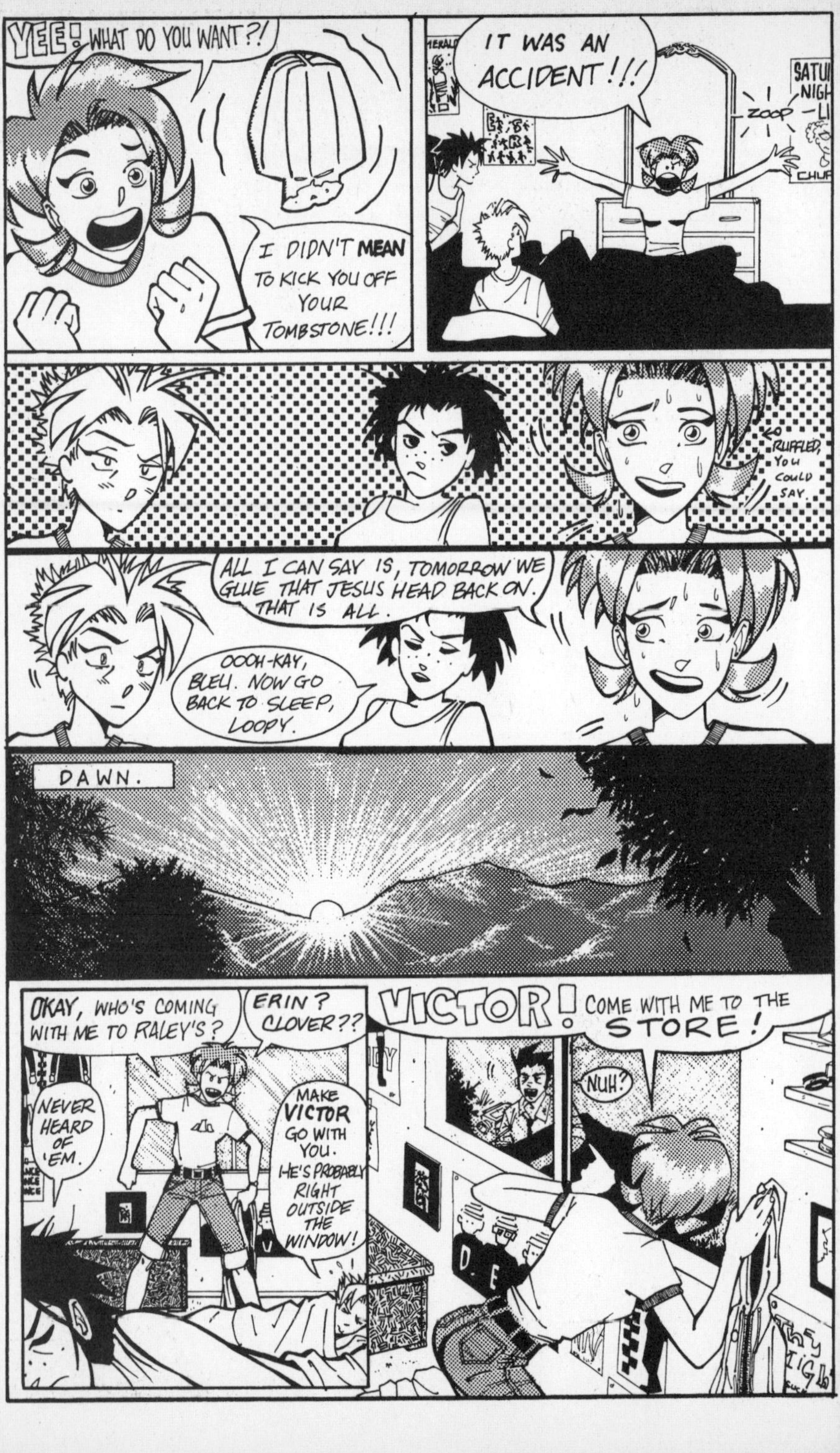
YEE! WHAT DO YOU WANT?!
I DIDN'T MEAN TO KICK YOU OFF YOUR TOMBSTONE!!!
IT WAS AN ACCIDENT!!!
ZOOP
RUFFLED, YOU COULD SAY.
ALL I CAN SAY IS, TOMORROW WE GLUE THAT JESUS HEAD BACK ON. THAT IS ALL.
OOOH-KAY, BLEU. NOW GO BACK TO SLEEP, LOOPY.
DAWN.
OKAY, WHO'S COMING WITH ME TO RALEY'S?
ERIN? CLOVER??
NEVER HEARD OF 'EM.
MAKE VICTOR GO WITH YOU. HE'S PROBABLY RIGHT OUTSIDE THE WINDOW!
VICTOR! COME WITH ME TO THE STORE!
NUH?

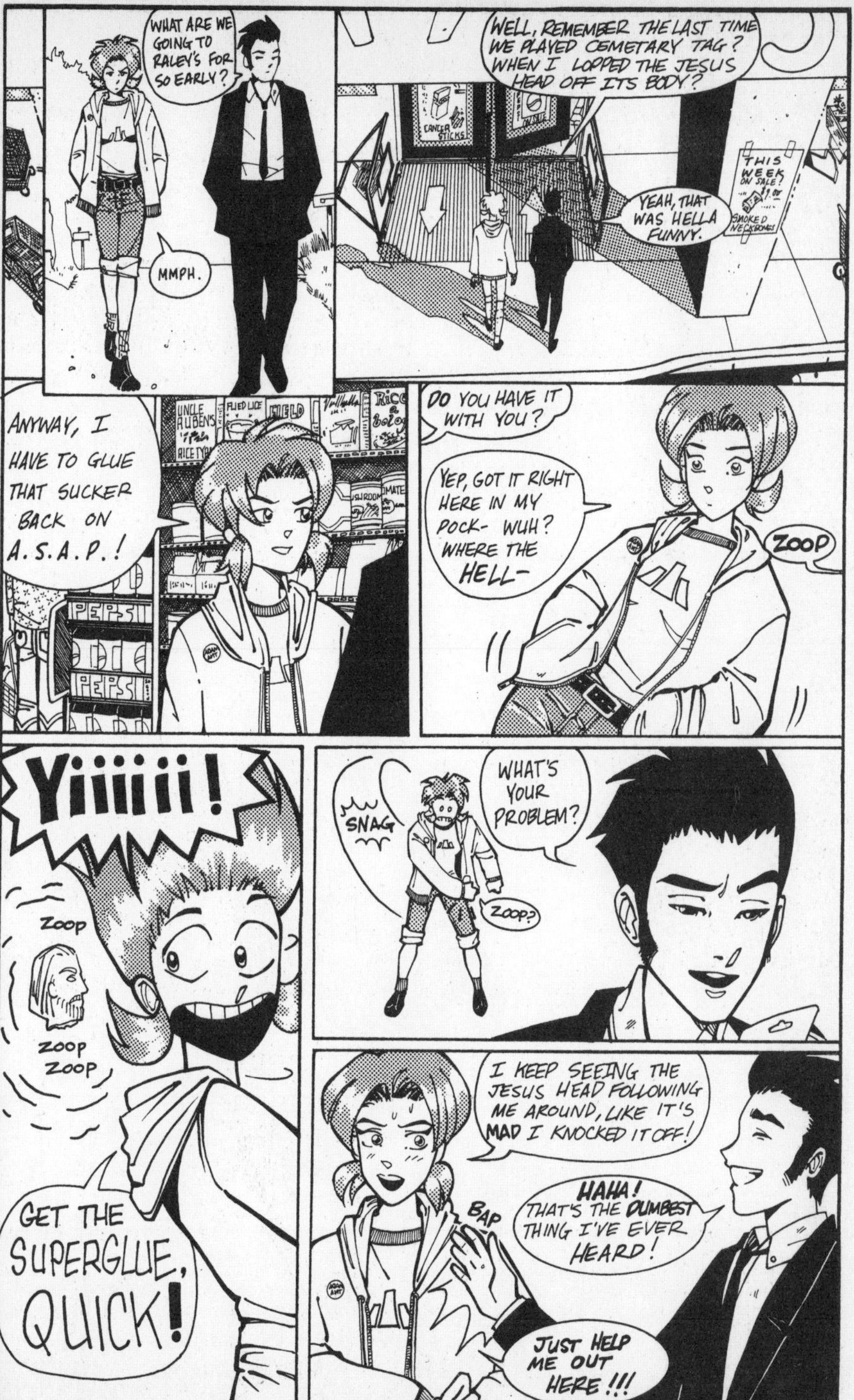
WHAT ARE WE GOING TO RALEY'S FOR SO EARLY?
MMPH.
WELL, REMEMBER THE LAST TIME WE PLAYED CEMETARY TAG? WHEN I LOPPED THE JESUS HEAD OFF ITS BODY?
YEAH, THAT WAS HELLA FUNNY.
CANCER STICKS
THIS WEEK ON SALE!
SMOKED NECKBONES
ANYWAY, I HAVE TO GLUE THAT SUCKER BACK ON A.S.A.P.!
PEPSI
DO YOU HAVE IT WITH YOU?
YEP, GOT IT RIGHT HERE IN MY POCK- WUH? WHERE THE HELL-
ZOOP
Yiiiiii!
ZOOP
ZOOP ZOOP
GET THE SUPERGLUE, QUICK!
SNAG
ZOOP?
WHAT'S YOUR PROBLEM?
I KEEP SEEING THE JESUS HEAD FOLLOWING ME AROUND, LIKE IT'S MAD I KNOCKED IT OFF!
BAP
HAHA! THAT'S THE DUMBEST THING I'VE EVER HEARD!
JUST HELP ME OUT HERE!!!

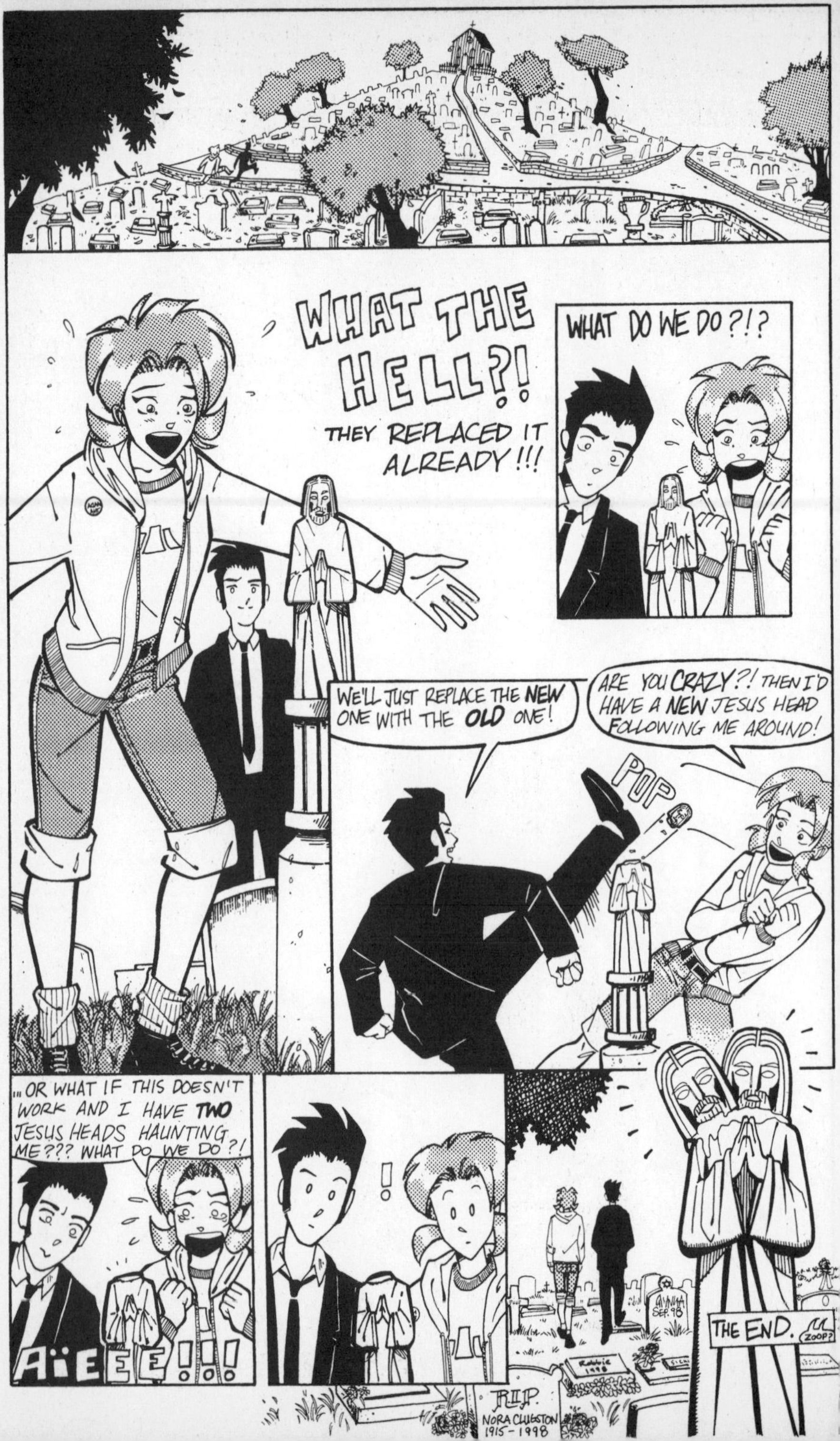
WHAT THE HELL?!
THEY REPLACED IT ALREADY!!!
WHAT DO WE DO?!?
WE'LL JUST REPLACE THE NEW ONE WITH THE OLD ONE!
ARE YOU CRAZY?! THEN I'D HAVE A NEW JESUS HEAD FOLLOWING ME AROUND!
POP
...OR WHAT IF THIS DOESN'T WORK AND I HAVE TWO JESUS HEADS HAUNTING ME??? WHAT DO WE DO?!
AïEEE!!!
!
Robbie 1998
THE END.
ZOOP?
R.I.P. NORA CLUGSTON 1915-1998

# BLUE MONDAY: "CONTAGIOUSLY YOURS"

A COMIC BY CHYNNA CLUGSTON-MAJOR ♪

FEB. 1999    SPECIAL THANKS TO JON "MUGSY" FLORES!    SOUNDTRACK: THE BEAT & DESMOND D.! ♪

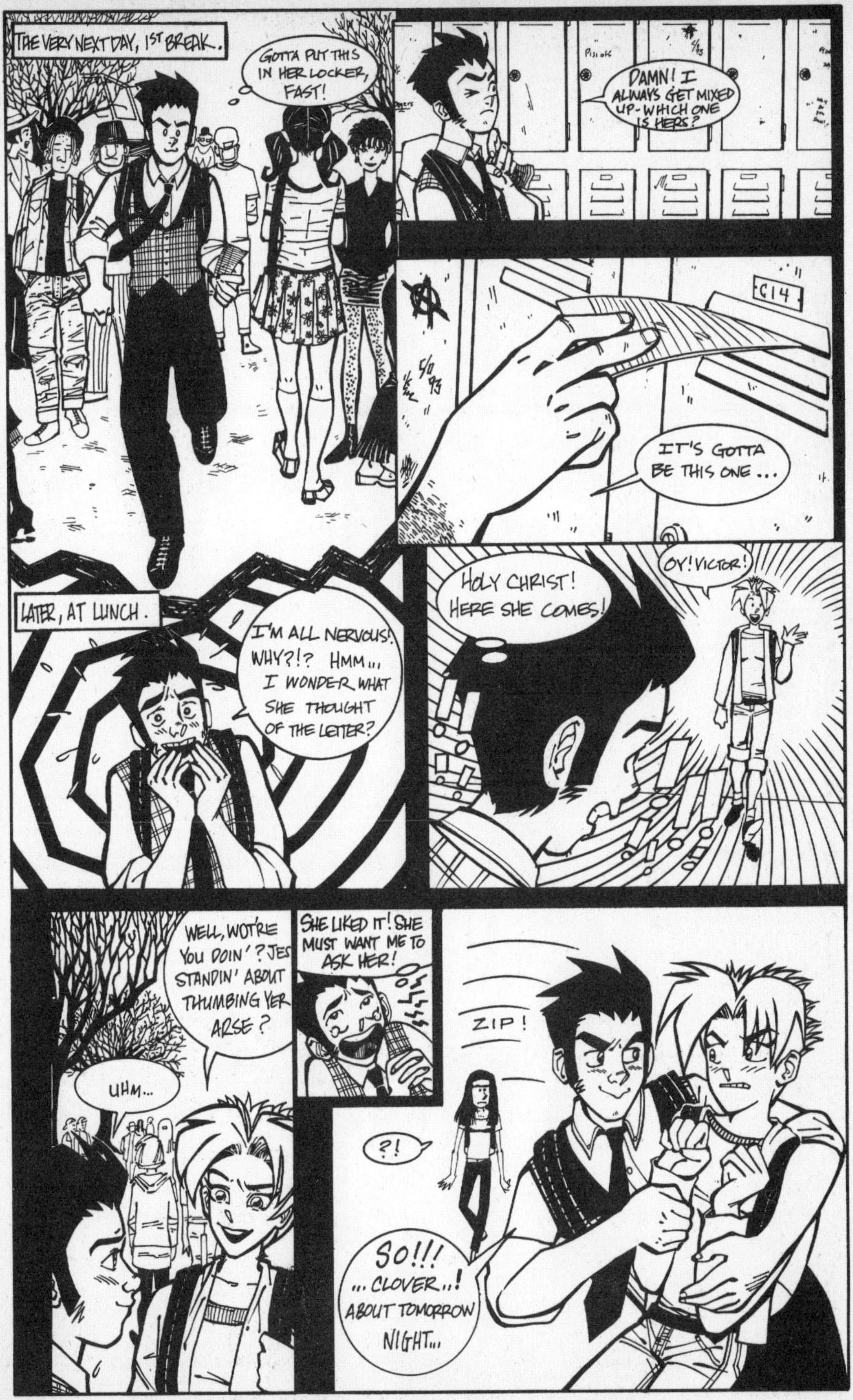
THE VERY NEXT DAY, 1ST BREAK.
GOTTA PUT THIS IN HER LOCKER, FAST!
DAMN! I ALWAYS GET MIXED UP-WHICH ONE IS HERS?
C14
IT'S GOTTA BE THIS ONE...
LATER, AT LUNCH.
I'M ALL NERVOUS! WHY?!? HMM... I WONDER WHAT SHE THOUGHT OF THE LETTER?
HOLY CHRIST! HERE SHE COMES!
OY! VICTOR!
WELL, WOT'RE YOU DOIN'? JES' STANDIN' ABOUT THUMBING YER ARSE?
UHM...
SHE LIKED IT! SHE MUST WANT ME TO ASK HER!
ZIP!
?!
SO!!! ...CLOVER...! ABOUT TOMORROW NIGHT...

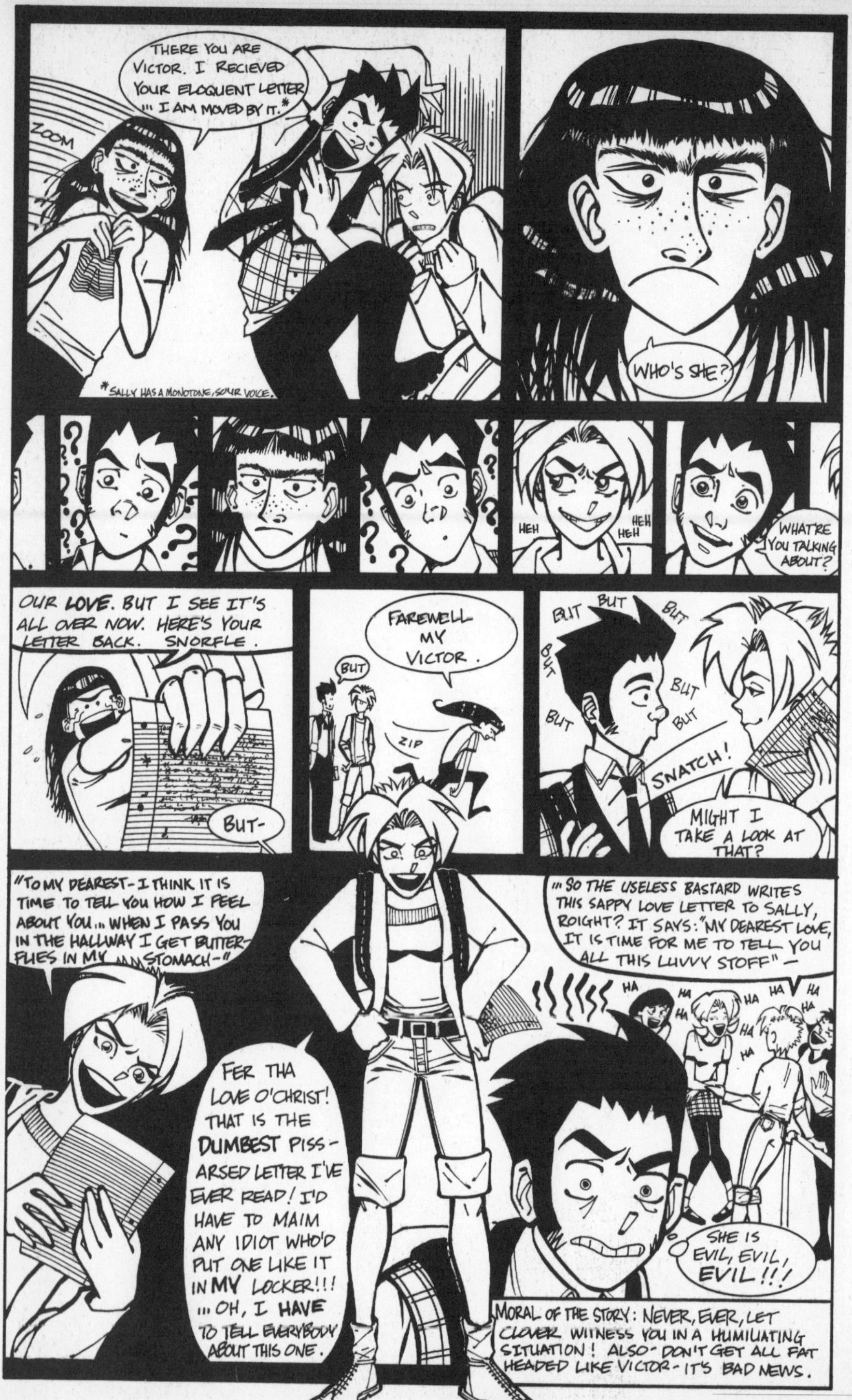
THERE YOU ARE VICTOR. I RECIEVED YOUR ELOQUENT LETTER ... I AM MOVED BY IT.*
ZOOM
*SALLY HAS A MONOTONE, SOUR VOICE.
WHO'S SHE?
HEH HEH HEH
WHAT'RE YOU TALKING ABOUT?
OUR LOVE. BUT I SEE IT'S ALL OVER NOW. HERE'S YOUR LETTER BACK. SNORFLE.
BUT-
FAREWELL MY VICTOR.
BUT
ZIP
BUT BUT BUT BUT BUT BUT BUT
SNATCH!
MIGHT I TAKE A LOOK AT THAT?
"TO MY DEAREST- I THINK IT IS TIME TO TELL YOU HOW I FEEL ABOUT YOU... WHEN I PASS YOU IN THE HALLWAY I GET BUTTER-FLIES IN MY STOMACH-"
FER THA LOVE O'CHRIST! THAT IS THE DUMBEST PISS-ARSED LETTER I'VE EVER READ! I'D HAVE TO MAIM ANY IDIOT WHO'D PUT ONE LIKE IT IN MY LOCKER!!! ... OH, I HAVE TO TELL EVERYBODY ABOUT THIS ONE.
... SO THE USELESS BASTARD WRITES THIS SAPPY LOVE LETTER TO SALLY, ROIGHT? IT SAYS: "MY DEAREST LOVE, IT IS TIME FOR ME TO TELL YOU ALL THIS LUVVY STOFF" -
HA HA HA HA HA HA HA HA HA
SHE IS EVIL, EVIL, EVIL!!!
MORAL OF THE STORY: NEVER, EVER, LET CLOVER WITNESS YOU IN A HUMILIATING SITUATION! ALSO- DON'T GET ALL FAT HEADED LIKE VICTOR- IT'S BAD NEWS.

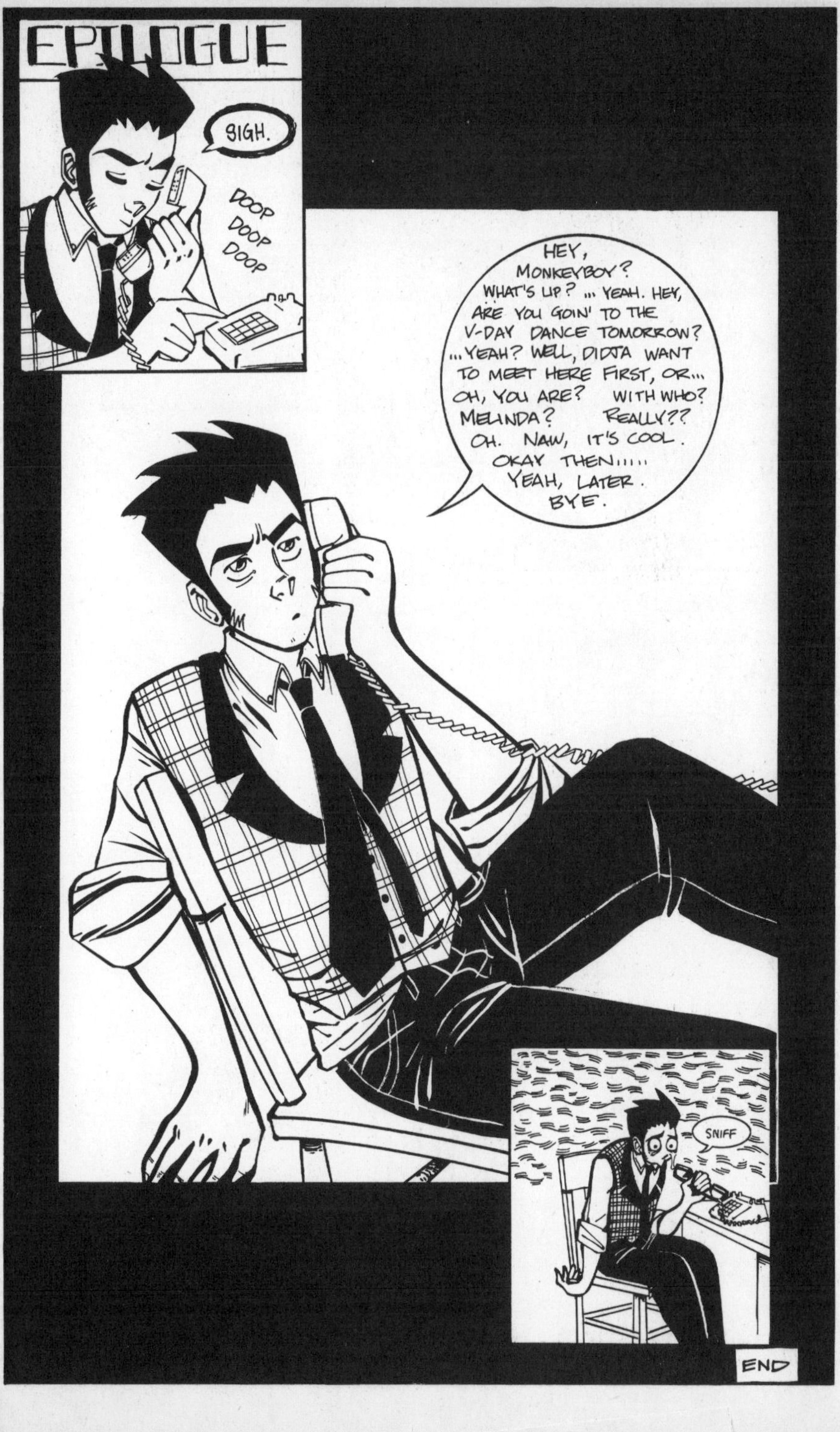
EPILOGUE
SIGH.
DOOP DOOP DOOP
HEY, MONKEYBOY? WHAT'S UP? ... YEAH. HEY, ARE YOU GOIN' TO THE V-DAY DANCE TOMORROW? ...YEAH? WELL, DIDJA WANT TO MEET HERE FIRST, OR... OH, YOU ARE? WITH WHO? MELINDA? REALLY?? OH. NAW, IT'S COOL. OKAY THEN..... YEAH, LATER. BYE.
SNIFF
END

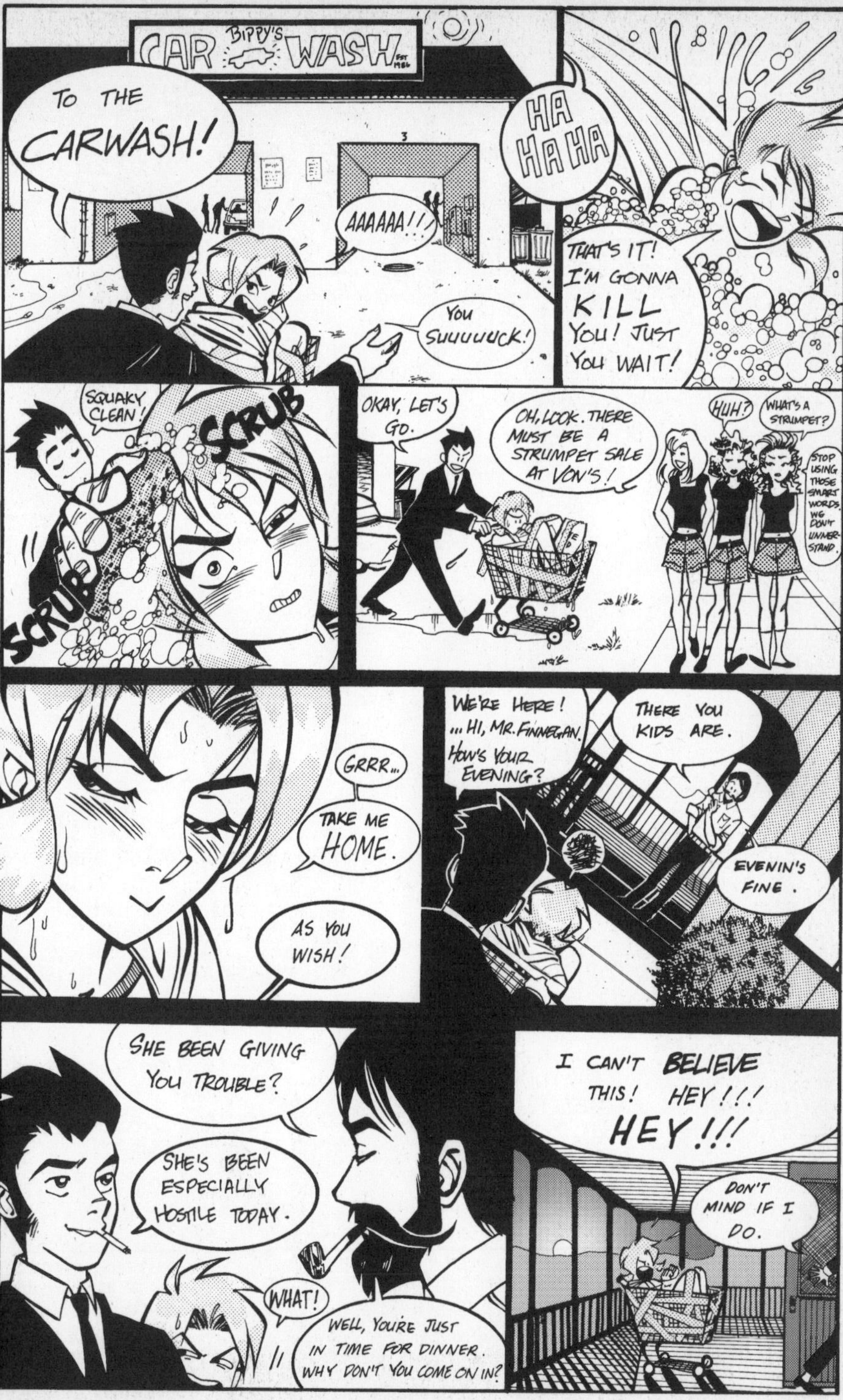
BIPPY'S CAR WASH EST 1986
TO THE CARWASH!
AAAAAA!!!
YOU SUUUUUCK!
HA HA HA HA
THAT'S IT! I'M GONNA KILL YOU! JUST YOU WAIT!
SQUAKY CLEAN!
SCRUB
SCRUB
OKAY, LET'S GO.
OH, LOOK. THERE MUST BE A STRUMPET SALE AT VON'S!
HUH?
WHAT'S A STRUMPET?
STOP USING THOSE SMART WORDS. WE DON'T UNDERSTAND.
GRRR...
TAKE ME HOME.
AS YOU WISH!
WE'RE HERE! ...HI, MR. FINNEGAN. HOW'S YOUR EVENING?
THERE YOU KIDS ARE.
EVENIN'S FINE.
SHE BEEN GIVING YOU TROUBLE?
SHE'S BEEN ESPECIALLY HOSTILE TODAY.
WHAT!
WELL, YOU'RE JUST IN TIME FOR DINNER. WHY DON'T YOU COME ON IN?
I CAN'T BELIEVE THIS! HEY!!! HEY!!!
DON'T MIND IF I DO.

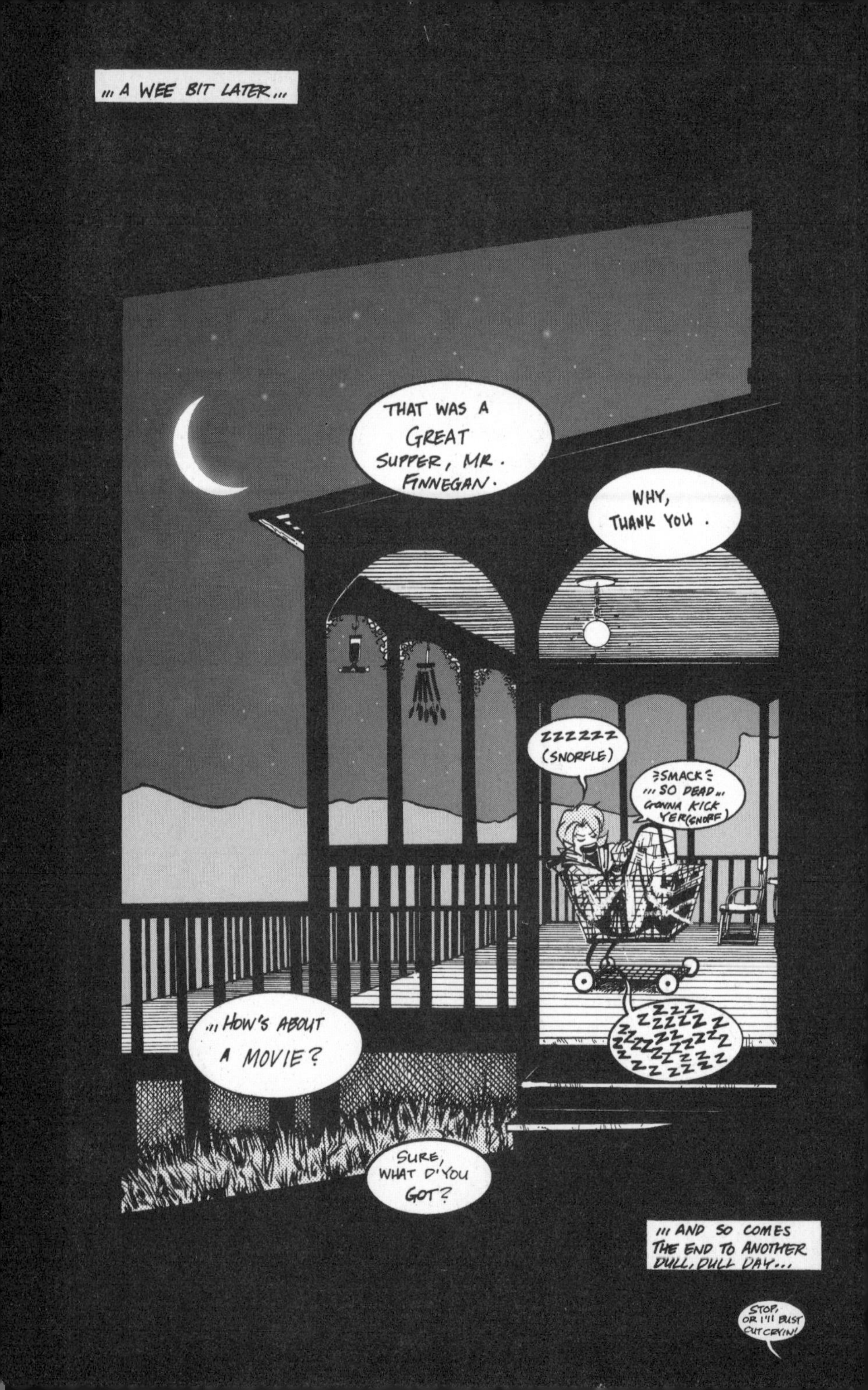
... A WEE BIT LATER ...
THAT WAS A GREAT SUPPER, MR. FINNEGAN.
WHY, THANK YOU.
ZZZZZZ (SNORFLE)
SMACK ... SO DEAD ... GONNA KICK YER (SNORF)
... HOW'S ABOUT A MOVIE?
SURE, WHAT D'YOU GOT?
... AND SO COMES THE END TO ANOTHER DULL, DULL DAY...
STOP, OR I'LL BUST OUT CRYIN!

# BLUE MONDAY: SHERLOCKETTE

## A TRIBUTE TO BUSTER KEATON

DEDICATED TO THE MEMORY OF
ERIC MAGARGEE OF CHECKMATE,
A GREAT GUY FROM A GREAT BAND

BY

CHYNNA CLUGSTON-MAJOR

LETTERING:
GARY KATO

SOUNDTRACK BY HEAVEN 17 & ELECTRONIC

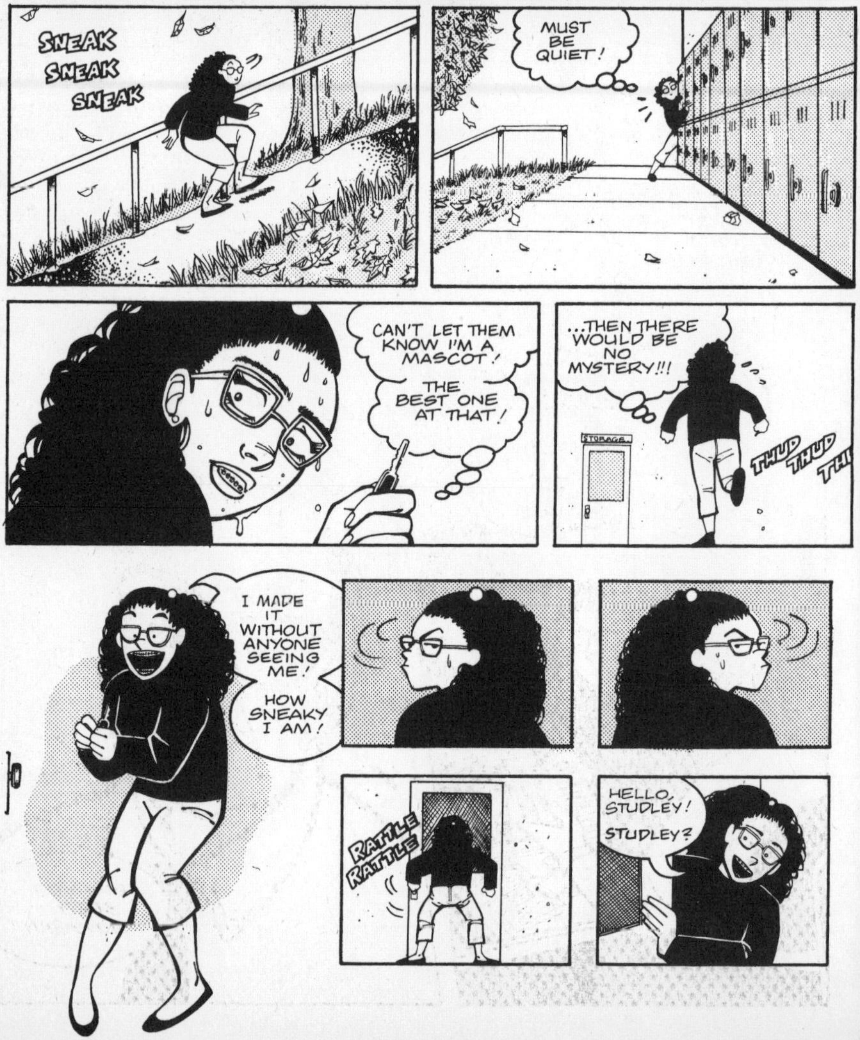
SNEAK
SNEAK
SNEAK
MUST BE QUIET!
CAN'T LET THEM KNOW I'M A MASCOT!
THE BEST ONE AT THAT!
...THEN THERE WOULD BE NO MYSTERY!!!
STORAGE
THUD THUD THU
I MADE IT WITHOUT ANYONE SEEING ME!
HOW SNEAKY I AM!
RATTLE RATTLE
HELLO, STUDLEY!
STUDLEY?

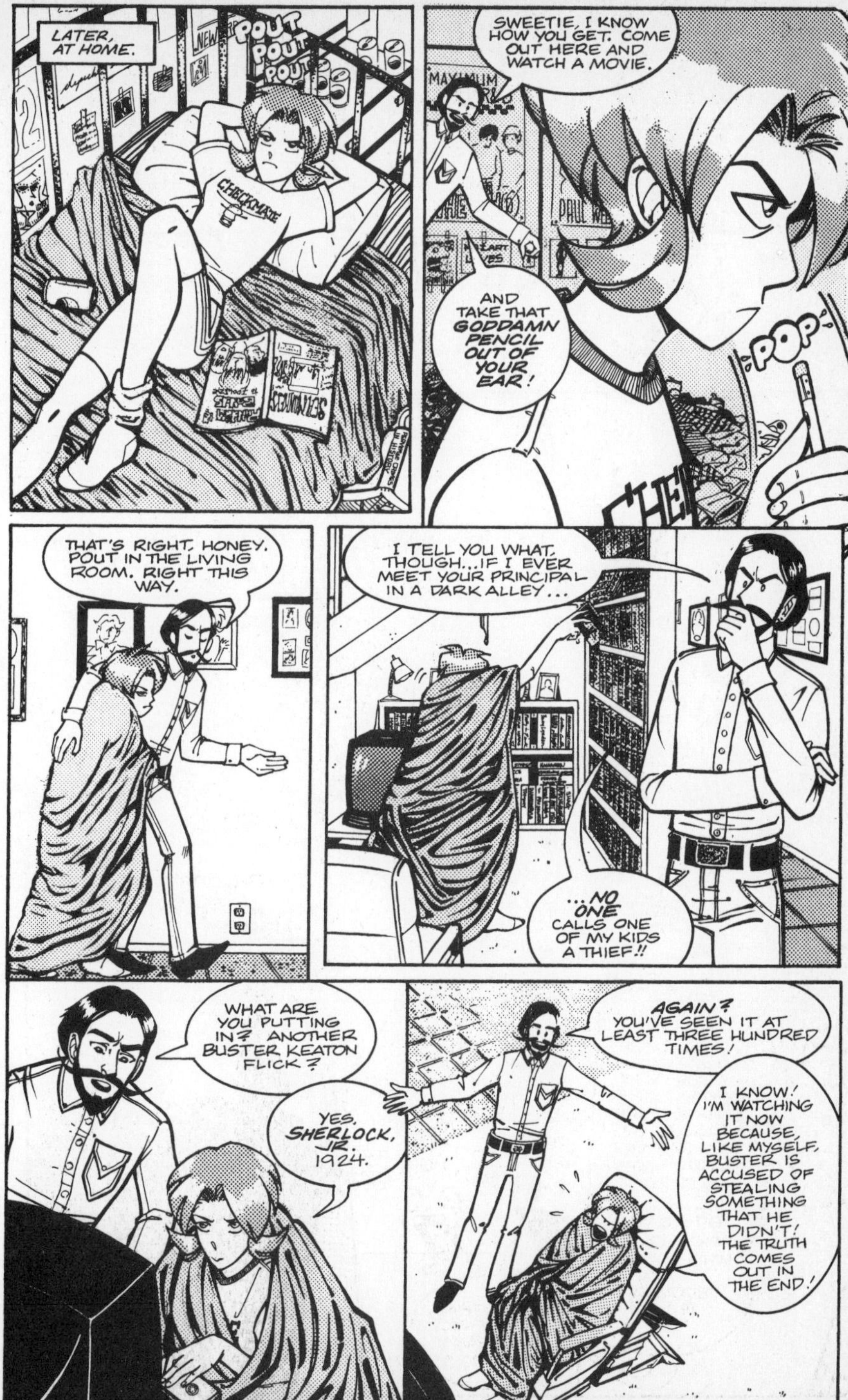
LATER, AT HOME.
POUT POUT POUT
CHECKMATE
SWEETIE, I KNOW HOW YOU GET. COME OUT HERE AND WATCH A MOVIE.
AND TAKE THAT GODDAMN PENCIL OUT OF YOUR EAR!
POP
THAT'S RIGHT, HONEY. POUT IN THE LIVING ROOM. RIGHT THIS WAY.
I TELL YOU WHAT, THOUGH... IF I EVER MEET YOUR PRINCIPAL IN A DARK ALLEY...
...NO ONE CALLS ONE OF MY KIDS A THIEF!!
WHAT ARE YOU PUTTING IN? ANOTHER BUSTER KEATON FLICK?
YES. SHERLOCK, JR. 1924.
AGAIN? YOU'VE SEEN IT AT LEAST THREE HUNDRED TIMES!
I KNOW! I'M WATCHING IT NOW BECAUSE, LIKE MYSELF, BUSTER IS ACCUSED OF STEALING SOMETHING THAT HE DIDN'T! THE TRUTH COMES OUT IN THE END!

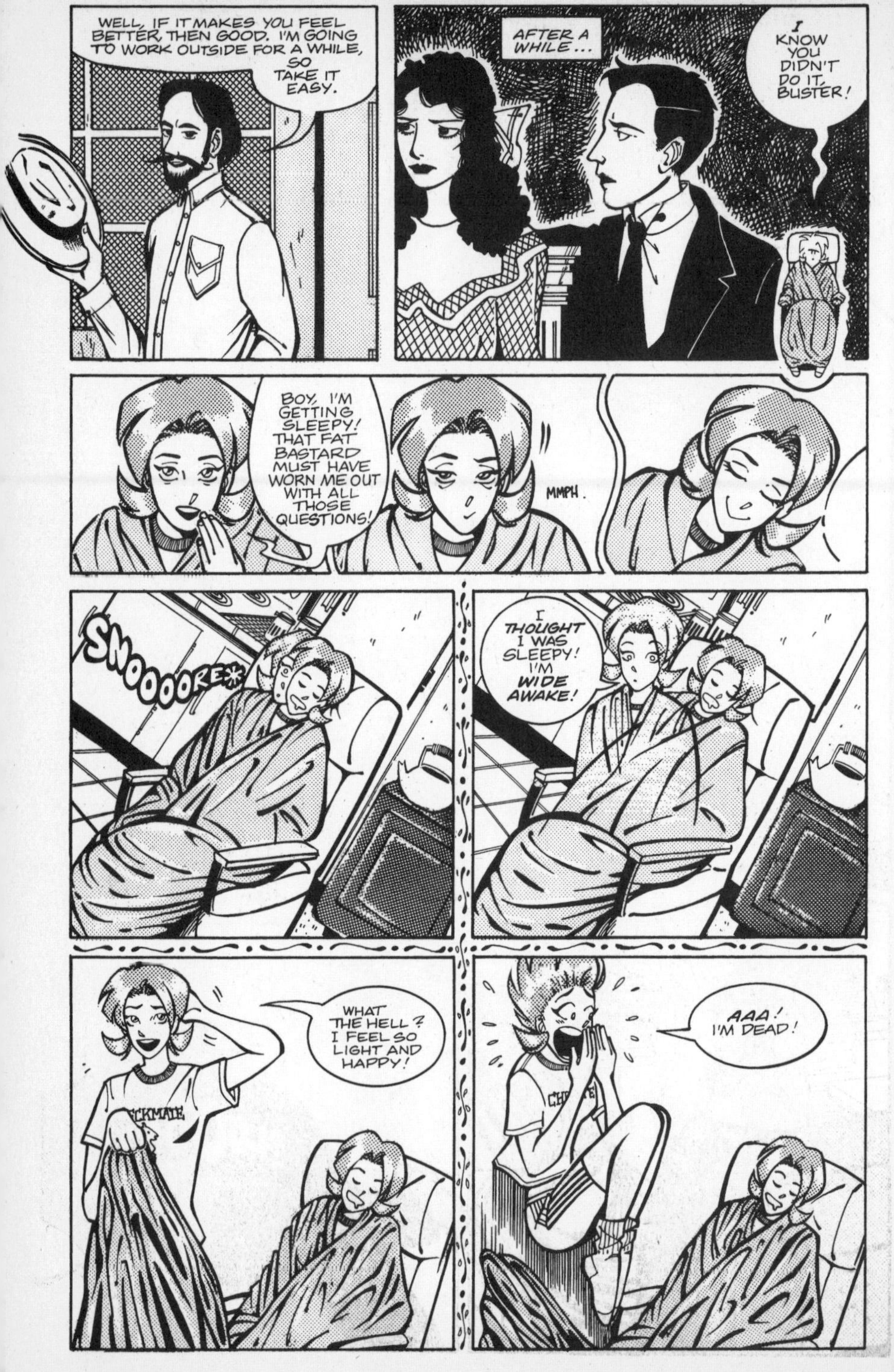
WELL, IF IT MAKES YOU FEEL BETTER, THEN GOOD. I'M GOING TO WORK OUTSIDE FOR A WHILE, SO TAKE IT EASY.
AFTER A WHILE...
I KNOW YOU DIDN'T DO IT, BUSTER!
BOY, I'M GETTING SLEEPY! THAT FAT BASTARD MUST HAVE WORN ME OUT WITH ALL THOSE QUESTIONS!
MMPH.
SNOOOORE
I THOUGHT I WAS SLEEPY! I'M WIDE AWAKE!
WHAT THE HELL? I FEEL SO LIGHT AND HAPPY!
AAA! I'M DEAD!

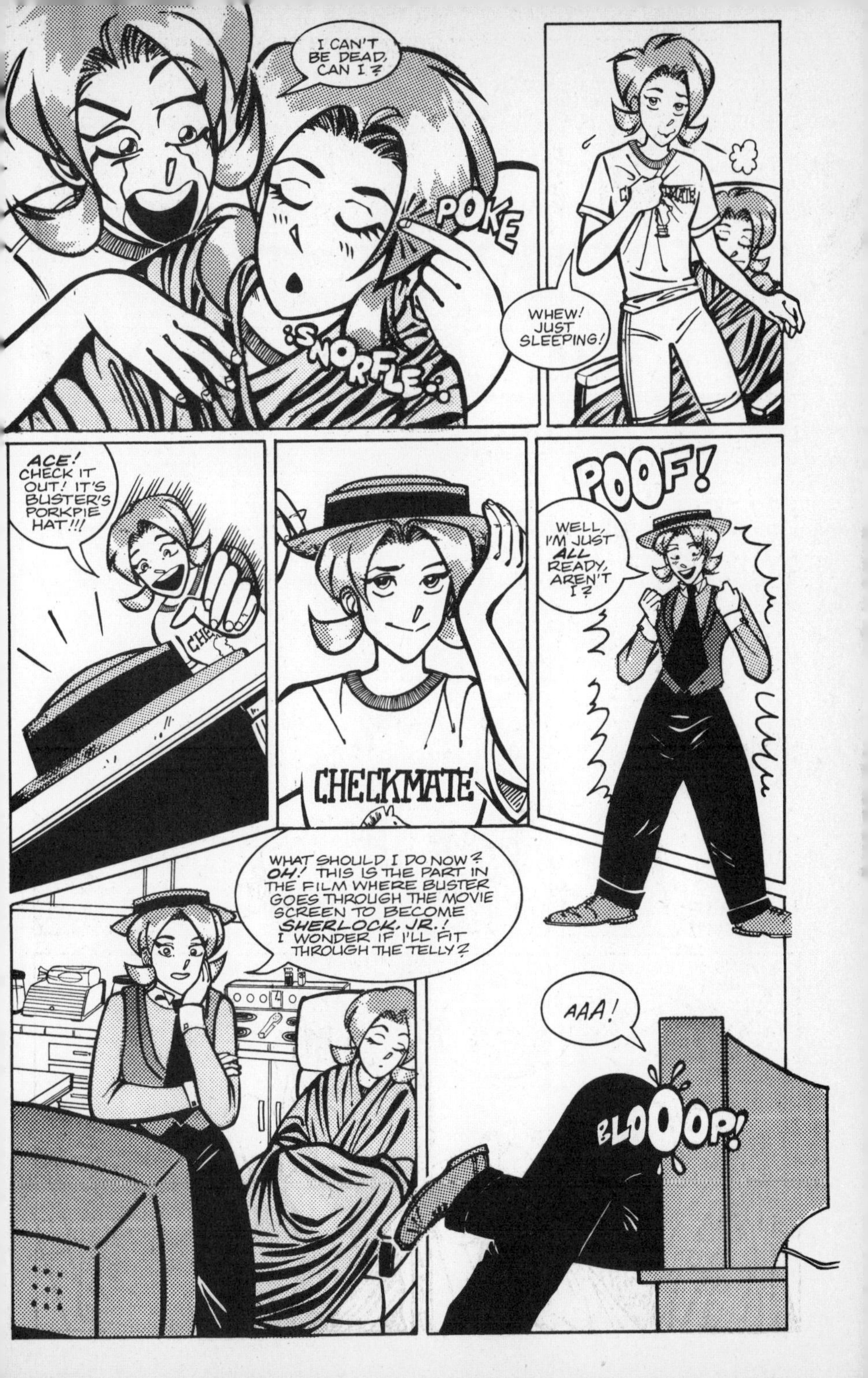
I CAN'T BE DEAD, CAN I?
POKE
SNORFLE...
WHEW! JUST SLEEPING!
ACE! CHECK IT OUT! IT'S BUSTER'S PORKPIE HAT!!!
CHECKMATE
POOF!
WELL, I'M JUST ALL READY, AREN'T I?
WHAT SHOULD I DO NOW? OH! THIS IS THE PART IN THE FILM WHERE BUSTER GOES THROUGH THE MOVIE SCREEN TO BECOME SHERLOCK, JR.! I WONDER IF I'LL FIT THROUGH THE TELLY?
AAA!
BLOOOP!

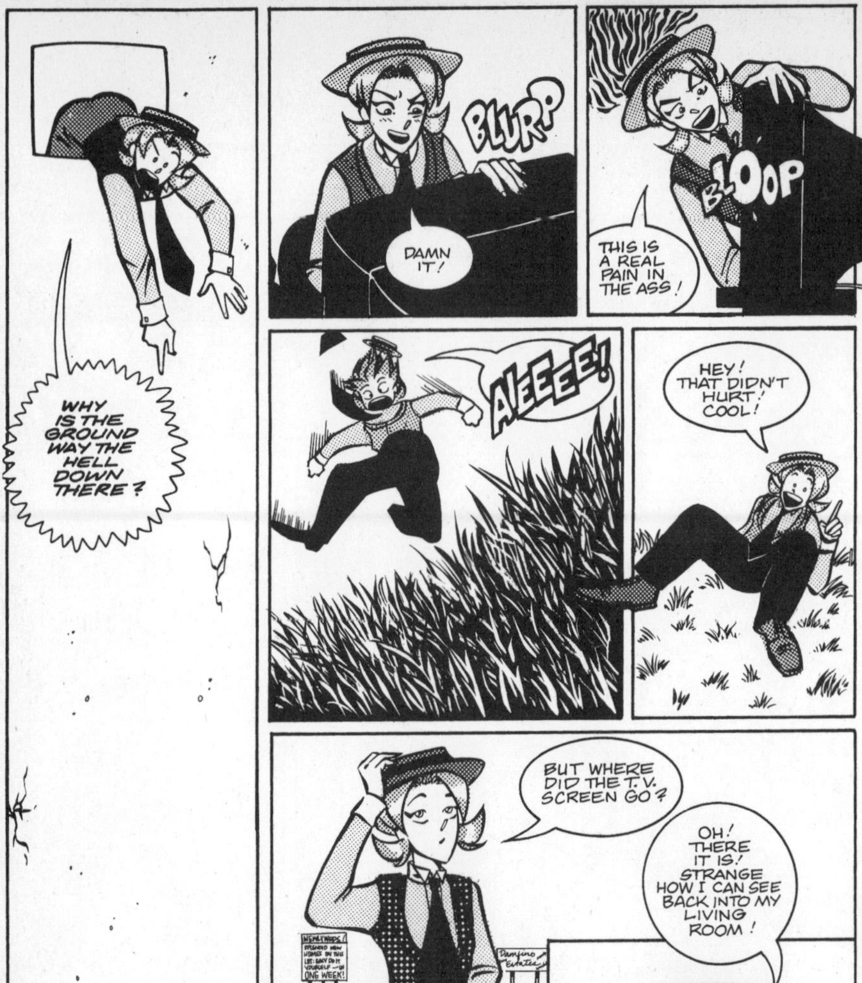
WHY IS THE GROUND WAY THE HELL DOWN THERE?
BLURP
DAMN IT!
BLOOP
THIS IS A REAL PAIN IN THE ASS!
AIEEEE!
HEY! THAT DIDN'T HURT! COOL!
BUT WHERE DID THE T.V. SCREEN GO?
OH! THERE IT IS! STRANGE HOW I CAN SEE BACK INTO MY LIVING ROOM!
ONE WEEK!

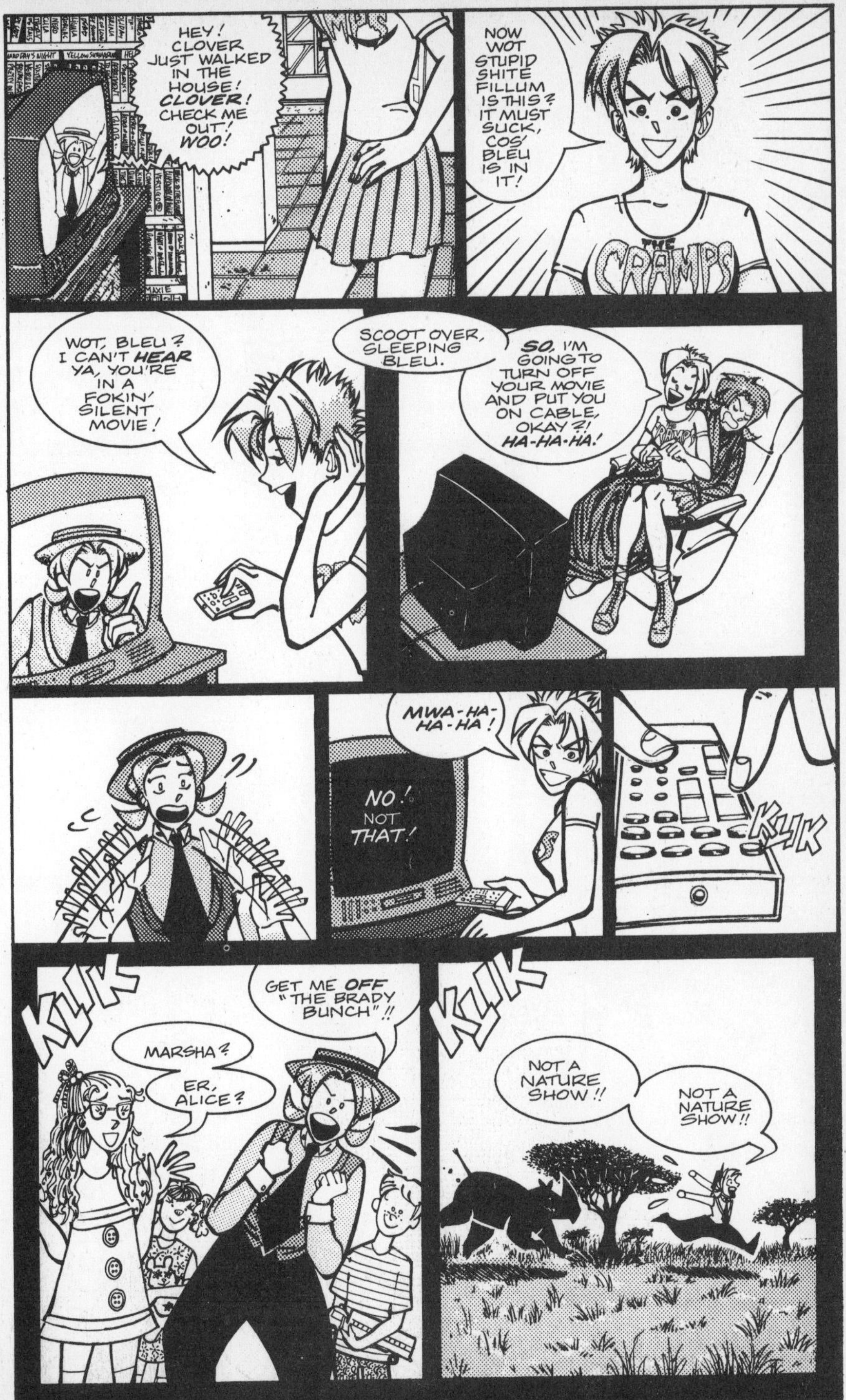
HEY! CLOVER JUST WALKED IN THE HOUSE! CLOVER! CHECK ME OUT! WOO!
NOW WOT STUPID SHITE FILLUM IS THIS?! IT MUST SUCK, COS' BLEU IS IN IT!
THE CRAMPS
WOT, BLEU?! I CAN'T HEAR YA, YOU'RE IN A FOKIN' SILENT MOVIE!
SCOOT OVER, SLEEPING BLEU.
SO, I'M GOING TO TURN OFF YOUR MOVIE AND PUT YOU ON CABLE, OKAY?! HA-HA-HA!
MWA-HA-HA-HA!
NO! NOT THAT!
KLIK
KLIK
GET ME OFF "THE BRADY BUNCH"!!
MARSHA?
ER, ALICE?
KLIK
NOT A NATURE SHOW!!
NOT A NATURE SHOW!!

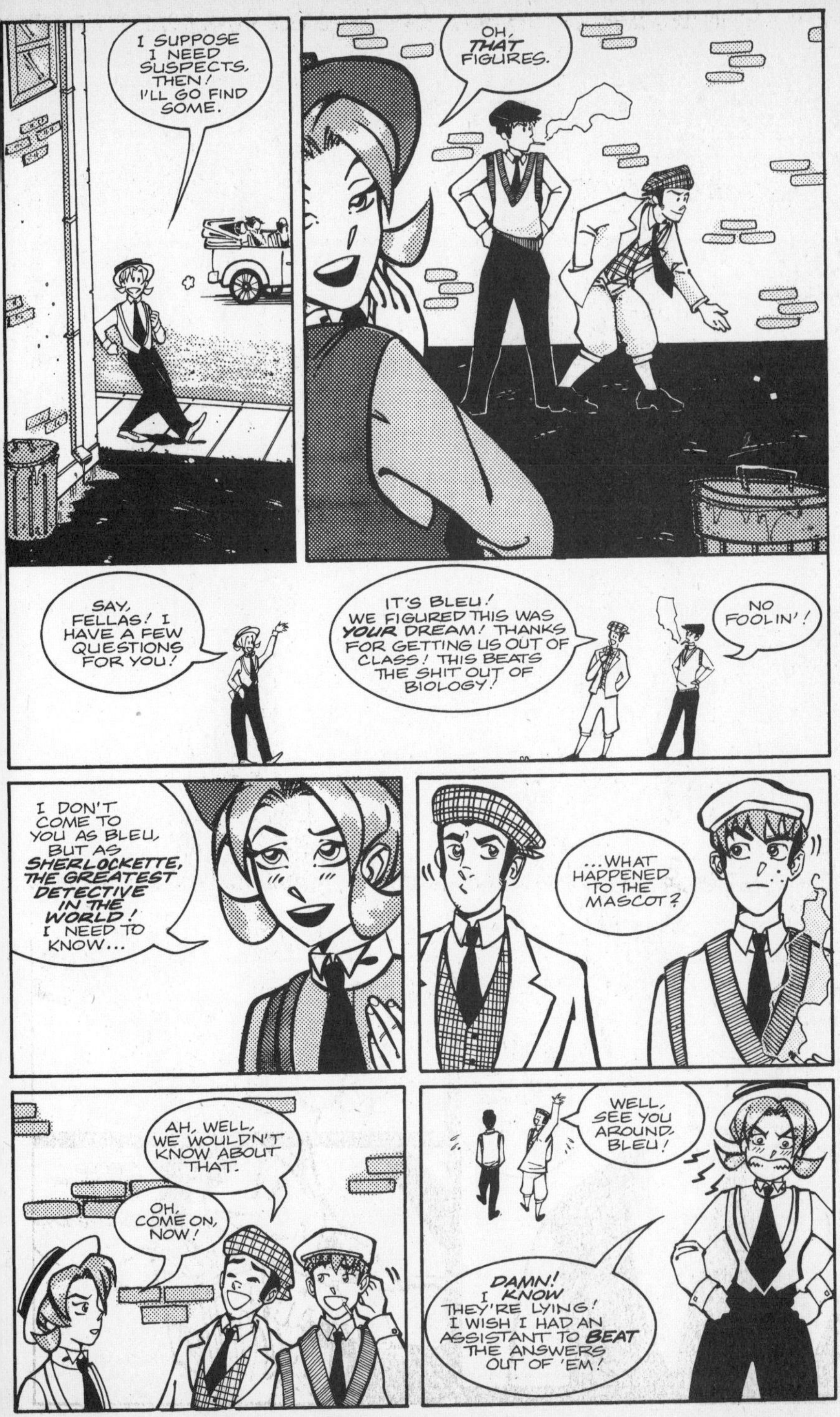
I SUPPOSE I NEED SUSPECTS, THEN! I'LL GO FIND SOME.
OH, THAT FIGURES.
SAY, FELLAS! I HAVE A FEW QUESTIONS FOR YOU!
IT'S BLEU! WE FIGURED THIS WAS YOUR DREAM! THANKS FOR GETTING US OUT OF CLASS! THIS BEATS THE SHIT OUT OF BIOLOGY!
NO FOOLIN'!
I DON'T COME TO YOU AS BLEU, BUT AS SHERLOCKETTE, THE GREATEST DETECTIVE IN THE WORLD! I NEED TO KNOW...
...WHAT HAPPENED TO THE MASCOT?
AH, WELL, WE WOULDN'T KNOW ABOUT THAT.
OH, COME ON, NOW!
WELL, SEE YOU AROUND, BLEU!
DAMN! I KNOW THEY'RE LYING! I WISH I HAD AN ASSISTANT TO BEAT THE ANSWERS OUT OF 'EM!

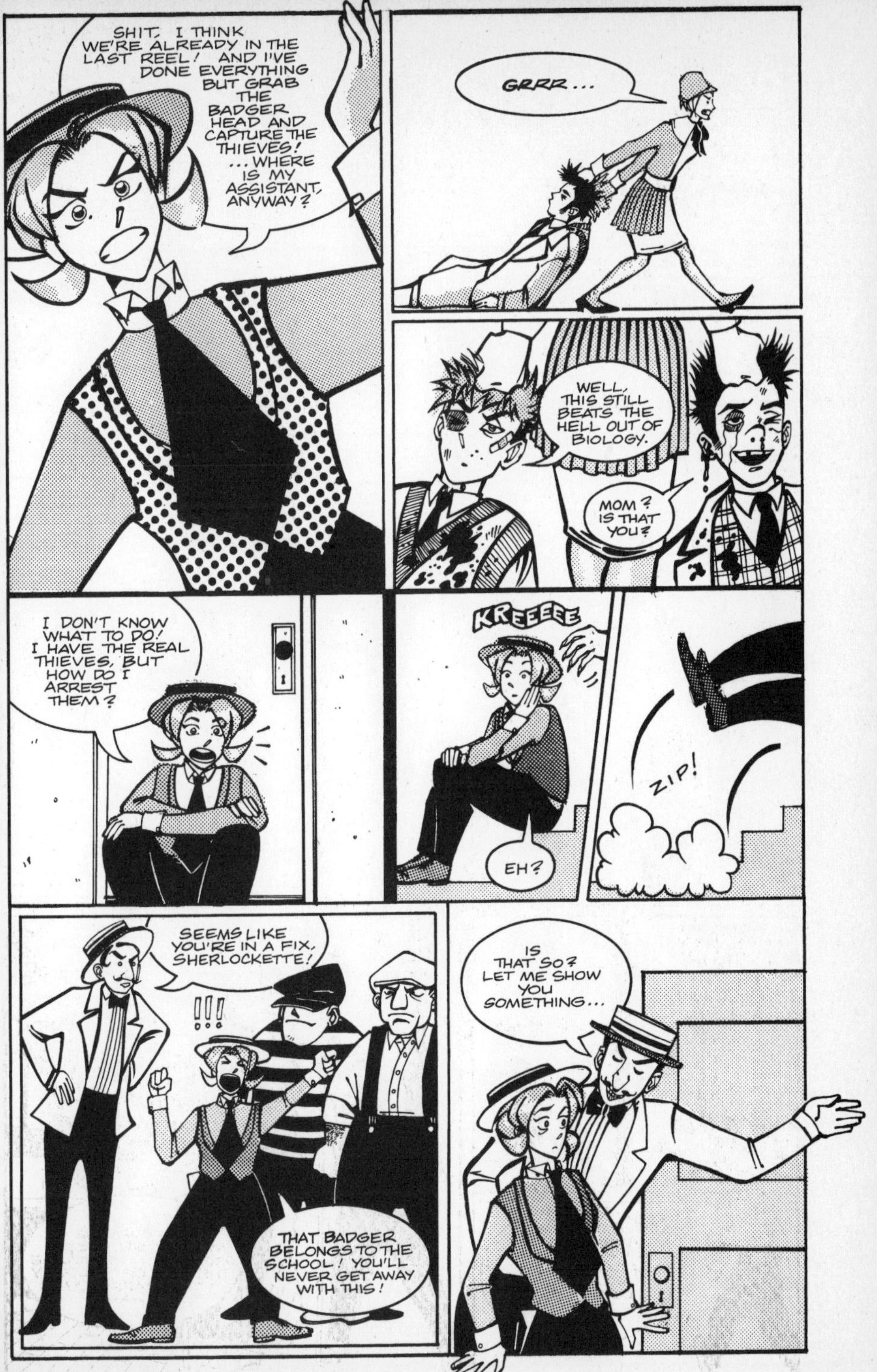
SHIT, I THINK WE'RE ALREADY IN THE LAST REEL! AND I'VE DONE EVERYTHING BUT GRAB THE BADGER HEAD AND CAPTURE THE THIEVES! ...WHERE IS MY ASSISTANT, ANYWAY?
GRRR...
WELL, THIS STILL BEATS THE HELL OUT OF BIOLOGY.
MOM? IS THAT YOU?
I DON'T KNOW WHAT TO DO! I HAVE THE REAL THIEVES, BUT HOW DO I ARREST THEM?
KREEEEE
EH?
ZIP!
SEEMS LIKE YOU'RE IN A FIX, SHERLOCKETTE!
!!!
THAT BADGER BELONGS TO THE SCHOOL! YOU'LL NEVER GET AWAY WITH THIS!
IS THAT SO? LET ME SHOW YOU SOMETHING...

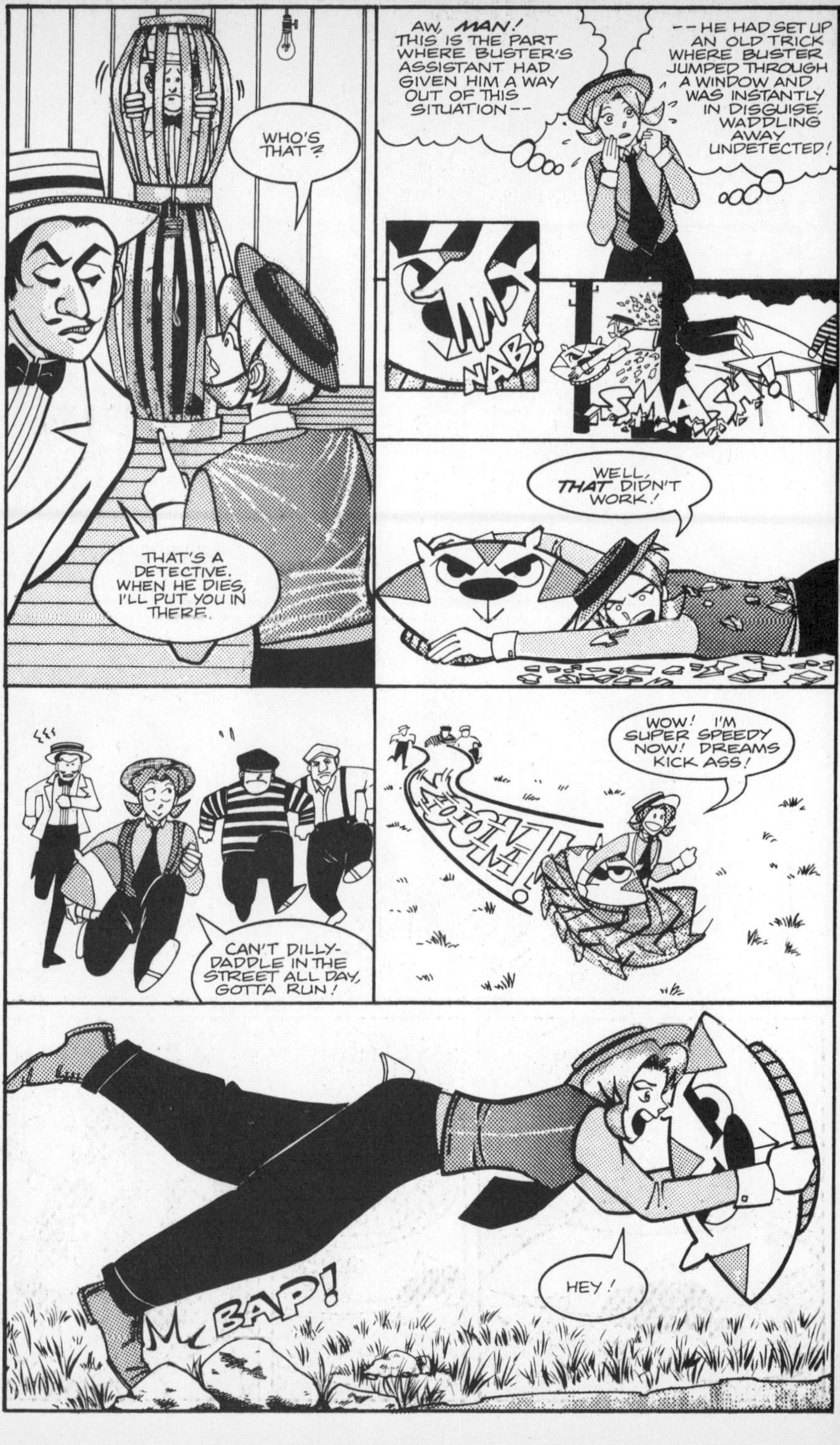
WHO'S THAT?!
THAT'S A DETECTIVE. WHEN HE DIES, I'LL PUT YOU IN THERE.
AW, MAN! THIS IS THE PART WHERE BUSTER'S ASSISTANT HAD GIVEN HIM A WAY OUT OF THIS SITUATION--
--HE HAD SET UP AN OLD TRICK WHERE BUSTER JUMPED THROUGH A WINDOW AND WAS INSTANTLY IN DISGUISE, WADDLING AWAY UNDETECTED!
NAB!
SMASH!
WELL, THAT DIDN'T WORK!
CAN'T DILLY-DADDLE IN THE STREET ALL DAY, GOTTA RUN!
WOW! I'M SUPER SPEEDY NOW! DREAMS KICK ASS!
HEY!
BAP!

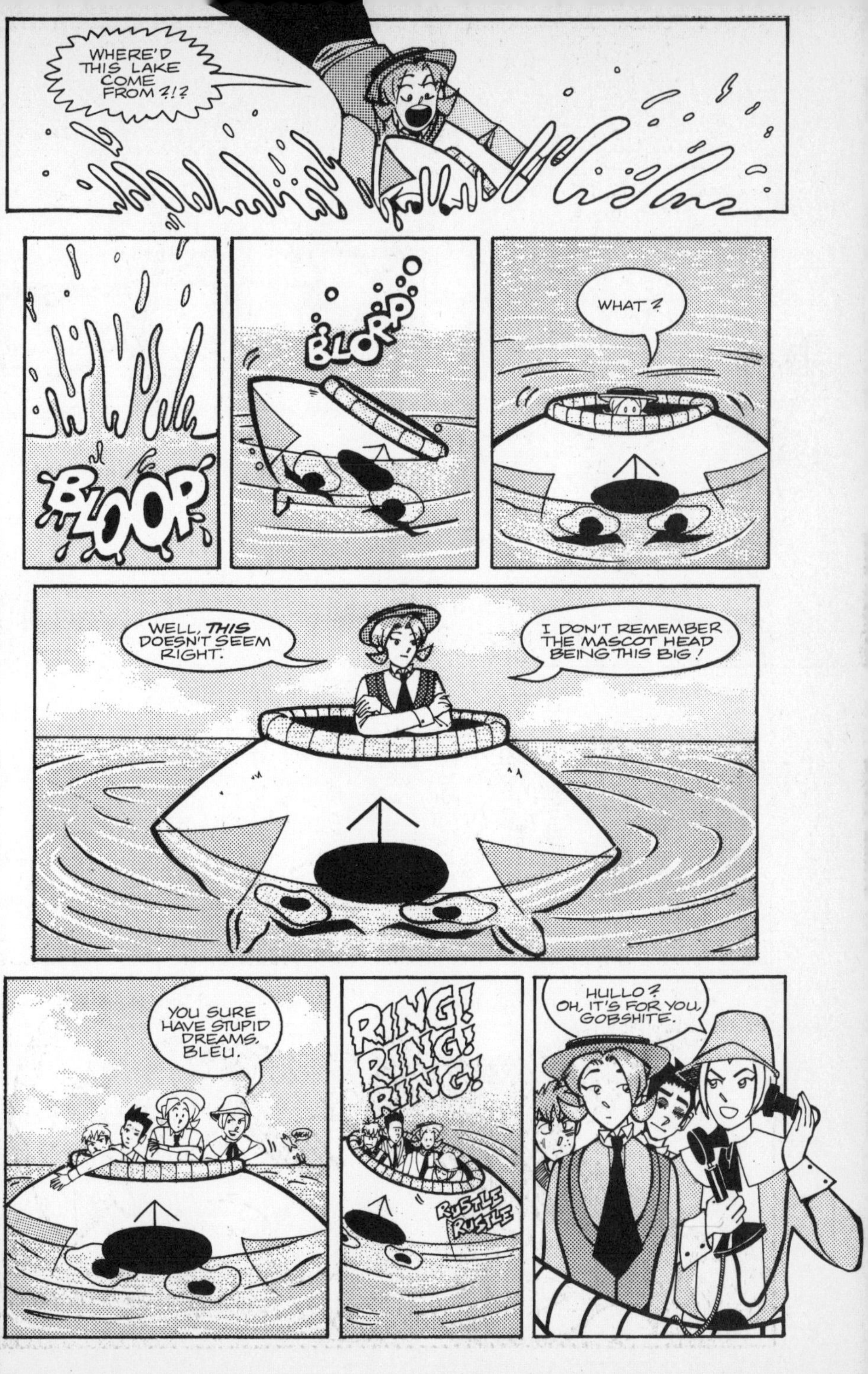
WHERE'D THIS LAKE COME FROM ?!?
BLOOP
BLORP
WHAT ?
WELL, THIS DOESN'T SEEM RIGHT.
I DON'T REMEMBER THE MASCOT HEAD BEING THIS BIG !
YOU SURE HAVE STUPID DREAMS, BLEU.
RING! RING! RING!
RUSTLE RUSTLE
HULLO ? OH, IT'S FOR YOU, GOBSHITE.

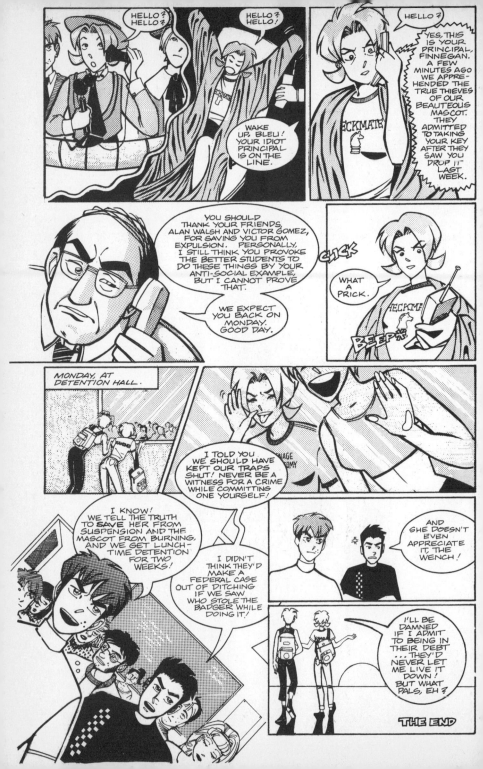

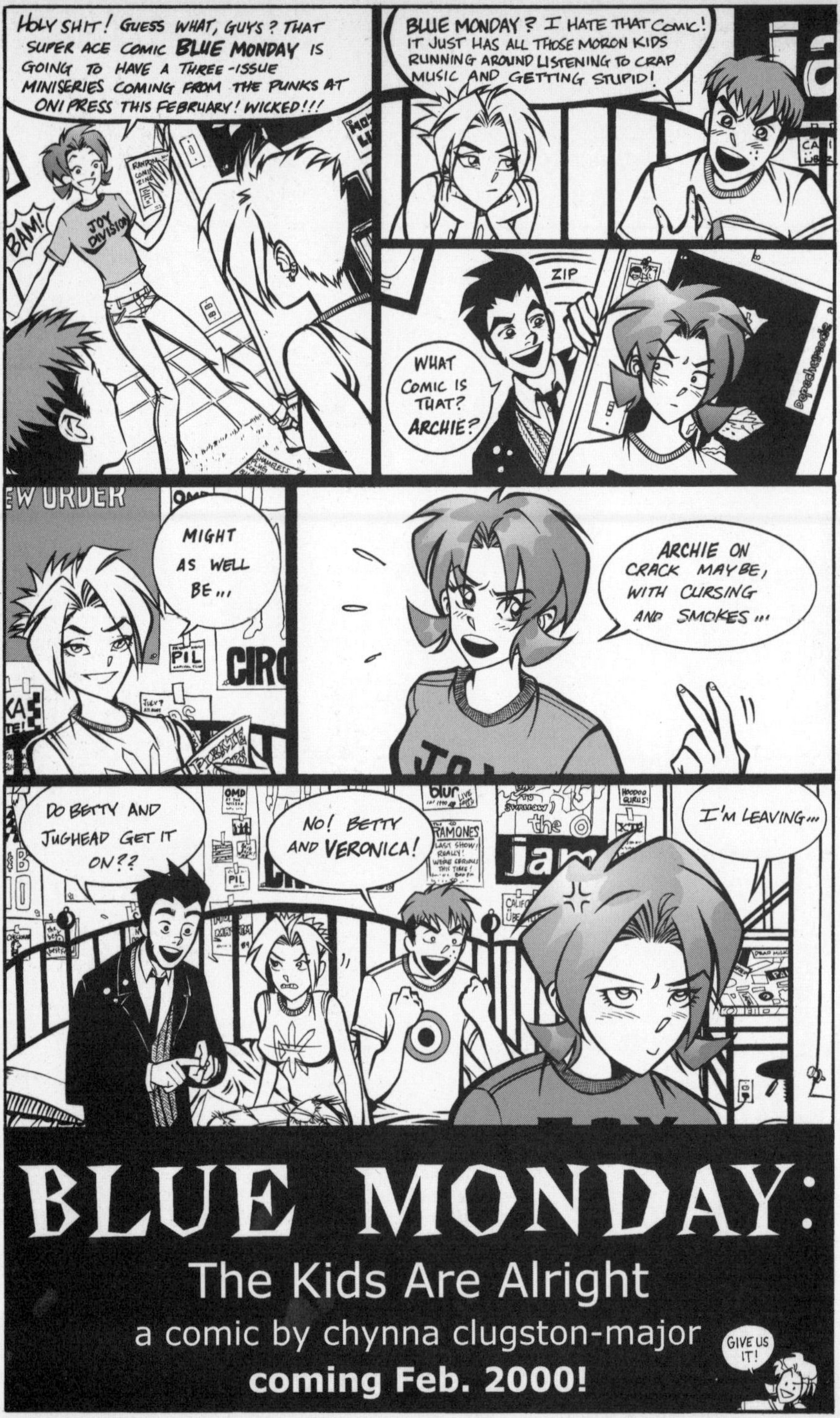
HOLY SHIT! GUESS WHAT, GUYS? THAT SUPER ACE COMIC BLUE MONDAY IS GOING TO HAVE A THREE-ISSUE MINISERIES COMING FROM THE PUNKS AT ONI PRESS THIS FEBRUARY! WICKED!!!
BAM!
JOY DIVISION
BLUE MONDAY? I HATE THAT COMIC! IT JUST HAS ALL THOSE MORON KIDS RUNNING AROUND LISTENING TO CRAP MUSIC AND GETTING STUPID!
ZIP
WHAT COMIC IS THAT? ARCHIE?
MIGHT AS WELL BE...
ARCHIE ON CRACK MAYBE, WITH CURSING AND SMOKES...
DO BETTY AND JUGHEAD GET IT ON??
NO! BETTY AND VERONICA!
I'M LEAVING...
BLUE MONDAY:
The Kids Are Alright
a comic by chynna clugston-major
coming Feb. 2000!
GIVE US IT!

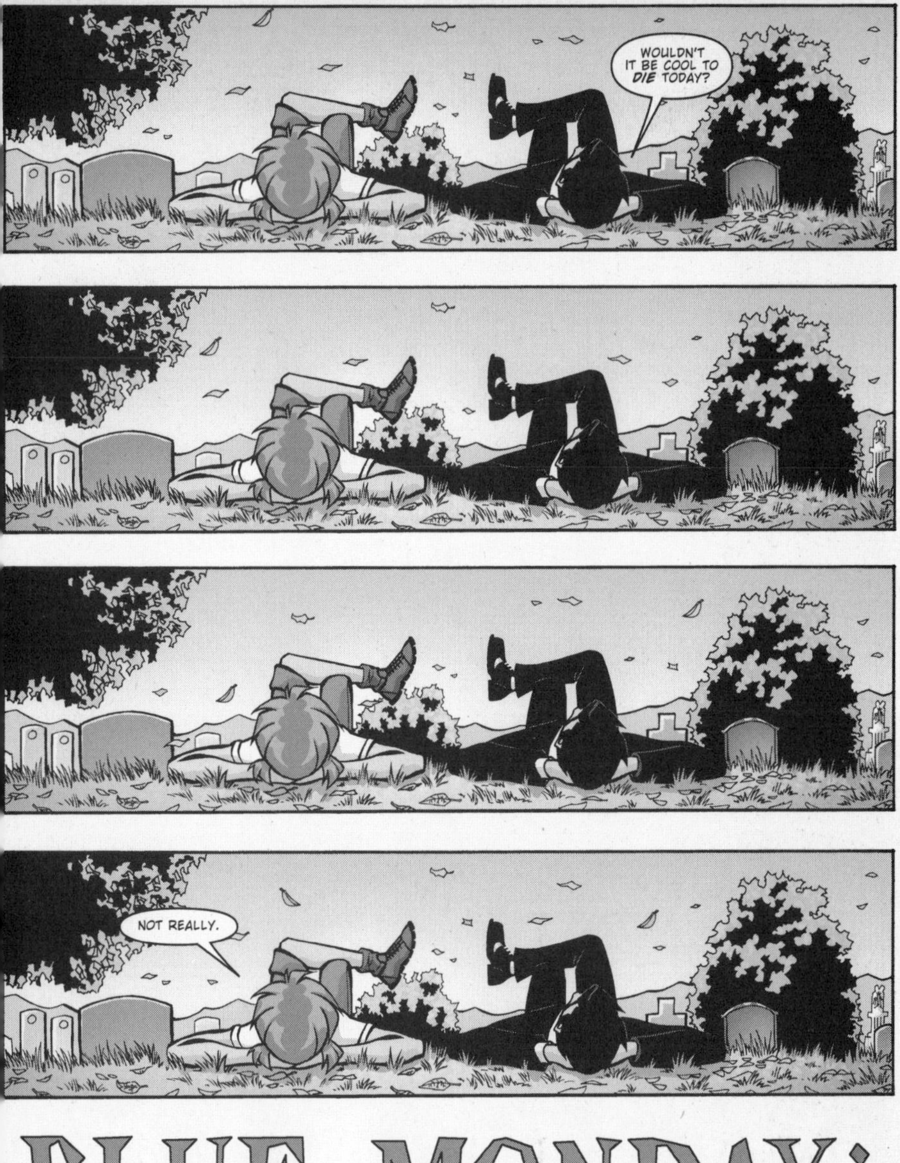
WOULDN'T IT BE COOL TO DIE TODAY?
NOT REALLY.

*This page: Comic done for an Italian anthology. Chynna has lost the script and doesn't remember what it says.*
*Next page: An unpublished cartoon illustrating the editor/creator relationship.*

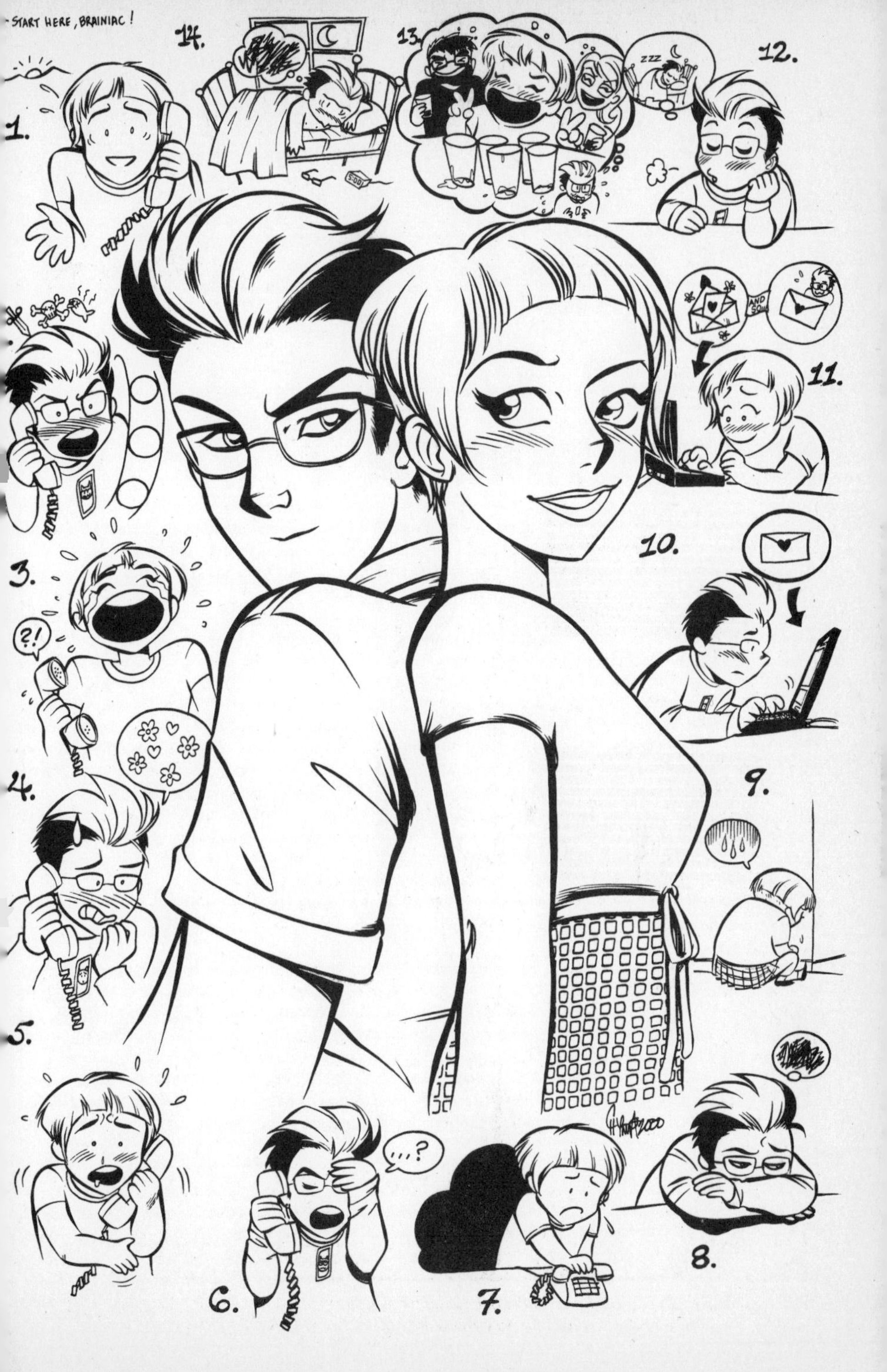
START HERE, BRAINIAC!
1.
?!
3.
4.
5.
6.
...?
7.
8.
9.
10.
11.
12.
ZZZ
13.
14.

## TO ELIZABETH ANN BORROR, A.K.A. BETH LINDSAY...

My motorcycle riding, stogie smoking, stubborn-assed, fiercely independent grandmother...who would risk getting into trouble at *The Fresno Bee* for using their equipment in order to help me make my horrible, porno-comedy minicomics (as long as I didn't put her name anywhere in the book.)

I miss you something terrible.

# SPECIAL THANKS:

(Excuse me while I cheese out here.) Obviously, I want to thank all the people that have been supportive and/or inspirational (art-wise, music-wise, otherwise-wise) while I've been trying to do comics for the last several years. There's a ton of 'em, so if I forget anyone, I'm sorry... but you see, while I was writing this. I had just eaten waaaay too many chili dogs and chips and I felt like I was going to die a pukey, explosive death. *Thank you*, whatever you did, whether you know it or not!

The Fresno/Oakhurst crew: Kaffy (my ace stepmom), Lissa Read, Jon Flores, Chris Denton, Dax Balzer, Dom Piper, Skye "Styles" Storey, Cherylyn Crill (from evil Sierra), Paul Durell, Josh Brenner, May Allen & family, Margo, David and Matt Read, Brian Kirkbride & co, Tom Van Houtrye (Fish Camel), Ronnie Dzerigian (look out, girls!), Chris Homen, Chris Felch, Katie Heitman, Ken Stone, Jay Swallow, Guy Welch, Mike & Rob Tyson, Shane and Jamie Lyster, D.J. Williams, Dave Majeno, Melissa Jones, Maria Ican'tevenspellyourlastname, Kelly Williams, Beth Minkler, Jennifer Heasley, Jonas, Pat Flanagan, Bill Rees, Holly Sendenko, Mr. Robison, Mr. Bartlett, Ms. Jackson, Mr. Smart, Mr. Zimmerman, Syd Claes, Julie Van Patten, Nathan Matheney, Andy, the nicer RHS kids (there weren't many), Laura Chute, The Catholic School Girls, Marty & Mary Nissen, Katie Reeves and family, Dennis & Laarni Cabuco, Jeff Martin, Eric Magargee & Checkmate, Eva, Eric, Suzy, Lynn, Rob Cross, John Yancura, Dave of Heroes Comics, Paul Pavelski, Ken & crew, Wendy Bair, Piemonte's, Charlie, Shane Hurley, Ashley Hurley, my uncles Dale' and Darrell & families, aunt Bobbi, Grandma Nora & Grandpa Ben Clugston, my little bro Quinten C., Lindsay Mosley (I miss you, kiddo), my crazy cousin Dave & family, Bruce & Eleanor Borror, Brian & family, Ashley Stearns & co, Carl & Mary Louise Major, and about a million other people from that area.

As for everyone else: Joe Nozemack, James Lucas Jones, Steve Birch (who has the amazing ability to make everything he touches look completely ace! Though I think he should still give me his car, whether he's more deserving of it or not), Benjamin Holcomb, Adam Warren, Bob Schreck, Andi Watson, Judd Winick, Jim Mahfood, Scott Morse, Evan Dorkin, Sarah Dyer, The Allreds, Jen Van Meter, Greg Rucka, Steve Rolston, Lawrence Marvit, C.B. Cebulski, Scott Allie, Bernie Wrightson, Jeromy Cox, Claudia LaRue, Matt Wagner, C.K., Chris Butcher, the boys at Wildstorm, Dan Vado, Bob Simpkins, my boy Travis O'Neil, Jhonen Vasquez, Maryanne "with the shaky hand" Huntzinger, Ben Abernathy, Diana, Lawrence Marvit, Lea Hernandez, Steve Lieber, Akemi Nakatani, Yuki Fukuyama, Sean Brighto, New Order, Tony, Tom, Pepsi, Chris from Gosh Comics, the Ken Club and Guinness in particular, Astrid & Birgit Amadori, Blur, RioYanez, Kit Fox, Brian Puckett, Awkward, Leah Friend, Paul Weller (yum), Michael & Smile, Hamanaka Sensei, that kid Jeremiah, Ernie the raddest mailman on earth, Dr. Donald Abbott, my gods Buster Keaton & Adam Ant, and above all others, my husband Guy Major and friend/editor Jamie S. Rich, without whose existence in my life I'm convinced none of this would ever have come about. Again, thanks.

Oni Press wants to thank Dan and Bob at Slave, as well as Anita and Lance at Dark Horse, for their assistance in making sure we had all the stories in this book we needed!

# BIO

Chynna Clugston-Major was born at Fresno Community Hospital in August 1975, the only child of an already doomed, nightmarish union. Whoever let those beasts copulate, she'll never know. Perhaps the gods were really drunk and playing truth or dare. Or maybe they were punishing her soul for something stupid she had done in a past life, and the gods thought it'd be funny to make her suffer the incessant irrational rants of two mentally unstable freaks of nature—the mother most of the time, and the father on the weekends. Either way, she does *Blue Monday* when she isn't busy loafing around, drinking Pepsi and watching "Wonder Years" reruns while her bulldog, Buster, passes gas and looks at her like she did it.

Since the publication of *The Kids Are Alright*, Chynna has done illustrations for Dark Horse's *Buffy The Vampire Slayer* comics, collaborated with Jen Van Meter on *Hopeless Savages*, contributed illustrations to *Cut My Hair* (a novel published by Crazyfish/MJ-12), and teamed her characters up with Paul Dini's in *Jingle Belle's All-Star Holiday Hullabaloo*. The year 2001 will bring a new story in *Buffy The Vampire Slayer: Lovers Walk*, collaborations with Adam Warren, more *Hopeless Savages*, and the second *Blue Monday* miniseries, *Absolute Beginners*—in addition to much dancing and the enjoyment of fine Irish beverages.

Chynna currently resides in San Diego, CA, and hopes to one day learn what she's doing.

# OTHER BOOKS FROM ONI PRESS...

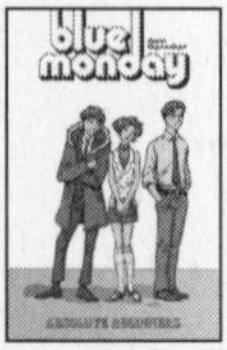
blue monday
ABSOLUTE BEGINNERS

***BLUE MONDAY, VOL. 2: ABSOLUTE BEGINNERS***
by Chynna Clugston-Major
128 pages, black-and-white interiors
$11.95 US, $17.95 CAN
ISBN: 1-929998-17-1

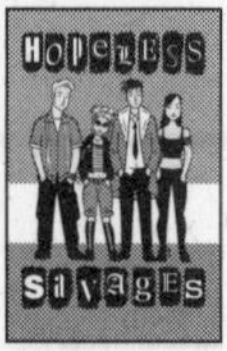
HOPELESS
SAVAGES

***HOPELESS SAVAGES, VOL. 1™***
by Jen Van Meter, Christine Norrie, & Chynna Clugston-Major
112 pages black & white,
16 pages color
$13.95 US, $21.95 CAN
ISBN: 1-929998-24-4

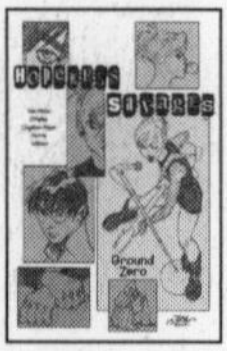
HOPELESS
SAVAGES
Ground Zero

***HOPELESS SAVAGES, VOL. 2: GROUND ZERO™***
by Jen Van Meter & Bryan O'Malley
w/ Chynna Clugston-Major, Christine Norrie, & Andi Watson
128 pages black-and-white interiors
$11.95 US, $17.95 CAN
ISBN: 1-929998-52-X

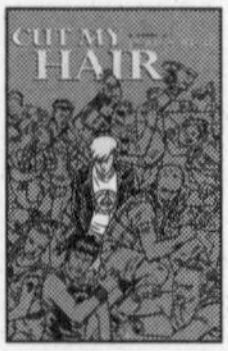
CUT MY
HAIR

***CUT MY HAIR™***
by Jamie S. Rich
w/ Chynna Clugston-Major, Scott Morse, Judd Winick, & Andi Watson
236 pages, black-and-white text with illustrations
$15.95 US, $23.95 CAN
ISBN: 0-9700387-0-4

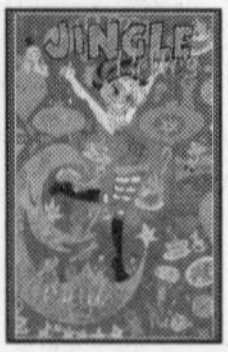
JINGLE

***JINGLE BELLE'S COOL YULE***
by Paul Dini, Chynna Clugston-Major, Jeff Smith, Jill Thompson, etc.
112 pages black & white, 8 pages color
$13.95 US, $21.95 CAN
ISBN: 1-929998-36-8

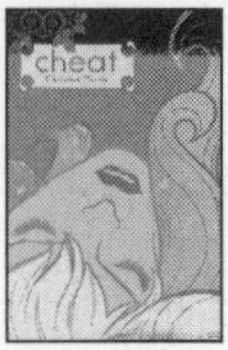
cheat

***CHEAT™***
by Christine Norrie
72 pages, black-and-white interiors
$5.95 US, $9.95 Can
ISBN: 1-929998-47-3

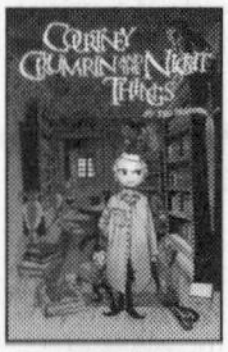
COURTNEY
CRUMRIN AND THE NIGHT
THINGS

***COURTNEY CRUMRIN & THE NIGHT THINGS™***
by Ted Naifeh
128 pages, black-and-white interiors
$11.95 US, $17.95 CAN
ISBN: 1-929998-42-2

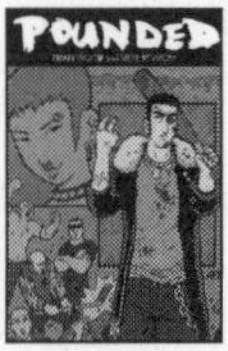
POUNDED

***POUNDED™***
by Brian Wood & Steve Rolston
88 pages, black-and-white interiors
$8.95 U.S., $12.95 CAN
ISBN: 1-929998-37-6

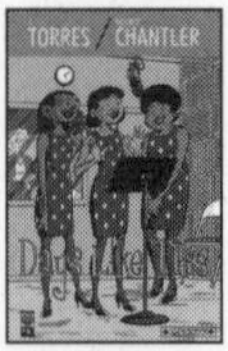
TORRES / CHANTLER

***DAYS LIKE THIS™***
by J. Torres & Scott Chantler
88 pages, black-and-white interiors
$8.95 US, $12.95 CAN
ISBN: 1-929998-48-1

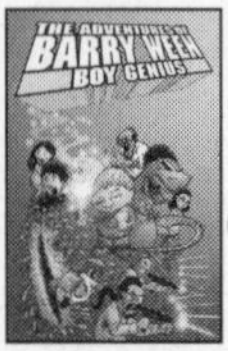
THE ADVENTURES OF
BARRY WEEN
BOY GENIUS

***THE ADVENTURES OF BARRY WEEN, BOY GENIUS™***
***Volume 1***
by Judd Winick
88 pages, black-and-white interiors
$8.95 US, $12.95 CAN.
ISBN 1-929998-00-7

***Available at finer comics shops everywhere. For a comics store near you, call 1-888-COMIC-BOOK.***

**For more information on more Oni Press titles go to: www.onipress.com**